Get the eBook FREE!
(PDF, ePub, Kindle, and liveBook all included)

We believe that once you buy a book from us, you should be able to read it in any format we have available. To get electronic versions of this book at no additional cost to you, purchase and then register this book at the Manning website.

Go to https://www.manning.com/freebook and follow the instructions to complete your pBook registration.

That's it!
Thanks from Manning!

GANs in Action

DEEP LEARNING WITH GENERATIVE ADVERSARIAL NETWORKS

JAKUB LANGR
VLADIMIR BOK

MANNING

SHELTER ISLAND

Manning Publications Co.
20 Baldwin Road
PO Box 761
Shelter Island, NY 11964

Acquisitions editor:	Brian Sawyer
Development editor:	Christina Taylor
Technical development editors:	John Hyaduck and
	Kostas Passadis
Review editor	Aleks Dragosavljević
Production editor:	Anthony Calcara
Copy editor:	Sharon Wilkey
Proofreader	Tiffany Taylor
Technical proofreader:	Karsten Strøbæk
Typesetter:	Dennis Dalinnik
Cover designer:	Marija Tudor

ISBN: 9781617295560
Printed in the United States of America

To those who will consider the jokes more of a pun-ishment than the math.
—Jakub Langr

To Michael Reitano, for helping me become a better writer;
to Simone Reitano, for helping me become a better person.
—Vladimir Bok

brief contents

contents

preface

Jakub Langr

When I first discovered GANs in 2015, I instantly fell in love with the idea. It was the kind of self-criticizing machine learning (ML) system that I always missed in other parts of ML. Even as humans, we constantly generate possible plans and then discriminate that just naively running into a door is not the best idea. GANs really made sense to me—to get to the next level of AI, we should take advantage of automatically learned representations and a machine learning feedback loop. After all, data was expensive, and compute was getting cheap.

The other thing I loved about GANs—though this realization came later—was its growth curve. No other part of ML is so "new." Most of computer vision was invented before 1998, whereas GANs were not working before 2014. Since that moment, we have had uninterrupted exponential growth until the time of this writing.

To date, we have achieved a great deal, cat meme vectors included. The first GAN paper has more than 2.5 times the number of citations the original TensorFlow paper got. GANs are frequently discussed by, for example, McKinsey & Company and most mainstream media outlets. In other words, GANs have an impact far beyond just tech.

It is a fascinating new world of possibilities, and I am honored and excited to be sharing this world with you. This book was close to two years in the making, and we hope it will be as exciting to you as it is to us. We can't wait to see what amazing inventions you bring to the community.

Vladimir Bok

In the words of science fiction writer Arthur C. Clarke, "Technology advanced enough is indistinguishable from magic." These words inspired me in my early years of exploring the impossible in computer science. However, after years of studying and working in machine learning, I found I had become desensitized to the advances in machine intelligence. When, in 2011, IBM's Watson triumphed over its flesh-and-bone rivals in Jeopardy, I was impressed; yet five years later, in 2016, when Google's AlphaGo did the same in the board game Go (computationally, an even more impressive achievement), I was hardly moved. The accomplishment felt somewhat underwhelming—even expected. The magic was gone.

Then, GANs came along.

I was first exposed to GANs during a research project at Microsoft Research. It was 2017 and, tired of hearing "Despacito" over and over again, my teammates and I set out to experiment with generative modeling for music using spectrograms (visual encodings of sound data). It quickly became apparent that GANs are vastly superior to other techniques in their ability to synthesize data. Spectrograms produced by other algorithms amounted to little more than white noise; those our GAN outputted were, quite literally, music to our ears. It is one thing to see machines triumph in areas where the objective is clear (as with Jeopardy and Go), and another to witness an algorithm create something novel and authentic independently.

I hope that, as you read our book, you will share my enthusiasm for GANs and rediscover the magic in AI. Jakub and I worked tirelessly to make this cutting-edge field accessible and comprehensive. We hope you will find our book enjoyable and informative—and our humor bearable.

acknowledgments

This book would not be possible without the support and guidance from the editorial team at Manning Publications. We are grateful to Christina Taylor for her hard work and dedication; we could not have hoped for a better development editor. We were also fortunate to work with John Hyaduck and Kostas Passadis, whose insightful feedback helped make this book the best it can be.

We also want to thank the Manning staff who worked behind the scenes on MEAP, promotion, and other essential aspects of making this publication a reality: Brian Sawyer, Christopher Kaufmann, Aleksandar Dragosavljević, Rebecca Rinehart, Melissa Ice, Candace Gillhoolley, and many others.

Above all, we are grateful to all our readers who provided invaluable feedback on the early drafts of the manuscript.

Jakub Langr

If this book is a success, I am forever grateful to my former team at Pearson, who have been great mentors and friends to this day—Andy, Kostas, Andreas, Dario, Marek, and Hubert. In 2013, they offered me my first data science internship, thus irrevocably changing the course of my life and career.

Words cannot express my gratitude to all the amazing people of Entrepreneur First, and especially to Dr. Pavan Kumar for being a wonderful friend, flatmate, and colleague.

I would also like to thank my friends and colleagues from Filtered.com, University of Oxford, ICP, and the R&D team at Mudano, who are all amazing people.

There are many more people I would like to thank who have been positive influences, but alas, word limit is a cruel lord. So, thank you to my friends and family for sticking by me through thick and thin.

If this book is not a success, I would like to dedicate the book to the foxes of Carminia Road because, first, what makes that kind of hellish noise at 2 a.m.? And second, I never have to wonder, what does the fox say?

Vladimir Bok

I am grateful to James McCaffrey, Roland Fernandez, Sayan Pathak, and the rest of the AI-611 staff at Microsoft Research for the opportunity and privilege to receive mentorship and instruction from some of the greatest minds in machine learning and AI. My gratitude also goes to my AI-611 teammates, Tim Balbekov and Rishav Mukherji, for joining me on the journey, and to our mentors, Nebojsa Jojic and Po-Sen Huang, for their guidance.

I would also like to thank my college advisor, Prof. Krzysztof Gajos, for allowing me to enroll in his graduate research seminar even though I had not fulfilled the course prerequisites; it was an invaluable first exposure to the world of hands-on computer science research.

Special thanks to my colleagues at Intent for their support and encouragement—and for bearing with my late-night email responses as many of my evenings were spent writing and doing research.

I am deeply grateful to Kimberly Pope for believing in the young Czech high school student all those years ago and selecting me for a scholarship that changed my life. It is a debt I can never repay.

Lastly, thank you to my family and friends for being there for me. Always.

about this book

The goal of this book is to provide the definitive guide for anyone interested in learning about Generative Adversarial Networks (GANs) from the ground up. Starting from the simplest examples, we advance to some of the most innovative GAN implementations and techniques. We make cutting-edge research accessible by providing the intuition behind these advances while sparing you all but the essential math and theory.

Ultimately, our goal is to give you the knowledge and tools necessary not only to understand what has been accomplished in GANs to date, but also to empower you to find new applications of your choosing. The generative adversarial paradigm is full of potential to be unraveled by enterprising individuals like you who can make an impact through academic and real-world applications alike. We are thrilled to have you join us on this journey.

Who should read this book

This book is intended for readers who already have some experience with machine learning and neural networks. The following list indicates what you should ideally know. Although we try our best to explain most things as we go, you should be confident about at least 70% of this list:

- We expect you to be able to run intermediate Python programs. You do not need to be a Python master, but you should have at least two years of Python experience (ideally as a full-time data scientist or software engineer).

- You should understand object-oriented programming, how to work with objects, and how to figure out their attributes and methods. You need to be able to understand reasonably typical Python objects (for example, Pandas Data-Frames) as well as atypical ones (for example, Keras layers).
- You should understand the basics of machine learning theory, such as train/test split, overfitting, weights, and hyperparameters, as well as the basics of supervised, unsupervised, and reinforcement learning. You should also be familiar with metrics such as accuracy and mean squared error.
- You should understand basic statistics and calculus, such as probability, density functions, probability distributions, differentiation, and simple optimization.
- You should understand elementary linear algebra, such as matrices, high-dimensional spaces, and, ideally, principal component analysis.
- You should understand the basics of deep learning—things such as feed-forward networks, weights and biases, activation functions, regularization, stochastic gradient descent, and backpropagation.
- You should also have elementary familiarity with, or willingness to independently learn, the Python-based machine learning library Keras.

We are not trying to scare you, but rather ensure that you will get the most out of this book. You may try to take a stab at it anyway, but the less you know, the more you should expect to search online on your own. However, if this list does not seem scary to you, you should be good to go.

About the code

This book contains many examples of source code, both in numbered listings and inline with normal text. In both cases, the source code is formatted in a `fixed-width font like this` to separate it from ordinary text. Sometimes the code is also in bold to highlight code that has changed from previous steps in the chapter, such as when a new feature adds to an existing line of code.

In many cases, the original source code has been reformatted; we've added line breaks and reworked indentation to accommodate the available page space in the book. In rare cases, even this was not enough, and listings include line-continuation markers (➥). Additionally, comments in the source code have often been removed from the listings when the code is described in the text. Code annotations accompany many of the listings, highlighting important concepts. The code for the examples in this book is available for download from the Manning website at www.manning.com/books/gans-in-action and from GitHub at https://github.com/GANs-in-Action/gans-in-action.

Throughout this book, we will be using Jupyter notebooks, as it the standard for data science education. Using Jupyter is also a prerequisite, but for intermediate Pythonistas, this should be easy to pick up. We are aware that sometimes it may be difficult to access GPUs or get everything working, especially on Windows. So for some chapters, we also provide Google Colaboratory notebooks (*Colab* for short), which are Google's free platform (available at https://colab.research.google.com) and come prepackaged with all the essential data science tools as well as a free GPU for a limited time. You can run all of these lessons straight from your browser! For the other chapters, feel free to upload them to Colab, as the two formats are made to be compatible.

liveBook discussion forum

Purchase of *GANs in Action* includes free access to a private web forum run by Manning Publications, where you can make comments about the book, ask technical questions, and receive help from the authors and from other users. To access the forum, go to https://livebook.manning.com/#!/book/gans-in-action/discussion. You can also learn more about Manning's forums and the rules of conduct at https://livebook.manning.com/#!/discussion.

Manning's commitment to our readers is to provide a venue where a meaningful dialogue between individual readers and between readers and the authors can take place. It is not a commitment to any specific amount of participation on the part of the authors, whose contribution to the forum remains voluntary (and unpaid). We suggest you try asking the authors some challenging questions lest their interest stray! The forum and the archives of previous discussions will be accessible from the publisher's website as long as the book is in print.

Other online resources

GANs are an active field with excellent (albeit fragmented) resources only a Google search away. Those with an academic bent can find the latest papers in *arXiv* (https://arxiv.org), an online repository of academic e-prints owned and operated by Cornell University. We hope that this book will equip you with all that is needed to keep up-to-date on the latest developments in this ever-changing field.

Both Jakub and Vladimir are active contributors to Medium (particularly the tech-focused publications *Towards Data Science* and *Hacker Noon*), where you can find the most recent content from the authors.

How this book is organized: a roadmap

GANs in Action strives to provide a balance of theory and practice. The book is organized into three parts:

PART 1, "INTRODUCTION TO GANS AND GENERATIVE MODELING"

Here, we introduce the foundational concepts behind generative learning and GANs and implement the most canonical GAN variants:

- *Chapter 1, "Introduction to GANs"*—We introduce Generative Adversarial Networks (GANs) and provide a high-level explanation of how they work. You will learn that GANs consist of two separate neural networks (the Generator and the Discriminator), and the networks are trained through a competitive dynamic.

The knowledge you will acquire in this chapter will provide the foundation for the remainder of this book.

- *Chapter 2, "Intro to generative modeling with autoencoders"*—We discuss autoencoders, which can be seen as precursors to GANs in many ways. Given the relative novelty of generative learning, we decided to include a chapter that helps set GANs in a broader context. This chapter also contains the first code tutorial, where we will build a variational autoencoder to generate handwritten digits—the same task we will be exploring in our GAN tutorials in later chapters. However, if you are already familiar with autoencoders or want to dive straight into GANs, feel free to skip this chapter.

- *Chapter 3, "Your first GAN: Generating handwritten digits"*—We dive deeper into the theory behind GANs and adversarial learning. We explore the key differences between GANs and traditional neural networks: namely, we discuss the differences in their cost functions and training processes. In a coding tutorial at the end of the chapter, you will apply what you've learned to implement a GAN in Keras and train it to generate handwritten digits.

- *Chapter 4, "Deep Convolutional GAN"*—We introduce convolutional neural networks and batch normalization. We then implement Deep Convolutional GAN (DCGAN), an advanced GAN architecture that uses convolutional networks as its Generator and Discriminator and takes advantage of batch normalization to stabilize the training process.

PART 2, "ADVANCED TOPICS IN GANS"

Building on the foundations, we dive deeper into the theory underlying GANs and implement a selection of advanced GAN architectures:

- *Chapter 5, "Training and common challenges: GANing for success"*—We discuss many of the theoretical and practical hurdles to training GANs and how to overcome them. We provide a comprehensive overview of the best practices for training a GAN based on relevant academic papers and presentations. We also cover options for evaluating GAN performance and why we need to worry about that.

- *Chapter 6, "Progressive growing of GANs"*—We explore the Progressive GAN (PGGAN, or ProGAN), a cutting-edge training methodology for the Generator and Discriminator. By adding new layers during the training process, the PGGAN achieves superior image quality and resolution. We explain how it all works in theory as well as in practice through hands-on code samples and by using the TensorFlow Hub (TFHub).

- *Chapter 7, "Semi-Supervised GAN"*—We continue to explore innovations based on the core GAN model. You will learn about the enormous practical importance of improving classification accuracy with only a small subset of labeled training examples through semi-supervised learning. Then, we implement the Semi-Supervised GAN (SGAN) and explain how it uses labels to turn the Discriminator into a robust multiclass classifier.

- *Chapter 8, "Conditional GAN"*—We present another GAN architecture that uses labels in training: Conditional GAN (CGAN). Conditional GAN addresses one of the main shortcomings of generative modeling—the inability to specify explicitly what example to synthesize—by using labels or other conditioning information while training its Generator and Discriminator. At the end of the chapter, we implement a CGAN to see targeted data generation firsthand.
- *Chapter 9, "CycleGAN"*—We discuss one of the most interesting GAN architectures: Cycle-Consistent Adversarial Networks (CycleGANs). This technique can be used to translate one image into another, such as turning a photo of a horse into a photo of a zebra. We walk through the CycleGAN architecture and explain its main components and innovations. As a coding tutorial, we then implement a CycleGAN to convert apples into oranges, and vice versa.

PART 3, "WHERE TO GO FROM HERE"

We discuss how and where we can apply our knowledge of GANs and adversarial learning:

- *Chapter 10, "Adversarial examples"*—We look at adversarial examples, a set of techniques to intentionally deceive a machine learning model into making a mistake. We discuss their significance through theory and practical examples and explore their connection to GANs.
- *Chapter 11, "Practical applications of GANs"*—We cover practical applications of GANs. We explore how to use techniques covered in earlier chapters for real-world use cases in medicine and fashion. In medicine, we look at how GANs can be used to augment a small dataset to improve classification accuracy. In fashion, we show how GANs can drive personalization.
- *Chapter 12, "Looking ahead"*—We wrap up our learning journey by summarizing the key takeaways and discussing the ethical considerations of GANs. We also mention emerging GAN techniques for those interested in continuing to explore this field beyond this book.

About the authors

Jakub Langr is a cofounder of a startup that uses GANs for creative and advertising applications. Jakub has worked in data science since 2013, most recently as a data science tech lead at Filtered.com and as an R&D data scientist at Mudano. He also designed and teaches data science courses at the University of Birmingham (UK) and at numerous private companies, and is a guest lecturer at the University of Oxford. He was an Entrepreneur in Residence at the seventh cohort of deep technology talent investor Entrepreneur First. Jakub is also a fellow at the Royal Statistical Society and an invited speaker at various international conferences. He graduated from the University of Oxford. Jakub is donating all of his proceeds from this publication to the nonprofit British Heart Foundation.

Vladimir Bok recognized the immense potential of GANs while pursuing an independent research project in musical style transfer at Microsoft Research. His work experience ranges from applied data science at a Y Combinator-backed startup to leading cross-functional initiatives at Microsoft. Most recently, Vladimir has been managing data science projects at a New York-based startup that provides machine learning services to online travel and e-commerce brands, including Fortune 500 companies. Vladimir graduated *cum laude* with a bachelor's degree in computer science from Harvard University. He is donating all of his proceeds from this book to the nonprofit organization Girls Who Code.

about the cover illustration

Saint-Sauveur

The figure on the cover of *GANs in Action* is captioned "Bourgeoise de Londre," or a bourgeoise woman from London. The illustration was originally issued in 1787 and is taken from a collection of dress costumes from various countries by Jacques Grasset de Saint-Sauveur (1757–1810). Each illustration is finely drawn and colored by hand. The rich variety of Grasset de Saint-Sauveur's collection vividly reminds us of how culturally distinct the world's towns and regions were just 200 years ago. Isolated from each other, people spoke different dialects and languages. In the streets or in the countryside, it was easy to identify where they lived and what their trade or station in life was just by their dress.

The way we dress has changed since then, and the regional diversity, so rich at the time, has faded away. It is now hard to tell apart the inhabitants of different continents, let alone different towns, regions, or countries. Perhaps we have traded cultural diversity for a more varied personal life—certainly for a more varied and fast-paced technological life.

At a time when it is hard to tell one computer book from another, Manning celebrates the inventiveness and initiative of the computer business with book covers based on the rich diversity of regional life of two centuries ago, brought back to life by Grasset de Saint-Sauveur's pictures.

Part 1

Introduction to GANs and generative modeling

Part 1 introduces the world of Generative Adversarial Networks (GANs) and walks through implementations of the most canonical GAN variants:

- In chapter 1, you will learn the basics of GANs and develop an intuitive understanding of how they work.
- In chapter 2, we will switch gears a little and look at autoencoders, so you can get a more holistic understanding of generative modeling. Autoencoders are some of the most important theoretical and practical precursors to GANs and continue to be widely used to this day.
- Chapter 3 starts where chapter 1 left off and dives deeper into the theory underlying GANs and adversarial learning. In this chapter, you will also implement and train your first, fully functional GAN.
- Chapter 4 continues your learning journey by exploring the Deep Convolutional GAN (DCGAN). This innovation on top of the original GAN uses convolutional neural networks to improve the quality of the generated images.

Introduction to GANs

This chapter covers

- An overview of Generative Adversarial Networks
- What makes this class of machine learning algorithms special
- Some of the exciting GAN applications that this book covers

The notion of whether machines can think is older than the computer itself. In 1950, the famed mathematician, logician, and computer scientist Alan Turing—perhaps best known for his role in decoding the Nazi wartime enciphering machine, Enigma—penned a paper that would immortalize his name for generations to come, "Computing Machinery and Intelligence."

In the paper, Turing proposed a test he called the *imitation game*, better known today as the *Turing test*. In this hypothetical scenario, an unknowing observer talks with two counterparts behind a closed door: one, a fellow human; the other, a computer. Turing reasons that if the observer is unable to tell which is the person and which is the machine, the computer passed the test and must be deemed intelligent.

Anyone who has attempted to engage in a dialogue with an automated chatbot or a voice-powered intelligent assistant knows that computers have a long way to go to pass this deceptively simple test. However, in other tasks, computers have not only matched human performance but also surpassed it—even in areas that were until recently considered out of reach for even the smartest algorithms, such as superhumanly accurate face recognition or mastering the game of Go.[1]

Machine learning algorithms are great at recognizing patterns in existing data and using that insight for tasks such as *classification* (assigning the correct category to an example) and *regression* (estimating a numerical value based on a variety of inputs). When asked to generate new data, however, computers have struggled. An algorithm can defeat a chess grandmaster, estimate stock price movements, and classify whether a credit card transaction is likely to be fraudulent. In contrast, any attempt at making small talk with Amazon's Alexa or Apple's Siri is doomed. Indeed, humanity's most basic and essential capacities—including a convivial conversation or the crafting of an original creation—can leave even the most sophisticated supercomputers in digital spasms.

This all changed in 2014 when Ian Goodfellow, then a PhD student at the University of Montreal, invented Generative Adversarial Networks (GANs). This technique has enabled computers to generate realistic data by using not one, but two, separate neural networks. GANs were not the first computer program used to generate data, but their results and versatility set them apart from all the rest. GANs have achieved remarkable results that had long been considered virtually impossible for artificial systems, such as the ability to generate fake images with real-world-like quality, turn a scribble into a photograph-like image, or turn video footage of a horse into a running zebra—all without the need for vast troves of painstakingly labeled training data.

A telling example of how far machine data generation has been able to advance thanks to GANs is the synthesis of human faces, illustrated in figure 1.1. As recently as

| 2014 | 2015 | 2016 | 2017 |

Figure 1.1 Progress in human face generation
(Source: "The Malicious Use of Artificial Intelligence: Forecasting, Prevention, and Mitigation," by Miles Brundage et al., 2018, https://arxiv.org/abs/1802.07228.)

---

[1] See "Surpassing Human-Level Face Verification Performance on LFW with GaussianFace," by Chaochao Lu and Xiaoou Tang, 2014, https://arXiv.org/abs/1404.3840. See also the *New York Times* article "Google's AlphaGo Defeats Chinese Go Master in Win for A.I.," by Paul Mozur, 2017, http://mng.bz/07WJ.

2014, when GANs were invented, the best that machines could produce was a blurred countenance—and even that was celebrated as a groundbreaking success. By 2017, just three years later, advances in GANs enabled computers to synthesize fake faces whose quality rivals high-resolution portrait photographs. In this book, we look under the hood of the algorithm that made all this possible.

1.1 What are Generative Adversarial Networks?

Generative Adversarial Networks (GANs) are a class of machine learning techniques that consist of two simultaneously trained models: one (the *Generator*) trained to generate fake data, and the other (the *Discriminator*) trained to discern the fake data from real examples.

The word *generative* indicates the overall purpose of the model: creating new data. The data that a GAN will learn to generate depends on the choice of the training set. For example, if we want a GAN to synthesize images that look like Leonardo da Vinci's, we would use a training dataset of da Vinci's artwork.

The term *adversarial* points to the game-like, competitive dynamic between the two models that constitute the GAN framework: the Generator and the Discriminator. The Generator's goal is to create examples that are indistinguishable from the real data in the training set. In our example, this means producing paintings that look just like da Vinci's. The Discriminator's objective is to distinguish the fake examples produced by the Generator from the real examples coming from the training dataset. In our example, the Discriminator plays the role of an art expert assessing the authenticity of paintings believed to be da Vinci's. The two networks are continually trying to outwit each other: the better the Generator gets at creating convincing data, the better the Discriminator needs to be at distinguishing real examples from the fake ones.

Finally, the word *networks* indicates the class of machine learning models most commonly used to represent the Generator and the Discriminator: neural networks. Depending on the complexity of the GAN implementation, these can range from simple feed-forward neural networks (as you'll see in chapter 3) to convolutional neural networks (as you'll see in chapter 4) or even more complex variants, such as the U-Net (as you'll see in chapter 9).

1.2 How do GANs work?

The mathematics underpinning GANs are complex (as you'll explore in later chapters, especially chapters 3 and 5); fortunately, many real-world analogies can make GANs easier to understand. Previously, we discussed the example of an art forger (the Generator) trying to fool an art expert (the Discriminator). The more convincing the fake paintings the forger makes, the better the art expert must be at determining their authenticity. This is true in the reverse situation as well: the better the art expert is at telling whether a particular painting is genuine, the more the forger must improve to avoid being caught red-handed.

Another metaphor often used to describe GANs—one that Ian Goodfellow himself likes to use—is that of a criminal (the Generator) who forges money, and a detective (the Discriminator) who tries to catch him. The more authentic-looking the counterfeit bills become, the better the detective must be at detecting them, and vice versa.

In more technical terms, the Generator's goal is to produce examples that capture the characteristics of the training dataset, so much so that the samples it generates look indistinguishable from the training data. The Generator can be thought of as an object recognition model in reverse. *Object recognition algorithms* learn the patterns in images to discern an image's content. Instead of recognizing the patterns, the Generator learns to create them essentially from scratch; indeed, the input into the Generator is often no more than a vector of random numbers.

The Generator learns through the feedback it receives from the Discriminator's classifications. The Discriminator's goal is to determine whether a particular example is real (coming from the training dataset) or fake (created by the Generator). Accordingly, each time the Discriminator is fooled into classifying a fake image as real, the Generator knows it did something well. Conversely, each time the Discriminator correctly rejects a Generator-produced image as fake, the Generator receives the feedback that it needs to improve.

The Discriminator continues to improve as well. Like any classifier, it learns from how far its predictions are from the true labels (real or fake). So, as the Generator gets better at producing realistic-looking data, the Discriminator gets better at telling fake data from the real, and both networks continue to improve simultaneously.

Table 1.1 summarizes the key takeaways about the two GAN subnetworks.

Table 1.1   Generator and Discriminator subnetworks

	Generator	Discriminator
Input	A vector of random numbers	The Discriminator receives input from two sources: ■ Real examples coming from the training dataset ■ Fake examples coming from the Generator
Output	Fake examples that strive to be as convincing as possible	Predicted probability that the input example is real
Goal	Generate fake data that is indistinguishable from members of the training dataset	Distinguish between the fake examples coming from the Generator and the real examples coming from the training dataset

1.3   GANs in action

Now that you have a high-level understanding of GANs and their constituent networks, let's take a closer look at the system in action. Imagine that our goal is to teach a GAN to produce realistic-looking handwritten digits. (You'll learn to implement such a model in chapter 3 and expand on it in chapter 4.) Figure 1.2 illustrates the core GAN architecture.

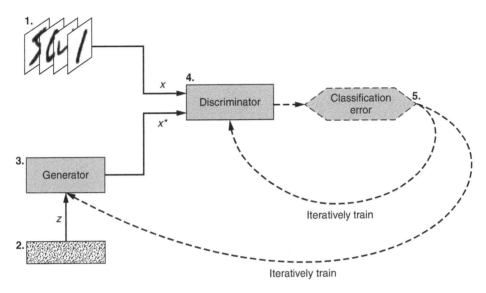

Figure 1.2 The two GAN subnetworks, their inputs and outputs, and their interactions

Let's walk through the details of the diagram:

1 *Training dataset*—The dataset of real examples that we want the Generator to learn to emulate with near-perfect quality. In this case, the dataset consists of images of handwritten digits. This dataset serves as input (x) to the Discriminator network.

2 *Random noise vector*—The raw input (z) to the Generator network. This input is a vector of random numbers that the Generator uses as a starting point for synthesizing fake examples.

3 *Generator network*—The Generator takes in a vector of random numbers (z) as input and outputs fake examples (x^*). Its goal is to make the fake examples it produces indistinguishable from the real examples in the training dataset.

4 *Discriminator network*—The Discriminator takes as input either a real example (x) coming from the training set or a fake example (x^*) produced by the Generator. For each example, the Discriminator determines and outputs the probability of whether the example is real.

5 *Iterative training/tuning*—For each of the Discriminator's predictions, we determine how good it is—much as we would for a regular classifier—and use the results to iteratively tune the Discriminator and the Generator networks through backpropagation:

– The Discriminator's weights and biases are updated to maximize its classification accuracy (maximizing the probability of correct prediction: x as real and x^* as fake).
– The Generator's weights and biases are updated to maximize the probability that the Discriminator misclassifies x^* as real.

1.3.1   GAN training

Learning about the purpose of the various GAN components may feel like looking at a snapshot of an engine: it cannot be understood fully until we see it in motion. That's what this section is all about. First, we present the GAN training algorithm; then, we illustrate the training process so you can see the architecture diagram in action.

GAN training algorithm

For each training iteration *do*

1 Train the Discriminator:

   a Take a random real example x from the training dataset.
   b Get a new random noise vector z and, using the Generator network, synthesize a fake example x^*.
   c Use the Discriminator network to classify x and x^*.
   d Compute the classification errors and backpropagate the total error to update the Discriminator's trainable parameters, seeking to *minimize* the classification errors.

2 Train the Generator:

   a Get a new random noise vector z and, using the Generator network, synthesize a fake example x^*.
   b Use the Discriminator network to classify x^*.
   c Compute the classification error and backpropagate the error to update the Generator's trainable parameters, seeking to *maximize* the Discriminator's error.

End for

GAN TRAINING VISUALIZED

Figure 1.3 illustrates the GAN training algorithm. The letters in the diagram refer to the list of steps in the GAN training algorithm.

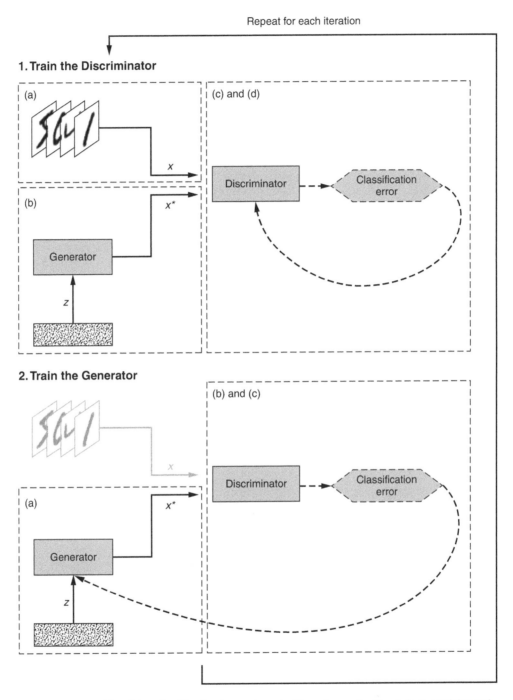

Figure 1.3 The GAN training algorithm has two main parts. These two parts, Discriminator training and Generator training, depict the same GAN network at different time snapshots in the corresponding stages of the training process.

Subdiagram legend

1 Train the Discriminator:

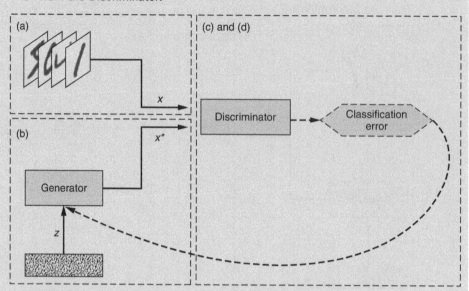

a Take a random real example *x* from the training dataset.

b Get a new random noise vector *z* and, using the Generator network, synthesize a fake example *x**.

c Use the Discriminator network to classify *x* and *x**.

d Compute the classification errors and backpropagate the total error to update the Discriminator weights and biases, seeking to *minimize* the classification errors.

2 Train the Generator:

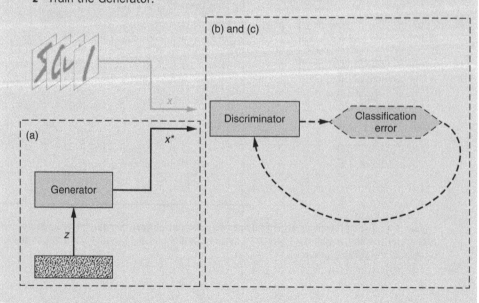

a   Get a new random noise vector *z* and, using the Generator network, synthesize a fake example *x**.

b   Use the Discriminator network to classify *x**.

c   Compute the classification error and backpropagate the error to update the Generator weights and biases, seeking to *maximize* the Discriminator's error.

1.3.2 Reaching equilibrium

You may wonder when the GAN training loop is meant to stop. More precisely, how do we know when a GAN is fully trained so that we can determine the appropriate number of training iterations? With a regular neural network, we usually have a clear objective to achieve and measure. For example, when training a classifier, we measure the classification error on the training and validation sets, and we stop the process when the validation error starts getting worse (to avoid overfitting). In a GAN, the two networks have competing objectives: when one network gets better, the other gets worse. How do we determine when to stop?

Those familiar with game theory may recognize this setup as a *zero-sum game*—a situation in which one player's gains equal the other player's losses. When one player improves by a certain amount, the other player worsens by the same amount. All zero-sum games have a *Nash equilibrium*, a point at which neither player can improve their situation or payoff by changing their actions.

GAN reaches Nash equilibrium when the following conditions are met:

- The Generator produces fake examples that are indistinguishable from the real data in the training dataset.
- The Discriminator can at best randomly guess whether a particular example is real or fake (that is, make a 50/50 guess whether an example is real).

NOTE   Nash equilibrium is named after the American economist and mathematician John Forbes Nash Jr., whose life story and career were captured in the biography titled *A Beautiful Mind* and inspired the eponymous film.

Let us convince you of why this is the case. When each of the fake examples (*x**) is truly indistinguishable from the real examples (*x*) coming from the training dataset, there is nothing the Discriminator can use to tell them apart from one another. Because half of the examples it receives are real and half are fake, the best the Discriminator can do is to flip a coin and classify each example as real or fake with 50% probability.

The Generator is likewise at a point where it has nothing to gain from further tuning. Because the examples it produces are already indistinguishable from the real ones, even a tiny change to the process it uses to turn the random noise vector (*z*) into a fake example (*x**) may give the Discriminator a cue for how to discern the fake example from the real data, making the Generator worse off.

With equilibrium achieved, GAN is said to have *converged*. Here is when it gets tricky. In practice, it is nearly impossible to find the Nash equilibrium for GANs because of the immense complexities involved in reaching convergence in nonconvex games (more on convergence in later chapters, particularly chapter 5). Indeed, GAN convergence remains one of the most important open questions in GAN research.

Fortunately, this has not impeded GAN research or the many innovative applications of generative adversarial learning. Even in the absence of rigorous mathematical guarantees, GANs have achieved remarkable empirical results. This book covers a selection of the most impactful ones, and the following section previews some of them.

1.4   Why study GANs?

Since their invention, GANs have been hailed by academics and industry experts as one of the most consequential innovations in deep learning. Yann LeCun, the director of AI research at Facebook, went so far as to say that GANs and their variations are "the coolest idea in deep learning in the last 20 years."[2]

The excitement is well justified. Unlike other advancements in machine learning that may be household names among researchers but would elicit no more than a quizzical look from anyone else, GANs have captured the imagination of researchers and the wider public alike. They have been covered by the *New York Times*, the BBC, *Scientific American*, and many other prominent media outlets. Indeed, it was one of those exciting GAN results that probably drove you to buy this book in the first place. (Right?)

Perhaps most notable is the capacity of GANs to create hyperrealistic imagery. None of the faces in figure 1.4 belongs to a real human; they are all fake, showcasing GANs' ability to synthesize images with photorealistic quality. The faces were produced using Progressive GANs, a technique covered in chapter 6.

Another remarkable GAN achievement is *image-to-image translation*. Similarly to the way a sentence can be translated from, say, Chinese to Spanish, GANs can translate an image from one domain to another. As shown in figure 1.5, GANs can turn an image of a horse into an image of zebra (and back!), and a photo into a Monet-like painting—all with virtually no supervision and no labels whatsoever. The GAN variant that made this possible is called *CycleGAN*; you'll learn all about it in chapter 9.

The more practically minded GAN use cases are just as fascinating. The online giant Amazon is experimenting with harnessing GANs for fashion recommendations: by analyzing countless outfits, the system learns to produce new items matching any given style.[3] In medical research, GANs are used to augment datasets with synthetic

---

[2] See "Google's Dueling Neural Networks Spar to Get Smarter," by Cade Metz, *Wired*, 2017, http://mng.bz/ KE1X.

[3] See "Amazon Has Developed an AI Fashion Designer," by Will Knight, *MIT Technology Review*, 2017, http:// mng.bz/9wOj.

Figure 1.4　These photorealistic but fake human faces were synthesized by a Progressive GAN trained on high-resolution portrait photos of celebrities.
(Source: "Progressive Growing of GANs for Improved Quality, Stability, and Variation," by Tero Karras et al., 2017, https://arxiv.org/abs/1710.10196.)

Figure 1.5　By using a GAN variant called CycleGAN, we can turn a Monet painting into a photograph or turn an image of a zebra into a depiction of a horse, and vice versa.
(Source: See "Unpaired Image-to-Image Translation Using Cycle-Consistent Adversarial Networks," by Jun-Yan Zhu et al., 2017, https://arxiv.org/abs/1703.10593.)

examples to improve diagnostic accuracy.[4] In chapter 11—after you've mastered the ins and outs of training GANs and their variants—you'll explore both of these applications in detail.

GANs are also seen as an important stepping stone toward achieving *artificial general intelligence*,[5] an artificial system capable of matching human cognitive capacity to acquire expertise in virtually any domain—from motor skills involved in walking, to language, to creative skills needed to compose sonnets.

But with the ability to generate new data and imagery, GANs also have the capacity to be dangerous. Much has been discussed about the spread and dangers of fake news, but the potential of GANs to create credible fake footage is disturbing. At the end of an aptly titled 2018 piece about GANs—"How an A.I. 'Cat-and-Mouse Game' Generates Believable Fake Photos"—the *New York Times* journalists Cade Metz and Keith Collins discuss the worrying prospect of GANs being exploited to create and spread convincing misinformation, including fake video footage of statements by world leaders. Martin Giles, the San Francisco bureau chief of *MIT Technology Review*, echoes their concern and mentions another potential risk in his 2018 article "The GANfather: The Man Who's Given Machines the Gift of Imagination": in the hands of skilled hackers, GANs can be used to intuit and exploit system vulnerabilities at an unprecedented scale. These concerns are what motivated us to discuss the ethical considerations of GANs in chapter 12.

GANs can do much good for the world, but all technological innovations have misuses. Here the philosophy has to be one of awareness: because it is impossible to "uninvent" a technique, it is crucial to make sure people like you are aware of this technique's rapid emergence and its substantial potential.

In this book, we are only able to scratch the surface of what is possible with GANs. However, we hope that this book will provide you with the necessary theoretical knowledge and practical skills to continue exploring any facet of this field that you find most interesting.

So, without further ado, let's dive in!

---

[4] See "Synthetic Data Augmentation Using GAN for Improved Liver Lesion Classification," by Maayan Frid-Adar et al., 2018, https://arxiv.org/abs/1801.02385.

[5] See "OpenAI Founder: Short-Term AGI Is a Serious Possibility," by Tony Peng, Synced, 2018, http://mng.bz/ j5Oa. See also "A Path to Unsupervised Learning Through Adversarial Networks," by Soumith Chintala, f Code, 2016, http://mng.bz/WOag.

Summary

- GANs are a deep learning technique that uses a competitive dynamic between two neural networks to synthesize realistic data samples, such as fake photorealistic imagery. The two networks that constitute a GAN are as follows:
  - The Generator, whose goal is to fool the Discriminator by producing data indistinguishable from the training dataset
  - The Discriminator, whose goal is to correctly distinguish between real data coming from the training dataset and the fake data produced by the Generator
- GANs have extensive applications across many different sectors, such as fashion, medicine, and cybersecurity.

Intro to generative modeling with autoencoders

2

This chapter covers

- Encoding data into a latent space (dimensionality reduction) and subsequent dimensionality expansion
- Understanding the challenges of generative modeling in the context of a variational autoencoder
- Generating handwritten digits by using Keras and autoencoders
- Understanding the limitations of autoencoders and motivations for GANs

I dedicate this chapter to my grandmother, Aurelie Langrova, who passed away as we were finishing the work on it. She will be missed dearly.

—Jakub

You might be wondering why we chose to include this chapter in the book. There are three core reasons:

- *Generative models are a new area for most.*

  Most people who come across machine learning typically become exposed to classification tasks in machine learning first and more extensively—perhaps because they tend to be more straightforward. Generative modeling, through which we are trying to produce a new example that looks realistic, is therefore less understood. So we decided to include a chapter that covers generative modeling in an easier setting before delving into GANs, especially given the wealth of resources and research on autoencoders—GANs' closest precursor. But if you want to dive straight into the new and exciting bits, feel free to skip this chapter.

- *Generative models are very challenging.*

  Because generative modeling has been underrepresented, most people are unaware of what a typical model looks like and its challenges. Although autoencoders are in many ways closer to the models that are most commonly taught (such as an explicit objective function, as we will discuss later), they still present many challenges that GANs face—such as how difficult it is to evaluate sample quality. Chapter 5 covers this in more depth.

- *Generative models are an important part of the literature today.*

  Autoencoders themselves have their own uses, as we discuss in this chapter. They are also still an active area of research, even state of the art in some areas, and are used explicitly by many GAN architectures. Other GAN architectures use them as implicit inspiration or a mental model—such as CycleGAN, covered in chapter 9.

2.1 Introduction to generative modeling

You should be familiar with how deep learning takes raw pixels and turns them into, for example, class predictions. For example, we can take three matrixes that contain pixels of an image (one for each color channel) and pass them through a system of transformations to get a single number at the end. But what if we want to go in the opposite direction?

We start with a prescription of what we want to produce and get the image at the other end of the transformations. That is *generative modeling* in its simplest, most informal form; we add more depth throughout the book.

A bit more formally, we take a certain prescription (z)—for this simple case, let's say it is a number between 0 and 9—and try to arrive at a generated sample (x^*). Ideally, this x^* would look as realistic as another real sample, x. The prescription, z, lives in a *latent space* and serves as an inspiration so that we do not always get the same output, x^*. This latent space is a learned representation—hopefully meaningful to people in ways we think of it ("disentangled"). Different models will learn a different latent representation of the same data.

The random noise vector we saw in chapter 1 is often referred to as a *sample from the latent space*. Latent space is a simpler, hidden representation of a data point. In our context, it is denoted by z, and *simpler* just means lower-dimensional—for example, a vector or array of 100 numbers rather than the 768 that is the dimensionality of the samples we will use. In many ways, a good latent representation of a data point will allow you to group things that are similar in this space. We will get to what *latent* means in the context of an autoencoder in figure 2.3 and show you how this affects our generated samples in figures 2.6 and 2.7, but before we can do that, we'll describe how autoencoders function.

2.2   *How do autoencoders function on a high level?*

As their name suggests, *autoencoders* help us encode data, well, automatically. Autoencoders are composed of two parts: encoder and decoder. For the purposes of this explanation, let's consider one use case: compression.

Imagine that you are writing a letter to your grandparents about your career as a machine learning engineer. You have only one page to explain everything that you do so that they understand, given their knowledge and beliefs about the world.

Now imagine that your grandparents suffer from acute amnesia and do not remember what you do at all. This already feels a lot harder, doesn't it? This may be because now you have to explain *all the terminology*. For example, they can still read and understand basic things in your letter, such as your description of what your cat did, but the notion of a machine learning engineer might be alien to them. In other words, their learned transformations from latent space z into $x*$ has been (almost) randomly initialized. You have to first retrain these mental structures in their heads before you can explain. You have to train their autoencoder by passing in concepts x and seeing whether they manage to reproduce them ($x*$) back to you in a meaningful way. That way, you can measure their error, called the *reconstruction loss* ($\| x - x* \|$).

Implicitly, we compress data—or information—every day so we do not spend ages explaining known concepts. Human communication is full of autoencoders, but they are context-dependent: what we explain to our grandparents, we do not have to explain to our engineering colleagues, such as what a machine learning model is. So some human latent spaces are more appropriate than others, depending on the context. We can just jump to the succinct representation that their autoencoder will already understand.

We can compress, because it is useful to simplify certain recurring concepts into abstractions that we have agreed on—for example, a job title. Autoencoders can systematically and automatically uncover these information-efficient patterns, define them, and use them as shortcuts to increase the information throughput. As a result, we need to transmit only the z, which is typically much lower-dimensional, thereby saving us bandwidth.

From an information theory point of view, you are trying to pass as much information through the "information bottleneck" (your letter or spoken communication) as possible without sacrificing too much of the understanding. You can almost imagine this as a secret shortcut that only you and your family understand but that has been optimized for the topics you frequently discussed.[1] For simplicity and to focus on compression, we chose to ignore the fact that words are an explicit model, although most words also have tremendous context-dependent complexity behind them.

> **DEFINITION** The *latent space* is the hidden representation of the data. Rather than expressing words or images (for example, *machine learning engineer* in our example, or JPEG codec for images) in their uncompressed versions, an autoencoder compresses and clusters them based on its understanding of the data.

2.3 What are autoencoders to GANs?

One of the key distinctions with autoencoders is that we end-to-end train the whole network with one loss function, whereas GANs have distinct loss functions for the Generator and the Discriminator. Let's now look at the context in which autoencoders sit compared to GANs. As you can see in figure 2.1, both are generative models that are subsets of artificial intelligence (AI) and machine learning (ML). In the case

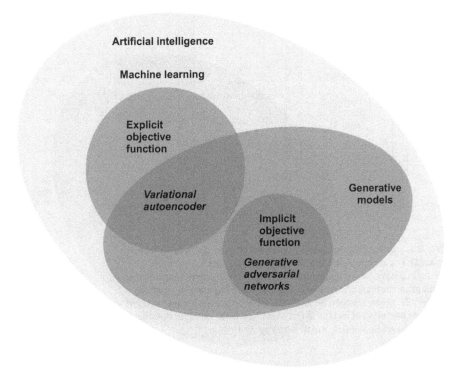

Figure 2.1 Placing GANs and autoencoders in the AI landscape. Different researchers might draw this differently, but we will leave this argument to academics.

---

[1] In fact, the Rothschilds, a famous European financier family, did this in their letters, which is why they were so successful in finance.

of autoencoders (or their variational alternative, VAEs), we have an explicitly written function that we are trying to optimize (a cost function); but in the case of GANs (as you will learn), we do not have an explicit metric as simple as mean squared error, accuracy, or area under the ROC curve to optimize.[2] GANs instead have two competing objectives that cannot be written in one function.

2.4   *What is an autoencoder made of?*

As we look at the structure of an autoencoder, we'll use images as an example, but this structure also applies in other cases (for instance, language, as in our example about the letter to your grandparents). Like many advancements in machine learning, the high-level idea of autoencoders is intuitive and follows these simple steps, illustrated in figure 2.2:

1 Encoder network: We take a representation x (for example, an image) and then reduce the dimension from y to z by using a learned encoder (typically, a one- or many-layer neural network).

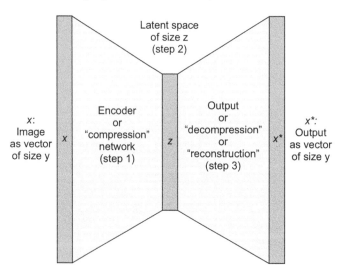

Figure 2.2   Using an autoencoder in our letter example follows these steps: (1) You compress all the things you know about a machine learning engineer, and then (2) compose that to the latent space (letter to your grandmother). When she, using her understanding of words as a decoder (3), reconstructs a (lossy) version of what that means, you get out a representation of an idea in the same space (in your grandmother's head) as the original input, which was your thoughts.

---

[2] A *cost function* (also known as a *loss function* or *objective function*) is what we are trying to optimize/minimize for. In statistics, for example, this would be the root mean squared error (RMSE). The *root mean squared error (RMSE)* is a mathematical function that gives an error by taking the root of the square of the difference between the true value of an example and our prediction.

In statistics, we typically want to evaluate a classifier across several combinations of false positives and negatives. The *area under the curve (AUC)* helps us do that. For more details, Wikipedia has an excellent explanation, as this concept is beyond the scope of this book.

2 Latent space (z): As we train, here we try to establish the latent space to have some meaning. Latent space is typically a representation of a smaller dimension and acts as an intermediate step. In this representation of our data, the autoencoder is trying to "organize its thoughts."

3 Decoder network: We reconstruct the original object into the original dimension by using the decoder. This is typically done by a neural network that is a mirror image of the encoder. This is the step from z to x^*. We apply the reverse process of the encoding to get back, for example, a 784 pixel-values long reconstructed vector (of a 28×28 image) from the 256 pixel-values long vector of the latent space.

Here's an example of autoencoder training:

1 We take images x and feed them through the autoencoder.

2 We get out x^*, reconstruction of the images.

3 We measure the reconstruction loss—the difference between x and x^*.

   – This is done using a distance (for example, mean average error) between the pixels of x and x^*.

   – This gives us an explicit objective function ($\| x - x^* \|$) to optimize via a version of gradient descent.

So we are trying to find the parameters of the encoder and the decoder that would minimize the reconstruction loss that we update by using gradient descent.

And that's it! We're done. Now you may be wondering why this is useful or important. You'd be surprised!

2.5 *Usage of autoencoders*

Despite their simplicity, there are many reasons to care about autoencoders:

- First of all, we get compression for free! This is because the intermediate step (2) from figure 2.2 becomes an intelligently reduced image or object at the dimensionality of the latent space. Note that in theory, this can be orders of magnitude less than the original input. It obviously is not lossless, but we are free to use this side effect, if we wish.

- Still using the latent space, we can think of many practical applications, such as a *one-class classifier* (an anomaly-detection algorithm), where we can see the items in a reduced, more quickly searchable latent space to check for similarity with the target class. This can work in search (information retrieval) or anomaly-detection settings (comparing closeness in the latent space).

- Another use case is data denoising or colorization of black-and-white images.[3] For example, if we have an old photo or video or a very noisy one—say, World

---

[3] For more information on coloring black-and-white images, see Emil Wallner's "Coloring Greyscale Images," on GitHub (http://mng.bz/6jWy).

War II images—we can make them less noisy and add color back in. Hence the similarity to GANs, which also tend to excel at these types of applications.

- Some GANs architectures—such as BEGAN[4]—use autoencoders as part of their architecture to help them stabilize their training, which is critically important, as you will discover later.

- Training of these autoencoders does not require labeled data. We will get to this and why unsupervised learning is so important in the next section. This makes our lives a lot easier, because it is only self-training and does not require us to look for labels.

- Last, but definitely not least, we can use autoencoders to generate new images. Autoencoders have been applied to anything from digits to faces to bedrooms, but usually the higher the resolution of the image, the worse the performance, as the output tends to look blurry. But for the MNIST dataset—as you will discover later—and other low-resolution images, autoencoders work great; you'll see what the code looks like in just a moment!

DEFINITION   The *Modified National Institute of Standards and Technology (MNIST) database* is a dataset of handwritten digits. Wikipedia has a great overview of this extremely popular dataset used in computer vision literature.

So all of these things can be done just because we found a new representation of the data we already had. This representation is useful because it brings out the core information, which is natively compressed, but it's also easier to manipulate or generate new data based on the latent representation!

2.6   *Unsupervised learning*

In the previous chapter, we already talked about unsupervised learning without using the term. In this section, we'll take a closer look.

DEFINITION   *Unsupervised learning* is a type of machine learning in which we learn from the data itself without additional labels as to what this data means. Clustering, for example, is unsupervised—because we are just trying to discover the underlying structure of the data; but anomaly detection is usually supervised, as we need human-labeled anomalies.

In this chapter, you will learn why unsupervised machine learning is different: we can use any data without having to label it for a *specific* purpose. We can throw in all images from the internet without having to annotate the data about the purpose of each sample, for *each representation* that we might care about. For example: Is there a dog in this picture? A car?

In supervised learning, on the other hand, if you don't have labels for that exact task, (almost) all of your labels could be unusable. If you're trying to make a classifier

---

[4] BEGAN is an acronym for Boundary Equilibrium Generative Adversarial Networks. This interesting GAN architecture was one of the first to use an autoencoder as part of the setup.

that would classify cars from Google Street View, but you do not have labels of those images for animals as well, training a classifier that would classify animals with the same dataset would be basically impossible. Even if the animals frequently feature in these samples, you would need to go back and ask your labelers to relabel the same Google Street View dataset for animals.

In essence, we need to think about the application of the data before we know the use case, which is difficult! But for a lot of compression-type tasks, you always have labeled data: your data. Some researchers, such as François Chollet (research scientist at Google and author of Keras), call this type of machine learning *self-supervised*. For much of this book, our only labels will be either the examples themselves or any other examples from the dataset.

Since our training data also acts as our labels, training many of these algorithms becomes far easier from one crucial perspective: we now have lots more data to work with, and we do not need to wait weeks and pay millions for enough labeled data.

2.6.1 *New take on an old idea*

Autoencoders themselves are a fairly old idea—at least when you look at the age of machine learning as a field. But seeing as everyone is working on *something* deep today, it should surprise exactly no one that people have successfully applied deep learning as part of both encoder and decoder.

An autoencoder is composed of two neural networks: an encoder and a decoder. In our case, both have activation functions,[5] and we will be using just one intermediate layer for each. This means we have two weight matrices in each network—one from input to intermediate and then one from intermediate to latent. Then again, we have one from latent to different intermediate and then one from intermediate to output. If we had just one weight matrix in each, our procedure would resemble a well-established analytical technique called *principal component analysis (PCA)*. If you have a background in linear algebra, you should be in broadly familiar territory.

> **NOTE** Some technical differences exist in how the solutions are learned—for example, PCA is numerically deterministic, whereas autoencoders are typically trained with a stochastic optimizer. There are also differences in the final form of the solution. But we're not going to give you a lecture about how one of them gives you an orthonormal basis and how fundamentally they still span the same vector space—though if you happen to know what that means, then more power to you.

---

[5] We feed any output from an earlier layer's computation through an *activation function* before passing it to the next one. Frequently, people pick a rectified linear unit (ReLU)—which is defined as *max(0, x)*. We don't go into too much depth on activation functions, because they alone could be a subject of a lengthy blog post.

2.6.2 *Generation using an autoencoder*

At the beginning of this chapter, we said that autoencoders can be used to generate data. Some of you who are really keen may have been thinking about the use of the latent space and whether it can be repurposed for something else . . . and it totally can! (If you got this right, you can give yourself an official, approved self-five!)

But you probably didn't buy this book to look silly, so let's get to the point. If we go back to the example with your grandparents and apply a slightly different lens, using autoencoders as a generative model might start to make sense. For example, imagine that your idea of what a *job* is becomes the input to the decoder network. Think of the word *job* written down on the piece of paper as the latent space input, and the idea of a job in your grandparents' head as the output.

In this case, we see that the latent space encoding (a written word, combined with your grandparents' ability to read and understand concepts) becomes a generative model that generates an idea in their heads. The written letter acts as an inspiration or some sort of latent vector, and the output—the ideas—are in the same high-dimensional space as the original input. Your grandparents' ideas are as complex—albeit slightly different—as yours.

Now let's switch back to the domain of images. We train our autoencoder on a set of images. So we tune the parameters of the encoder and the decoder to find appropriate parameters for the two networks. We also get a sense for the way the examples are represented in the latent space. For generation, we cut off the encoder part and use only the latent space and the decoder. Figure 2.3 shows a schematic of the generation process.

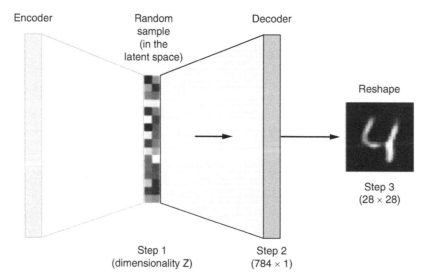

Figure 2.3 Because we know from training where our examples get placed in the latent space, we can easily generate examples similar to the ones that the model has seen. Even if not, we can easily iterate or grid-search through the latent space to determine the kinds of representations that our model can generate.

(Image adapted from Mat Leonard's simple autoencoder project on GitHub, http://mng.bz/oNXM.)

2.6.3 *Variational autoencoder*

You may be wondering: what is the difference between a variational autoencoder and a "regular" one? It all has to do with the magical latent space. In the case of a variational autoencoder, we choose to represent the latent space as a distribution with a learned mean and standard deviation rather than just a set of numbers. Typically, we choose multivariate Gaussian, but exactly what that is or why we choose this distribution over another is not that important right now. If you would like a refresher on what that might look like, take a look at figure 2.5.

As the more statistically inclined of you may have realized at this point, the variational autoencoder is a technique based on Bayesian machine learning. In practice, this means we have to learn the distribution, which adds further constraints. In other words, frequentist autoencoders would try to learn the latent space as an array of numbers, but Bayesian—for example, variational—autoencoders would try to find the right parameters defining a distribution.

We then sample from the latent distribution and get some numbers. We feed these numbers through the decoder. We get back an example that looks like something from the original dataset, except it has been newly created by the model. Ta-da!

2.7 *Code is life*

In this book, we use a popular, deep learning, high-level API called *Keras*. We highly suggest that you familiarize yourself with it. If you are not already comfortable with it, plenty of good free resources are available online, including outlets such as Towards Data Science (http://towardsdatascience.com), where we frequently contribute. If you want to learn more about Keras from a book, several good resources exist, including another great Manning book, *Deep Learning with Python* by François Chollet—the author and creator of Keras.

Keras is a high-level API for several deep learning frameworks—TensorFlow, Microsoft Cognitive Toolkit (CNTK), and Theano. It is easy to use and allows you to work on a much higher level of abstraction, so you can focus on the concepts rather than recording every standard block of multiplication, biasing, activation, and then pooling[6] or having to worry about variable scopes too much.

To show the true power of Keras and how it simplifies the process of writing a neural network, we will look at the variational autoencoder example in its simplest form.[7] In this tutorial, we use the *functional API* that Keras has for a more function-oriented approach to writing deep learning code, but we will show you the sequential API (the other way) in later tutorials as things get more difficult.

The goal of this exercise is to generate handwritten digits based on the latent space. We are going to create an object, generator or decoder, that can use the

---

[6] A *pooling block* is an operation on a layer that allows us to pool several inputs into fewer—for example, having a matrix of four numbers and getting the maximum value as a single number. This is a common operation in computer vision to reduce complexity.

[7] This example was highly modified by the authors for simplicity, from http://mng.bz/nQ4K.

predict() method to generate new examples of handwritten digits, given an input seed, which is just the latent space vector. And of course, we have to use MNIST because we wouldn't want anyone getting any ideas that there could be other datasets out there; see figure 2.4.

Figure 2.4   How computer vision researchers think. Enough said.
(Source: Artificial Intelligence Memes for Artificial Intelligence Teens on Facebook, http://mng.bz/vNjM.)

In our code, we first have to import all dependencies, as shown in the following listing. For reference, this code was checked with Keras as late as 2.2.4 and TensorFlow as late as 1.12.0.

Listing 2.1   Standard imports

```
from keras.layers import Input, Dense, Lambda
from keras.models import Model
from keras import backend as K
from keras import objectives
from keras.datasets import mnist
import numpy as np
```

The next step is to set global variables and hyperparameters, as shown in listing 2.2. They should all be familiar: the original dimensions are 28 × 28, which is the standard size. We then flatten the images from the MNIST dataset, to get a vector of 784 (28 × 28) dimensions. And we will also have a single intermediate layer of, say, 256 nodes. But do experiment with other sizes; that's why it's a hyperparameter!

Listing 2.2   Setting hyperparameters

```
batch_size = 100
original_dim = 28*28        ◁── Height × width of
                                 MNIST image
```

```
latent_dim = 2
intermediate_dim = 256
nb_epoch = 5          ⟵┘  Number of epochs
epsilon_std = 1.0
```

In listing 2.3, we start constructing the encoder. To achieve this, we use the functional API from Keras.

NOTE The *functional API* uses lambda functions in Python to return constructors for another function, which takes another input, producing the final result.

The short version is that we will simply declare each layer, mentioning the previous input as a *second group of arguments* after the regular arguments. For example, the layer h takes x as an input. At the end, when we compile the model and indicate where it starts (*x*) and where it ends ([z_mean, z_log_var and z]), Keras will understand how the starting input and the final list output are linked together. Remember from the diagrams that z is our latent space, which in this case is a normal distribution defined by mean and variance. Let's now define the encoder.[8]

Listing 2.3 Creating the encoder

Defines the mean of the latent space   **Input to our encoder**   **Intermediate layer**

```
x = Input(shape=(original_dim,), name="input")  ⟵
h = Dense(intermediate_dim, activation='relu', name="encoding")(x)  ⟵
z_mean = Dense(latent_dim, name="mean")(h)
z_log_var = Dense(latent_dim, name="log-variance")(h)          ⟵  Defines the
z = Lambda(sampling, output_shape=(latent_dim,))([z_mean, z_log_var])   log variance
encoder = Model(x, [z_mean, z_log_var, z], name="encoder")  ⟵       of the latent
                                                                     space
```

Note that output_shape isn't necessary with the TensorFlow backend.   **Defines the encoder as a Keras model**

Now comes the tricky part, where we sample from the latent space and then feed this information through to the decoder. But think for a bit how z_mean and z_log_var are connected: they are both connected to h with a dense layer of two nodes, which are the defining characteristics of a normal distribution: mean and variance. The preceding sampling function is implemented as shown in the following listing.

Listing 2.4 Creating the sampling helper function

```
def sampling(args):
    z_mean, z_log_var = args
    epsilon = K.random_normal(shape=(batch_size, latent_dim), mean=0.)
    return z_mean + K.exp(z_log_var / 2) * epsilon
```

---

[8] This idea is inspired by Branko Blagojevic in our book forums. Thank you for this suggestion.

In other words, we learn the mean (μ) and the variance (σ). This overall implementation, where we have one z connected through a sampling function as well as z_mean and z_log_var, allows us to both train and subsequently sample efficiently to get some neat-looking figures at the end. During generation, we sample from this distribution according to these learned parameters, and then we feed these values through the decoder to get the output, as you will see in the figures later. For those of you who are a bit rusty on distributions—or probability density functions in this case—we have included several examples of unimodal two-dimensional Gaussians in figure 2.5.

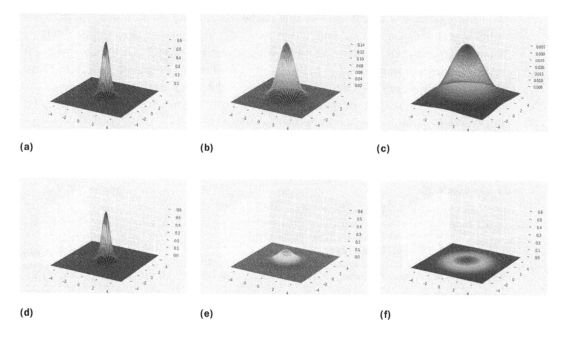

Figure 2.5   As a reminder of what a multivariate (2D) distribution looks like, we've plotted probability density functions of bivariate (2D) Gaussians. They are uncorrelated 2D normal distributions, except with different variances. (a) has a variance of 0.5, (b) of 1, and (c) of 2. (d), (e), and (f) are the exact same distributions as (a), (b), and (c), respectively, but plotted with a set z-axis limit at 0.7. Intuitively, this is just a function that for each point says how likely it is to occur. So (a) and (d) are much more concentrated, whereas (c) and (f) are making it possible for values far away from the origin (0,0) to occur, but each given value is not as likely.

Now that you understand what defines our latent space and what these distributions look like, we'll write the decoder. In this case, we write the layers as variables first so we can reuse them later for the generation.

Listing 2.5   Writing the decoder

Input to the decoder

Takes the latent space to the intermediate dimension

```
input_decoder = Input(shape=(latent_dim,), name="decoder_input")
decoder_h = Dense(intermediate_dim, activation='relu',
name="decoder_h")(input_decoder)
x_decoded = Dense(original_dim, activation='sigmoid',
name="flat_decoded")(decoder_h)
decoder = Model(input_decoder, x_decoded, name="decoder")
```

Gets the mean from the original dimension

Defines the decoder as a Keras model

We can now combine the encoder and the decoder into a single VAE model.

Listing 2.6   Combining the model

```
output_combined = decoder(encoder(x)[2])
vae = Model(x, output_combined)
vae.summary()
```

Grabs the output. Recall that we need to grab the third element, our sampling z.

Links the input and the overall output

Prints out what the overall model looks like

Next, we get to the more familiar parts of machine learning: defining a loss function so our autoencoder can train.

Listing 2.7   Defining our loss function

```
def vae_loss(x, x_decoded_mean, z_log_var, z_mean,
    original_dim=original_dim):
    xent_loss = original_dim * objectives.binary_crossentropy(
        x, x_decoded_mean)
    kl_loss = - 0.5 * K.sum(
        1 + z_log_var - K.square(z_mean) - K.exp(z_log_var),
        axis=-1)
    return xent_loss + kl_loss

vae.compile(optimizer='rmsprop', loss=vae_loss)
```

Finally compiles our model

Here you can see where using binary cross-entropy and KL divergence add together to form overall loss. *KL divergence* measures the difference between distributions; imagine the two blobs from figure 2.5 and then measuring the volume of overlap. Binary cross-entropy is one of the common loss functions for two-class classification: here we simply compare each grayscale pixel value of x to the value in x_decoded_mean, which is the reconstruction we were talking about earlier. If you are still confused about this paragraph after the following definition, chapter 5 provides more details on measuring differences between distributions.

DEFINITION   For those interested in more detail and who are familiar with information theory, the *Kullback–Leibler divergence (KL divergence)*, aka *relative* *entropy*, is the difference between cross-entropy of two distributions and their own entropy. For everyone else, imagine drawing out the two distributions, and wherever they do not overlap will be an area proportional to the KL divergence.

Then we define the model to start at x and end at x_decoded_mean. The model is compiled using RMSprop, but we could use Adam or vanilla stochastic gradient descent (SGD). As with any deep learning system, we are using backpropagated errors to navigate the parameter space. We are always using some type of gradient descent, but in general, people rarely try any other than the three mentioned here: Adam, SGD, or RMSprop.

> **DEFINITION** *Stochastic gradient descent (SGD)* is an optimization technique that allows us to train complex models by figuring out the contribution of any given weight to an error and updating this weight (no update if the prediction is 100% correct). We recommend brushing up on this in, for example, *Deep Learning with Python*.

We train the model by using the standard procedure of train-test split and input normalization.

Listing 2.8 Creating the train/test split

```
(x_train, y_train), (x_test, y_test) = mnist.load_data()

x_train = x_train.astype('float32') / 255.
x_test = x_test.astype('float32') / 255.
x_train = x_train.reshape((len(x_train), np.prod(x_train.shape[1:])))
x_test = x_test.reshape((len(x_test), np.prod(x_test.shape[1:])))
```

We normalize the data and reshape the train set and test set to be one 784-digit-long array per example instead of a 28×28 matrix.

Then we apply the fit function, using shuffling to get a realistic (nonordered) dataset. We also use validation data to monitor progress as we train:

```
vae.fit(x_train, x_train,
        shuffle=True,
        nb_epoch=nb_epoch,
        batch_size=batch_size,
        validation_data=(x_test, x_test),verbose=1)
```

We're done!

The full version of the code provides a fun visualization of the latent space; however, for that, look into the accompanying Jupyter/Google Colaboratory notebook. Now we get to kick back, relax, and watch those pretty progress bars. After we are done, we can even take a look at what the values of the latent space look like on a 2D plane, as shown in figure 2.6.

We can also compute the values at fixed increments of a latent space grid to take a look at the generated output. For example, going from 0.05 to 0.95 in 0.15 linear increments across both dimensions gives us the visualization in figure 2.7. Remember

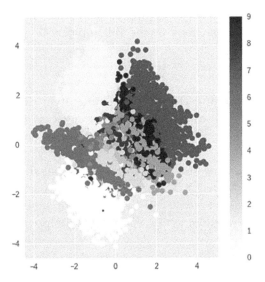

Figure 2.6 2D projection of all the points from the test set into the latent space and their class. In this figure, we display the 2D latent space onto the graph. We then map out the classes of these generated examples and color them accordingly, as per the legend on the right. Here we can see that the classes tend to be neatly grouped together, which tells us that this is a good representation. A color version is available in the GitHub repository for this book.

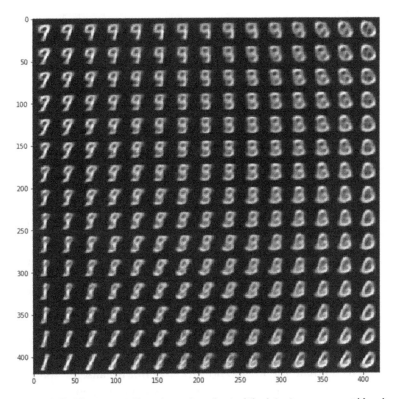

Figure 2.7 We map out the values of a subset of the latent space on a grid and pass each of those latent space values through the generator to produce this figure. This gives us a sense of how much the resulting picture changes as we vary *z*.

that we're using a bivariate Gaussian in this case, giving us two axes to iterate over. Again, for the code for this visualization, look at the full Jupyter/Google Colab notebook.

2.8   *Why did we try aGAN?*

It would seem that the book could almost stop at this point. After all, we have successfully generated images of MNIST, and that will be our test case for several examples. So before you call it quits, let us explain our motivation for the chapters to come.

To appreciate the challenges, imagine that we have a simple one-dimensional bimodal distribution—as pictured in figure 2.8. (As before, just think of it as a simple mathematical function that is bounded between 0 and 1 and that represents probability at any given point. The higher the value of the function, the more points we sampled at that exact point before.)

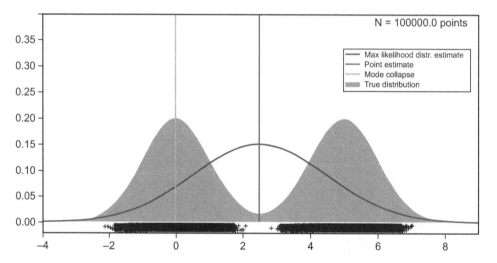

Figure 2.8   Maximum likelihood, point estimates, and true distributions. The gray (theoretical) distribution is bimodal rather than having a single mode. But because we have assumed this, our model is catastrophically wrong. Alternatively, we can get mode collapse, which is worth keeping in mind for chapter 5. This is especially true when we are using flavors of the KL, such as the VAE or early GANs.

Suppose we draw a bunch of samples from this true distribution, but we do not know the underlying model. We are now trying to infer what distribution generated these samples, but for some reason we assume that the true distribution is a simple Gaussian and we just need to estimate the mean and variance. But because we did not specify the model correctly (in this case, we put in wrong assumptions about the modality of these samples), we get into loads of trouble. For example, if we apply a traditional statistical technique called *maximum likelihood estimation* to estimate this distribution as unimodal—in some ways, that is what VAE is trying to do—we get out the wrong estimate. Because we have misspecified the model,[9] it will estimate a normal distribution around the average of the two distributions—called the *point estimate*. Maximum likelihood is a technique that does not know and cannot figure out that there are two distinct distributions. So to minimize the error, it creates a "fat-tailed" normal around the point estimate. Here, it can seem trivial, but always remember, we are trying to specify models in very high-dimensional spaces, which is not easy!

> **DEFINITION** *Bimodal* means having two peaks, or modes. This notion will be useful in chapter 5. In this case, we made the overall distribution to be composed of two normals with means of 0 and 5.

Interestingly, the point estimate will also be wrong and can even live in an area where there is no actual data sampled from the true distribution. When you look at the samples (black crosses), no real samples occur where we have estimated our mean. This is, again, quite troubling. To tie it back to the autoencoder, see how in figure 2.6 we learned 2D normal distribution in the latent space centered around the origin? But what if we had thrown images of celebrity faces into the training data? We would no longer have an easy center to estimate, because the two data distributions would have more modalities than we thought we would have. As a result, even around the center of the distribution, the VAE could produce odd hybrids of the two datasets, because the VAE would try to somehow separate the two datasets.

So far, we have discussed only the hypothetical impact of a statistical mistake. To connect this aspect all the way to autoencoder-generated images, we should think about what our Gaussian latent space z allows us to do. The VAE uses the Gaussian as a way to build representations of the data it sees. But because Gaussians have 99.7% of the probability mass within three standard deviations of the middle, the VAE will also opt for the safe middle. Because VAEs are, in a way, trying to come up directly with the underlying model based on Gaussians, but the reality can be pretty complex, VAEs do not scale up as well as GANs, which can pick up "scenarios."

You can see what happens when your VAE opts for the "safe middle" in figure 2.9. On the CelebA dataset, which features aligned and cropped celebrity faces, the VAE models the consistently present facial features well, such as eyes or mouth, but makes mistakes in the background.

On the other hand, GANs have an implicit and hard-to-analyze understanding of the real data distribution. As you will discover in chapter 5, VAEs live in the directly estimated maximum likelihood model family.

---

[9] See *Pattern Recognition and Machine Learning*, by Christopher Bishop (Springer, 2011).

Figure 2.9   In these images of fake celebrity faces generated by a VAE, the edges are quite blurry and blend into the background. This is because the CelebA dataset has centered and aligned images with consistent features around eyes and mouth, but the backgrounds tend to vary. The VAE picks the safe path and makes the background blurry by choosing a "safe" pixel value, which minimizes the loss, but does not provide good images.
(Source: VAE-TensorFlow by Zhenliang He, GitHub, https://github.com/LynnHo/VAE-Tensorflow.)

This section hopefully made you comfortable with thinking about the distributions of the target data and how these distributional implications manifest themselves in our training process. We will look into these assumptions much more in chapter 10, where the model has assumed how to fill in the distributions and that becomes a problem that adversarial examples will be able to exploit to make our machine learning models fail.

Summary

- Autoencoders on a high level are composed of an encoder, a latent space, and a decoder. An autoencoder is trained by using a common objective function that measures the distance between the reproduced and original data.

- Autoencoders have many applications and can also be used as a generative model. In practice, this tends not to be their primary use because other methods, especially GANs, are better at the generative task.
- We can use Keras (a high-level API for TensorFlow) to write a simple variational autoencoder that produces handwritten digits.
- VAEs have limitations that motivate us to move on to GANs.

Your first GAN:
Generating handwritten digits

This chapter covers

- Exploring the theory behind GANs and adversarial training
- Understanding how GANs differ from conventional neural networks
- Implementing a GAN in Keras, and training it to generate handwritten digits

In this chapter, we explore the foundational theory behind GANs. We introduce the commonly used mathematical notation you may encounter if you choose to dive deeper into this field, perhaps by reading a more theoretically focused publication or even one of the many academic papers on this topic. This chapter also provides background knowledge for the more advanced chapters, particularly chapter 5.

From a strictly practical standpoint, however, you don't have to worry about many of these formalisms—much as you don't need to know how an internal combustion engine works to drive a car. Machine learning libraries such as Keras and TensorFlow abstract the underlying mathematics away from us and neatly package them into importable lines of code.

This will be a recurring theme throughout this book; it is also true for machine learning and deep learning in general. So, if you are someone who prefers to dive straight into practice, feel free to skim through the theory section and skip ahead to the coding tutorial.

3.1 *Foundations of GANs: Adversarial training*

Formally, the Generator and the Discriminator are represented by differentiable functions, such as neural networks, each with its own cost function. The two networks are trained by backpropagation by using the Discriminator's loss. The Discriminator strives to minimize the loss for both the real and the fake examples, while the Generator tries to maximize the Discriminator's loss for the fake examples it produces.

This dynamic is summarized in figure 3.1. It is a more general version of the diagram from chapter 1, where we first explained what GANs are and how they work. Instead of the concrete example of handwritten digits, in this diagram, we have a general training dataset which, in theory, could be anything.

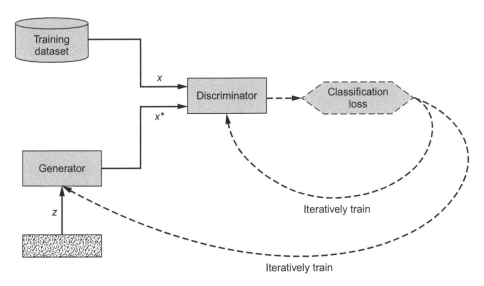

Figure 3.1 In this GAN architecture diagram, both the Generator and the Discriminator are trained using the Discriminator's loss. The Discriminator strives to minimize the loss; the Generator seeks to maximize the loss for the fake examples it produces.

Importantly, the training dataset determines the kind of examples the Generator will learn to emulate. If, for instance, our goal is to produce realistic-looking images of cats, we would supply our GAN with a dataset of cat images.

In more technical terms, the Generator's goal is to produce examples that capture the data distribution of the training dataset.[1] Recall that to a computer, an image is

---

[1] See "Generative Adversarial Networks," by Ian J. Goodfellow et al., 2014, https://arxiv.org/abs/1406.2661.

just a matrix of values: two-dimensional for grayscale and three-dimensional for color (RGB) images. When rendered onscreen, the pixel values within these matrices manifest all the visual elements of an image—lines, edges, contours, and so forth. These values follow a complex distribution across each image in a dataset; after all, if no distribution is followed, an image will be no more than random noise. Object recognition models learn the patterns in images to discern an image's content. The Generator can be thought of as the reverse of the process: rather than recognizing these patterns, it learns to synthesize them.

3.1.1 Cost functions

Following the standard notation, let $J^{(G)}$ denote the Generator's cost function and $J^{(D)}$ the Discriminator's cost function. The trainable parameters (weights and biases) of the two networks are represented by the Greek letter theta: $\theta^{(G)}$ for the Generator and $\theta^{(D)}$ for the Discriminator.

GANs differ from conventional neural networks in two key respects. First, the cost function, J, of a traditional neural network is defined exclusively in terms of its own trainable parameters, θ. Mathematically, this is expressed as $J(\theta)$. In contrast, GANs consist of two networks whose cost functions are dependent on *both* of the networks' parameters. That is, the Generator's cost function is $J^{(G)}(\theta^{(G)}, \theta^{(D)})$, and the Discriminator's cost function is $J^{(D)}(\theta^{(G)}, \theta^{(D)})$.[2]

The second (related) difference is that a traditional neural network can tune *all* its parameters, θ, during the training process. In a GAN, each network can tune only its own weights and biases. The Generator can tune only $\theta^{(G)}$, and the Discriminator can tune only $\theta^{(D)}$ during training. Accordingly, each network has control over only a part of what determines its loss.

To make this a little less abstract, consider the following analogy. Imagine we are choosing which route to drive home from work. If there is no traffic, the fastest option is the highway. During rush hour, however, we may be better off taking one of the side roads. Despite being longer and windier, they might get us home faster when the highway is all clogged up with traffic.

Let's phrase it as a math problem. Let J be our cost function, defined as the amount of time it takes us to get home. Our goal is to minimize J. For simplicity, let's assume we have a set time to leave the office, so we cannot leave early to get ahead of rush hour or stay late to avoid it. The only parameter, θ, we can change is our route.

If ours were the only car on the road, our cost would be similar to a regular neural network's: it would depend only on the route, and it would be entirely within our power to optimize, $J(\theta)$. However, as soon as we introduce other drivers into the equation, the situation gets more complicated. Suddenly, the time it will take us to get home depends not only on our decisions but also on other drivers' course of action,

---

[2] See "NIPS 2016 Tutorial: Generative Adversarial Networks," by Ian Goodfellow, 2016, https://arxiv.org/abs/1701.00160.

$J(\theta^{(us)}, \theta^{(other\ drivers)})$. Much like the Generator and Discriminator networks, our "cost function" will depend on an interplay of factors, some of which are under our control and others of which are not.

3.1.2   *Training process*

The two differences we've described have far-reaching implications on the GAN training process. The training of a traditional neural network is an optimization problem. We seek to minimize the cost function by finding a set of parameters such that moving to any neighboring point in the parameter space would increase the cost. This could be either a local or a global minimum in the parameter space, as determined by the cost function we are seeking to minimize. Figure 3.2 illustrates the optimization process of minimizing a cost function.

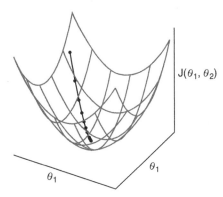

$J(\theta_1, \theta_2)$

Figure 3.2   The bowl-shaped mesh represents the loss J in the parameter space θ_1 and θ_2. The black dotted line illustrates the minimization of the loss in the parameter space through optimization.
(Source: "Adversarial Machine Learning," by Ian Goodfellow, ICLR Keynote, 2019, www.iangoodfellow.com/slides/2019-05-07.pdf.)

Because the Generator and Discriminator can tune only their own parameters and not each other's, GAN training can be better described as a game, rather than optimization.[3] The players in this game are the two networks that the GAN comprises.

Recall from chapter 1 that GAN training ends when the two networks reach Nash equilibrium, a point in a game at which neither player can improve their situation by changing their strategy. Mathematically, this occurs when the Generator cost $J^{(G)}(\theta^{(G)}, \theta^{(D)})$ is minimized with respect to the Generator's trainable parameters $\theta^{(G)}$ and, simultaneously, the Discriminator cost $J^{(D)}(\theta^{(G)}, \theta^{(D)})$ is minimized with respect to the parameters under this network's control, $\theta^{(D)}$.[4] Figure 3.3 illustrates the setup of a two-player zero-sum game and the process of reaching Nash equilibrium.

Coming back to our analogy, Nash equilibrium would occur when every route home takes exactly the same amount of time—for us and all other drivers we may encounter on the way. Any faster route would be offset by a proportional increase in traffic, slowing everyone down just the right amount. As you may imagine, this state is virtually unattainable in real life. Even with tools like Google Maps that

---

[3] Ibid.
[4] Ibid.

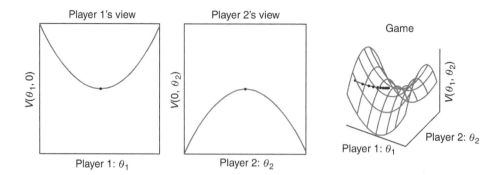

Figure 3.3   **Player 1 (left) seeks to minimize V by tuning θ_1. Player 2 (middle) seeks to minimize −V (maximize V) by tuning θ_2. The saddle-shaped mesh (right) shows the combined loss in the parameter space $V(\theta_1, \theta_2)$. The dotted line shows the convergence to Nash equilibrium at the center of the saddle.** (Source: Goodfellow, 2019, www.iangoodfellow.com/slides/2019-05-07.pdf.)

provide real-time traffic updates, it is often impossible to perfectly evaluate the optimal path home.

The same is true in the high-dimensional, nonconvex world of training GANs. Even small 28 × 28-pixel grayscale images like the ones in the MNIST dataset have 28 × 28 = 784 dimensions. If they were colored (RGB), their dimensionality would increase threefold, to 2,352. Capturing this distribution across all images in the training dataset is extremely difficult, especially when the best approach to learn is from an adversary (the Discriminator).

Training GANs successfully requires trial and error, and although there are best practices, it remains as much an art as it is a science. Chapter 5 revisits the topic of GAN convergence in more detail. For now, you can rest assured that the situation is not as bad as it may sound. As we previewed in chapter 1, and as you will see throughout this book, neither the enormous complexities in approximating the generative distribution nor our lack of complete understanding of what conditions make GANs converge has impeded GANs' practical usability and their ability to generate realistic data samples.

3.2   *The Generator and the Discriminator*

Let's recap what you've learned by introducing more notation. The Generator (G) takes in a random noise vector z and produces a fake example x^*. Mathematically, $G(z) = x^*$. The Discriminator (D) is presented either with a real example x or with a fake example x^*; for each input, it outputs a value between 0 and 1 indicating the probability that the input is real. Figure 3.4 depicts the GAN architecture by using the terminology and notation we just presented.

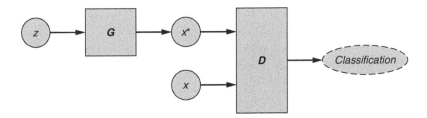

Figure 3.4 The Generator network G transforms the random vector z into a fake example x*: G(z) = x*. The Discriminator network D outputs a classification of whether the input example is real. For the real examples x, the Discriminator strives to output values as close to 1 as possible. For the fake examples x*, the Discriminator strives to output values as close to 0 as possible. In contrast, the Generator wants D(x*) to be as close as possible to 1, indicating that the Discriminator was fooled into classifying a fake example as real.

3.2.1 Conflicting objectives

The Discriminator's goal is to be as accurate as possible. For the real examples x, $D(x)$ seeks to be as close as possible to 1 (label for the positive class). For fake examples x^*, $D(x^*)$ strives to be as close as possible to 0 (label for the negative class).

The Generator's goal is the opposite. It seeks to fool the Discriminator by producing fake examples x^* that are indistinguishable from the real data in the training dataset. Mathematically, the Generator strives to produce fake examples x^* such that $D(x^*)$ is as close to 1 as possible.

3.2.2 Confusion matrix

The Discriminator's classifications can be expressed in terms of a confusion matrix, a tabular representation of all the possible outcomes in binary classification. In the case of the Discriminator, these are as follows:

- *True positive*—Real example correctly classified as real; $D(x) \approx 1$
- *False negative*—Real example incorrectly classified as fake; $D(x) \approx 0$
- *True negative*—Fake example correctly classified as fake; $D(x^*) \approx 0$
- *False positive*—Fake example incorrectly classified as real; $D(x^*) \approx 1$

Table 3.1 presents these outcomes.

Table 3.1 Confusion matrix of Discriminator outcomes

Input	Discriminator output	
	Close to 1 (real)	Close to 0 (fake)
Real (x)	True positive	False negative
Fake (x*)	False positive	True negative

Using the confusion matrix terminology, the Discriminator is trying to maximize true positive and true negative classifications or, equivalently, minimize false positive and false negative classifications. In contrast, the Generator's goal is to maximize the Discriminator's false positive classifications—these are the instances in which the Generator successfully fools the Discriminator into believing a fake example is real. The Generator is not concerned with how well the Discriminator classifies the real examples; it cares only about the Discriminator's classifications of the fake data samples.

3.3   GAN training algorithm

Let's revisit the GAN training algorithm from chapter 1 and formalize it by using the notation introduced in this chapter. Unlike the algorithm in chapter 1, this one uses mini-batches rather than one example at a time.

GAN training algorithm

For each training iteration **do**

1   Train the Discriminator:
   a   Take a random mini-batch of real examples: x.
   b   Take a mini-batch of random noise vectors z and generate a mini-batch of fake examples: $G(z) = x^*$.
   c   Compute the classification losses for $D(x)$ and $D(x^*)$, and backpropagate the total error to update $\theta^{(D)}$ to *minimize* the classification loss.
2   Train the Generator:
   a   Take a mini-batch of random noise vectors z and generate a mini-batch of fake examples: $G(z) = x^*$.
   b   Compute the classification loss for $D(x^*)$, and backpropagate the loss to update $\theta^{(G)}$ to *maximize* the classification loss.

End for

Notice that in step 1, the Generator's parameters are kept intact while we train the Discriminator. Similarly, in step 2, we keep the Discriminator's parameters fixed while the Generator is trained. The reason we allow updates only to the weights and biases of the network being trained is to isolate all changes to only the parameters that are under the network's control. This ensures that each network gets relevant signals about the updates to make, without interference from the other's updates. You can almost think of it as two players taking turns.

Of course, you can imagine a scenario in which each player merely undoes the other's progress, so not even a turn-based game is guaranteed to yield a useful outcome. (Have we said yet that GANs are notoriously tricky to train?) More on this in chapter 5, where we also discuss techniques to maximize our chances of success.

That's it for theory, for the time being. Let's now put what we learned into practice and implement our first GAN.

3.4   *Tutorial: Generating handwritten digits*

In this tutorial, we will implement a GAN that learns to produce realistic-looking handwritten digits. We will use the Python neural network library Keras with a TensorFlow backend. Figure 3.5 shows a high-level architecture of the GAN we will implement.

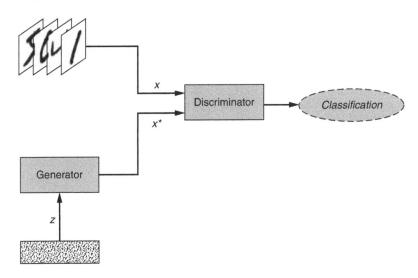

Figure 3.5   Over the course of the training iterations, the Generator learns to turn random noise input into images that look like members of the training data: the MNIST dataset of handwritten digits. Simultaneously, the Discriminator learns to distinguish the fake images produced by the Generator from the genuine ones coming from the training dataset.

Much of the code used in this tutorial—especially the boilerplate code used in the training loop—was adapted from the open source GitHub repository of GAN implementations in Keras, *Keras-GAN*, created by Erik Linder-Norén (https://github.com/eriklindernoren/Keras-GAN). The repository also includes several advanced GAN variants, some of which will be covered later in this book. We revised and simplified the implementation considerably, in terms of both code and network architecture, and we renamed variables so that they are consistent with the notation used in this book.

A Jupyter notebook with the full implementation, including added visualizations of the training progress, is available on the book's website at www.manning.com/books/gans-in-action and in the GitHub repository for this book at https://github.com/GANs-in-Action/gans-in-action under the chapter-3 folder. The code was tested with Python 3.6.0, Keras 2.1.6, and TensorFlow 1.8.0.

3.4.1   *Importing modules and specifying model input dimensions*

First, we import all the packages and libraries needed to run the model. Notice we also import the MNIST dataset of handwritten digits directly from `keras.datasets`.

Listing 3.1   Import statements

```
%matplotlib inline

import matplotlib.pyplot as plt
import numpy as np

from keras.datasets import mnist
from keras.layers import Dense, Flatten, Reshape
from keras.layers.advanced_activations import LeakyReLU
from keras.models import Sequential
from keras.optimizers import Adam
```

Second, we specify the input dimensions of our model and dataset. Each image in MNIST is 28 × 28 pixels with a single channel (because the images are grayscale). The variable `z_dim` sets the size of the noise vector, *z*.

Listing 3.2   Model input dimensions

```
img_rows = 28
img_cols = 28
channels = 1

img_shape = (img_rows, img_cols, channels)    ⟵⎯|  Input image
                                                  dimensions

z_dim = 100    ⟵⎯|  Size of the noise vector, used
                    as input to the Generator
```

Next, we implement the Generator and the Discriminator networks.

3.4.2   *Implementing the Generator*

For simplicity, the Generator is a neural network with only a single hidden layer. It takes in *z* as input and produces a 28 × 28 × 1 image. In the hidden layer, we use the *Leaky ReLU* activation function. Unlike a regular ReLU function, which maps any negative input to 0, Leaky ReLU allows a small positive gradient. This prevents gradients from dying out during training, which tends to yield better training outcomes.

At the output layer, we employ the *tanh* activation function, which scales the output values to the range [−1, 1]. The reason for using *tanh* (as opposed to, say, *sigmoid*, which would output values in the more typical 0 to 1 range) is that *tanh* tends to produce crisper images.

The following listing implements the Generator.

Listing 3.3   Generator

```
def build_generator(img_shape, z_dim):
    model = Sequential()

    model.add(Dense(128, input_dim=z_dim))      <─┐  Fully connected
                                                   │  layer
    model.add(LeakyReLU(alpha=0.01))            <─┘
                                                      Leaky ReLU
                                                      activation
    model.add(Dense(28 * 28 * 1, activation='tanh'))  <─┐  Output layer
                                                         │  with tanh
    model.add(Reshape(img_shape))      <─┐               │  activation
                                         │  Reshapes the
    return model                            Generator output to
                                            image dimensions
```

3.4.3   Implementing the Discriminator

The Discriminator takes in a $28 \times 28 \times 1$ image and outputs a probability indicating whether the input is deemed real rather than fake. The Discriminator is represented by a two-layer neural network, with 128 hidden units and a *Leaky ReLU* activation function at the hidden layer.

For simplicity, our Discriminator network looks almost identical to the Generator. This does not have to be the case; indeed, in most GAN implementations, the Generator and Discriminator network architectures vary greatly in both size and complexity.

Notice that unlike for the Generator, in the following listing we apply the *sigmoid* activation function at the Discriminator's output layer. This ensures that our output value will be between 0 and 1, so it can be interpreted as the probability the Generator assigns that the input is real.

Listing 3.4   Discriminator

```
def build_discriminator(img_shape):

    model = Sequential()
                                                      Flattens the
    model.add(Flatten(input_shape=img_shape))  <─┐   input image
                                                  │
    model.add(Dense(128))      <─────────────────┘   Fully connected
                                                      layer

    model.add(LeakyReLU(alpha=0.01))   <─┐  Leaky ReLU activation

    model.add(Dense(1, activation='sigmoid'))   <─┐  Output layer with
                                                   │  sigmoid activation
    return model
```

3.4.4   Building the model

In listing 3.5, we build and compile the Generator and Discriminator models implemented previously. Notice that in the combined model used to train the Generator, we keep the Discriminator parameters fixed by setting `discriminator.trainable` to `False`. Also note that the combined model, in which the Discriminator is set to untrainable, is used to train the Generator only. The Discriminator is trained as an independently compiled model. (This will become apparent when we review the training loop.)

We use binary cross-entropy as the loss function we are seeking to minimize during training. *Binary cross-entropy* is a measure of the difference between computed probabilities and actual probabilities for predictions with only two possible classes. The greater the cross-entropy loss, the further away our predictions are from the true labels.

To optimize each network, we use the *Adam optimization algorithm.* This algorithm, whose name is derived from *adaptive moment estimation,* is an advanced gradient-descent-based optimizer. The inner workings of this algorithm are beyond the scope of this book, but it suffices to say that Adam has become the go-to optimizer for most GAN implementations thanks to its often superior performance.

Listing 3.5   Building and compiling the GAN

```
def build_gan(generator, discriminator):

    model = Sequential()

    model.add(generator)              Combined Generator +
    model.add(discriminator)          Discriminator model

    return model


discriminator = build_discriminator(img_shape)       Builds and compiles
discriminator.compile(loss='binary_crossentropy',    the Discriminator
                optimizer=Adam(),
                metrics=['accuracy'])         Builds the Generator

generator = build_generator(img_shape, z_dim)      Keeps Discriminator's
                                                   parameters constant
discriminator.trainable = False                    for Generator training

gan = build_gan(generator, discriminator)           Builds and compiles
gan.compile(loss='binary_crossentropy', optimizer=Adam())   GAN model with fixed
                                                    Discriminator to
                                                    train the Generator
```

3.4.5   *Training*

The training code in listing 3.6 implements the GAN training algorithm. We get a random mini-batch of MNIST images as real examples and generate a mini-batch of fake images from random noise vectors z. We then use those to train the Discriminator network while keeping the Generator's parameters constant. Next, we generate a mini-batch of fake images and use those to train the Generator network while keeping the Discriminator's parameters fixed. We repeat this for each iteration.

We use one-hot-encoded labels: 1 for real images and 0 for fake ones. To generate z, we sample from the standard normal distribution (a bell curve with 0 mean and a standard deviation of 1). The Discriminator is trained to assign *fake* labels to the fake images and *real* labels to real images. The Generator is trained such that the Discriminator assigns *real* labels to the fake examples it produces.

Notice that we are rescaling the real images in the training dataset from –1 to 1. As you saw in the preceding example, the Generator uses the *tanh* activation function at the output layer, so the fake images will be in the range (–1, 1). Accordingly, we have to rescale all the Discriminator's inputs to the same range.

Listing 3.6   GAN training loop

```
losses = []
accuracies = []
iteration_checkpoints = []


def train(iterations, batch_size, sample_interval):

    (X_train, _), (_, _) = mnist.load_data()

    X_train = X_train / 127.5 - 1.0
    X_train = np.expand_dims(X_train, axis=3)

    real = np.ones((batch_size, 1))

    fake = np.zeros((batch_size, 1))

    for iteration in range(iterations):

        idx = np.random.randint(0, X_train.shape[0], batch_size)
        imgs = X_train[idx]

        z = np.random.normal(0, 1, (batch_size, 100))
        gen_imgs = generator.predict(z)

        d_loss_real = discriminator.train_on_batch(imgs, real)
        d_loss_fake = discriminator.train_on_batch(gen_imgs, fake)
        d_loss, accuracy = 0.5 * np.add(d_loss_real, d_loss_fake)


        z = np.random.normal(0, 1, (batch_size, 100))
        gen_imgs = generator.predict(z)

        g_loss = gan.train_on_batch(z, real)

        if (iteration + 1) % sample_interval == 0:

            losses.append((d_loss, g_loss))
            accuracies.append(100.0 * accuracy)
            iteration_checkpoints.append(iteration + 1)
```

Annotations:
- **Loads the MNIST dataset** → `(X_train, _), (_, _) = mnist.load_data()`
- **Rescales [0, 255] grayscale pixel values to [–1, 1]** → `X_train = X_train / 127.5 - 1.0`
- **Labels for real images: all 1s** → `real = np.ones((batch_size, 1))`
- **Labels for fake images: all 0s** → `fake = np.zeros((batch_size, 1))`
- **Gets a random batch of real images** → `idx = np.random.randint(0, X_train.shape[0], batch_size)`
- **Generates a batch of fake images** → `z = np.random.normal(0, 1, (batch_size, 100))`
- **Trains the Discriminator** → `d_loss_real = discriminator.train_on_batch(imgs, real)`
- **Generates a batch of fake images** → `z = np.random.normal(0, 1, (batch_size, 100))`
- **Trains the Generator** → `g_loss = gan.train_on_batch(z, real)`
- **Saves losses and accuracies so they can be plotted after training** → `losses.append((d_loss, g_loss))`

Outputs training progress

```
print("%d [D loss: %f, acc.: %.2f%%] [G loss: %f]" %
       (iteration + 1, d_loss, 100.0 * accuracy, g_loss))

sample_images(generator)
```

Outputs a sample of generated images

3.4.6   Outputting sample images

In the Generator training code, you may notice an invocation of the `sample_images()` function. This function gets called every `sample_interval` iterations and outputs a 4 × 4 grid of images synthesized by the Generator in the given iteration. After we run our model, we will use these images to inspect interim and final outputs.

Listing 3.7   Displaying generated images

```
def sample_images(generator, image_grid_rows=4, image_grid_columns=4):
```

Sample random noise

```
    z = np.random.normal(0, 1, (image_grid_rows * image_grid_columns, z_dim))

    gen_imgs = generator.predict(z)
```

Generates images from random noise

Rescales image pixel values to [0, 1]

```
    gen_imgs = 0.5 * gen_imgs + 0.5

    fig, axs = plt.subplots(image_grid_rows,
                            image_grid_columns,
                            figsize=(4, 4),
                            sharey=True,
                            sharex=True)
```

Sets image grid

```
    cnt = 0
    for i in range(image_grid_rows):
        for j in range(image_grid_columns):
            axs[i, j].imshow(gen_imgs[cnt, :, :, 0], cmap='gray')
            axs[i, j].axis('off')
            cnt += 1
```

Outputs a grid of images

3.4.7   Running the model

That brings us to the final step, shown in listing 3.8. We set the training hyperparameters—the number of iterations and the batch size—and train the model. There is no tried-and-true method to determine the right number of iterations or the right batch size; we determine them experimentally through trial and error as we observe the training progress.

That said, there are important practical constraints to these numbers: each minibatch must be small enough to fit inside the processing memory (typical batch sizes people use are powers of 2: 32, 64, 128, 256, and 512). The number of iterations also has a practical constraint: the more iterations we have, the longer the training process takes. With complex deep learning models like GANs, this can get out of hand quickly, even with significant computing power.

To determine the right number of iterations, we monitor the training loss and set the iteration number around the point when the loss plateaus, indicating that we are getting little to no incremental improvement from further training. (Because this is a generative model, overfitting is as much a concern as it is for supervised learning algorithms.)

Listing 3.8 Running the model

```
iterations = 20000            ⊲┐   Sets
batch_size = 128                │   hyperparameters
sample_interval = 1000          │                          Trains the GAN for
                                                           the specified
train(iterations, batch_size, sample_interval)   ⊲┘       number of iterations
```

3.4.8 Inspecting the results

Figure 3.6 shows example images produced by the Generator over the course of training iterations, from earliest to latest.

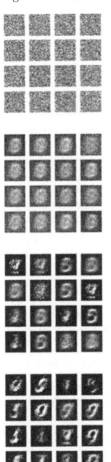

Figure 3.6 Starting from what looks to be no more than random noise, the Generator gradually learns to emulate the features of the training dataset: in our case, images of handwritten digits.

As you can see, the Generator starts out by producing little more than random noise. Over the course of the training iterations, it gets better and better at emulating the features of the training data. Each time the Discriminator rejects a generated image as false or accepts one as real, the Generator improves a little. Figure 3.7 shows examples of images the Generator can synthesize after it is fully trained.

Figure 3.7   Although far from perfect, our simple two-layer Generator learned to produce realistic-looking numerals, such as 9 and 1.

For comparison, figure 3.8 shows a randomly selected sample of real images from the MNIST dataset.

Figure 3.8   Example of real handwritten digits from the MNIST dataset used to train our GAN. Although the Generator made impressive progress toward emulating the training data, the difference between the numerals it produces and the real, human-written numerals remains clear.

3.5   Conclusion

Although the images our GAN generated are far from perfect, many of them are easily recognizable as real numerals—an impressive achievement, given that we used only a simple two-layer network architecture for both the Generator and the Discriminator. In the following chapter, you will learn how to improve the quality of the generated images by using a more complex and powerful neural network architecture for the Generator and Discriminator: convolutional neural networks.

Summary

- GANs consist of two networks: the Generator (G) and the Discriminator (D), each with its own loss function: $J^{(G)}(\theta^{(G)}, \theta^{(D)})$ and $J^{(D)}(\theta^{(G)}, \theta^{(D)})$, respectively.
- During training, the Generator and the Discriminator can tune only their own parameters: $\theta^{(G)}$ and $\theta^{(D)}$, respectively.
- The two GAN networks are trained simultaneously via a game-like dynamic. The Generator seeks to maximize the Discriminator's false-positive classifications (classifying a generated image as real), while the Discriminator seeks to minimize its false-positive and false-negative classifications.

Deep Convolutional GAN

4

This chapter covers

- Understanding key concepts behind convolutional neural networks
- Using batch normalization
- Implementing Deep Convolutional GAN, an advanced GAN architecture

In the previous chapter, we implemented a GAN whose Generator and Discriminator were simple feed-forward neural networks with a single hidden layer. Despite this simplicity, many of the images of handwritten digits that the GAN's Generator produced after being fully trained were remarkably convincing. Even the ones that were not recognizable as human-written numerals had many of the hallmarks of handwritten symbols, such as discernible line edges and shapes—especially when compared to the random noise used as the Generator's raw input.

Imagine what we could accomplish with more powerful network architecture. In this chapter, we will do just that: instead of simple two-layer feed-forward networks, both our Generator and Discriminator will be implemented as convolutional neural networks (CNNs, or ConvNets). The resulting GAN architecture is known as *Deep Convolutional GAN*, or *DCGAN* for short.

Before delving into the nitty-gritty of the DCGAN implementation, we will review the key concepts underlying ConvNets, review the history behind the discovery of the DCGAN, and cover one of the key breakthroughs that made complex architectures like DCGAN possible in practice: batch normalization.

4.1 Convolutional neural networks

We expect that you've already been exposed to convolutional networks; that said, if this technique is new to you, don't worry. In this section, we review all the key concepts you need for this chapter and the rest of this book.

4.1.1 Convolutional filters

Unlike a regular feed-forward neural network whose neurons are arranged in flat, fully connected layers, layers in a ConvNet are arranged in three dimensions (width × height × depth). Convolutions are performed by sliding one or more *filters* over the input layer. Each filter has a relatively small receptive field (width × height) but always extends through the entire depth of the input volume.

At every step as it slides across the input, each filter outputs a single activation value: the dot product between the input values and the filter entries. This process results in a two-dimensional activation map for each filter. The activation maps produced by each filter are then stacked on top of one another to produce a three-dimensional output layer; the output depth is equal to the number of filters used.

4.1.2 Parameter sharing

Importantly, filter parameters are shared by all the input values to the given filter. This has both intuitive and practical advantages. Intuitively, parameter sharing allows us to efficiently learn visual features and shapes (such as lines and edges) regardless of where they are located in the input image. From a practical perspective, parameter sharing drastically reduces the number of trainable parameters. This decreases the risk of overfitting and allows this technique to scale up to higher-resolution images without a corresponding exponential increase in trainable parameters, as would be the case with a traditional, fully connected network.

4.1.3 ConvNets visualized

If all this sounds confusing, let's make these concepts a little less abstract by visualizing them. Diagrams make everything easier to understand for most people (us included!). Figure 4.1 shows a single convolution operation; figure 4.2 illustrates the convolution operation in the context of the input and output layers in a ConvNet.

Figure 4.1 depicts the convolution operation for a single filter over a two-dimensional input. In practice, the input volume is usually three-dimensional, and we use several stacked filters. The underlying mechanics, however, remain the same: each filter produces a single value per step, regardless of the depth of the input volume. The number of filters we use determines the depth of the output volume, as their resulting activation maps are stacked on top of one another. All this is illustrated in figure 4.2.

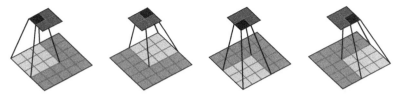

Figure 4.1   A 3 × 3 convolutional filter as it slides over a 5 × 5 input—left to right, top to bottom. At each step, the filter moves by two strides; accordingly, it makes a total of four steps, resulting in a 2 × 2 activation map. Notice how at each step, the entire filter produces a single activation value.
(Source: "A Guide to Convolution Arithmetic for Deep Learning," by Vincent Dumoulin and Francesco Visin, 2016, https://arxiv.org/abs/1603.07285.)

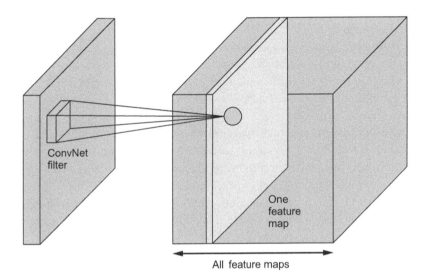

ConvNet filter

One feature map

All feature maps

Figure 4.2   An activation value for a single convolutional step within the context of the activation map (feature map) and the input and output volumes. Notice that the ConvNet filter extends through the full depth of the input volume and that the depth of the output volume is determined by stacking together activation maps.
(Source: "Convolutional Neural Network," by Nameer Hirschkind et al., Brilliant.org, retrieved November 1, 2018, http://mng.bz/8zJK.)

NOTE   If you would like to dive deeper into convolutional networks and the underlying concepts, we recommend reading the relevant chapters in François Chollet's *Deep Learning with Python* (Manning, 2017), which provides an outstanding, hands-on introduction to all the key concepts and techniques in deep learning, including ConvNets. For those with a more academic bent, a great resource is Andrej Karpathy's excellent lecture notes from his Stanford University class on Convolutional Neural Networks for Visual Recognition (http://cs231n.github.io/convolutional-networks/).

4.2   *Brief history of the DCGAN*

Introduced in 2016 by Alec Radford, Luke Metz, and Soumith Chintala, DCGAN marked one of the most important early innovations in GANs since the technique's inception two years earlier.[1] This was not the first time a group of researchers tried harnessing ConvNets for use in GANs, but it was the first time they succeeded at incorporating ConvNets directly into a full-scale GAN model.

The use of ConvNets exacerbates many of the difficulties plaguing GAN training, including instability and gradient saturation. Indeed, these challenges proved so daunting that some researchers resorted to alternative approaches, such as the LAPGAN, which uses a cascade of convolutional networks within a Laplacian pyramid, with a separate ConvNet being trained at each level using the GAN framework.[2] If none of this makes sense to you, don't worry. Superseded by superior methods, LAPGAN has been largely relegated to the dustbin of history, so it is not important to understand its internals.

Although inelegant, complex, and computationally taxing, LAPGAN yielded the highest-quality images to date at the time of its publication, with fourfold improvement over the original GAN (40% versus 10% of generated images mistaken for real by human evaluators). As such, LAPGAN demonstrated the enormous potential of marrying GANs with ConvNets.

With DCGAN, Radford and his collaborators introduced techniques and optimizations that allowed ConvNets to scale up to the full GAN framework without the need to modify the underlying GAN architecture and without reducing GAN to a subroutine of a more complex model framework, like LAPGAN. One of the key techniques Radford et al. used is batch normalization, which helps stabilize the training process by normalizing inputs at each layer where it is applied. Let's take a closer look at what batch normalization is and how it works.

4.3   *Batch normalization*

Batch normalization was introduced by Google scientists Sergey Ioffe and Christian Szegedy in 2015.[3] Their insight was as simple as it was groundbreaking. Just as we normalize network inputs, they proposed to normalize the inputs to each layer, for each training mini-batch as it flows through the network.

---

[1] See "Unsupervised Representation Learning with Deep Convolutional Generative Adversarial Networks," by Alec Radford et al., 2015, https://arxiv.org/abs/1511.06434.

[2] See "Deep Generative Image Models Using a Laplacian Pyramid of Adversarial Networks," by Emily Denton et al., 2015, https://arxiv.org/abs/1506.05751.

[3] See "Batch Normalization: Accelerating Deep Network Training by Reducing Internal Covariate Shift," by Sergey Ioffe and Christian Szegedy, 2015, https://arxiv.org/abs/1502.03167.

4.3.1 *Understanding normalization*

It helps to remind ourselves what normalization is and why we bother normalizing the input feature values in the first place. *Normalization* is the scaling of data so that it has zero mean and unit variance. This is accomplished by taking each data point x, subtracting the mean μ, and dividing the result by the standard deviation, σ, as shown in equation 4.1:

$$\hat{x} = \frac{x - \mu}{\sigma}$$

Equation 4.1

Normalization has several advantages. Perhaps most important, it makes comparisons between features with vastly different scales easier and, by extension, makes the training process less sensitive to the scale of the features. Consider the following (rather contrived) example. Imagine we are trying to predict the monthly expenditures of a family based on two features: the family's annual income and the family size. We would expect that, in general, the more a family earns, the more they spend; and the bigger a family is, the more they spend.

However, the scales of these features are vastly different—an extra \$10 in annual income probably wouldn't influence how much a family spends, but an additional 10 members would likely wreak havoc on any family's budget. Normalization solves this problem by scaling each feature value onto a standardized scale, such that each data point is expressed not as its face value but as a relative "score" indicating how many standard deviations the given data point is from the mean.

The insight behind batch normalization is that normalizing inputs alone may not go far enough when dealing with deep neural networks with many layers. As the input values flow through the network, from one layer to the next, they are scaled by the trainable parameters in each of those layers. And as the parameters get tuned by backpropagation, the distribution of each layer's inputs is prone to change in subsequent training iterations, which destabilizes the learning process. In academia, this problem is known as *covariate shift*. Batch normalization solves it by scaling values in each minibatch by the mean and variance of that mini-batch.

4.3.2 *Computing batch normalization*

The way batch normalization is computed differs in several respects from the simple normalization equation we presented earlier. This section walks through it step by step.

Let μ_B be the mean of the mini-batch B, and σ_B^2 be the variance (mean squared deviation) of the mini-batch B. The normalized value $\hat{x}$ is computed as shown in equation 4.2:

$$\hat{x} = \frac{x - \mu_B}{\sqrt{\sigma^2 + \varepsilon}}$$

Equation 4.2

The term ε (epsilon) is added for numerical stability, primarily to avoid division by zero. It is set to a small positive constant value, such as 0.001.

In batch normalization, we do not use these normalized values directly. Instead, we multiply them by γ (gamma) and add β (beta) before passing them as inputs to the next layer; see equation 4.3.

$$y = \gamma\hat{x} + \beta$$

Equation 4.3

Importantly, the terms γ and β are trainable parameters, which—just like weights and biases—are tuned during network training. The reason for this is that it may be beneficial for the intermediate input values to be standardized around a mean other than 0 and have a variance other than 1. Because γ and β are trainable, the network can learn what values work best.

Fortunately for us, we don't have to worry about any of this. The Keras function `keras.layers.BatchNormalization` handles all the mini-batch computations and updates behind the scenes for us.

Batch normalization limits the amount by which updating the parameters in the previous layers can affect the distribution of inputs received by the current layer. This decreases any unwanted interdependence between parameters across layers, which helps speed up the network training process and increase its robustness, especially when it comes to network parameter initialization.

Batch normalization has proven essential to the viability of many deep learning architectures, including the DCGAN, which you will see in action in the following tutorial.

4.4 *Tutorial: Generating handwritten digits with DCGAN*

In this tutorial, we will revisit the MNIST dataset of handwritten digits from chapter 3. This time, however, we will use the DCGAN architecture and represent both the Generator and the Discriminator as convolutional networks, as shown in figure 4.3. Besides this change, the rest of the network architecture remains unchanged. At the end of the tutorial, we will compare the quality of the handwritten numerals produced by the two GANs (traditional versus DCGAN) so you can see the improvement made possible by the use of a more advanced network architecture.

As in chapter 3, much of the code in this tutorial was adapted from Erik Linder-Norén's open source GitHub repository of GAN models in Keras (https://github .com/eriklindernoren/Keras-GAN), with numerous modifications and improvements spanning both the implementation details and network architectures. A Jupyter notebook with the full implementation, including added visualizations of the training progress, is available in the GitHub repository for this book at https://github.com/ GANs-in-Action/gans-in-action, under the chapter-4 folder. The code was tested with Python 3.6.0, Keras 2.1.6, and TensorFlow 1.8.0. To speed up the training time, it is recommended to run the model on a GPU.

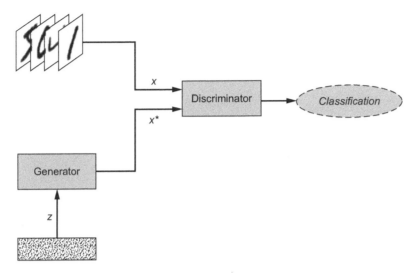

Figure 4.3 The overall model architecture for this chapter's tutorial is the same as the GAN we implemented in chapter 3. The only differences (not visible on this high-level diagram) are the internal representations of the Generator and Discriminator networks (the insides of the Generator and Discriminator boxes). These networks are covered in detail later in this tutorial.

4.4.1 Importing modules and specifying model input dimensions

First, we import all the packages, modules, and libraries we need to train and run the model. Just as in chapter 3, the MNIST dataset of handwritten digits is imported directly from `keras.datasets`.

Listing 4.1 Import statements

```
%matplotlib inline

import matplotlib.pyplot as plt
import numpy as np

from keras.datasets import mnist
from keras.layers import (
    Activation, BatchNormalization, Dense, Dropout, Flatten, Reshape)
from keras.layers.advanced_activations import LeakyReLU
from keras.layers.convolutional import Conv2D, Conv2DTranspose
from keras.models import Sequential
from keras.optimizers import Adam
```

We also specify the model input dimensions: the image shape and the length of the noise vector *z*.

Listing 4.2   Model input dimensions

```
img_rows = 28
img_cols = 28
channels = 1

img_shape = (img_rows, img_cols, channels)      Input image
                                                 dimensions

z_dim = 100           Size of the noise vector, used
                      as input to the Generator
```

4.4.2   *Implementing the Generator*

ConvNets have traditionally been used for image classification tasks, in which the network takes in an image with the dimensions *height × width × number of color channels* as input and—through a series of convolutional layers—outputs a single vector of class scores, with the dimensions $1 \times n$, where n is the number of class labels. To generate an image by using the ConvNet architecture, we reverse the process: instead of taking an image and processing it into a vector, we take a vector and upsize it to an image.

Key to this process is the *transposed convolution.* Recall that regular convolution is typically used to reduce input width and height while increasing its depth. Transposed convolution goes in the reverse direction: it is used to increase the width and height while reducing depth, as you can see in the Generator network diagram in figure 4.4.

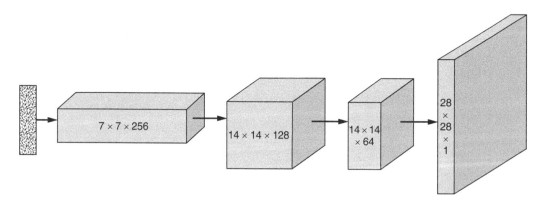

Figure 4.4   The Generator takes in a random noise vector as input and produces a 28 × 28 × 1 image. It does so by multiple layers of transposed convolutions. Between the convolutional layers, we apply batch normalization to stabilize the training process. (Image is not to scale.)

The Generator starts with a noise vector z. Using a fully connected layer, we reshape the vector into a three-dimensional hidden layer with a small base (width × height) and large depth. Using transposed convolutions, the input is progressively reshaped such that its base grows while its depth decreases until we reach the final layer with the shape of the image we are seeking to synthesize, 28 × 28 × 1. After each transposed convolution layer, we apply batch normalization and the *Leaky ReLU* activation function. At the final layer, we do not apply batch normalization and, instead of ReLU, we use the *tanh* activation function.

Putting all the steps together, we do the following:

1 Take a random noise vector and reshape it into a 7 × 7 × 256 tensor through a fully connected layer.
2 Use transposed convolution, transforming the 7 × 7 × 256 tensor into a 14 × 14 × 128 tensor.
3 Apply batch normalization and the *Leaky ReLU* activation function.
4 Use transposed convolution, transforming the 14 × 14 × 128 tensor into a 14 × 14 × 64 tensor. Notice that the width and height dimensions remain unchanged; this is accomplished by setting the stride parameter in Conv2DTranspose to 1.
5 Apply batch normalization and the *Leaky ReLU* activation function.
6 Use transposed convolution, transforming the 14 × 14 × 64 tensor into the output image size, 28 × 28 × 1.
7 Apply the *tanh* activation function.

The following listing shows what the Generator network looks like when implemented in Keras.

Listing 4.3 DCGAN Generator

```
def build_generator(z_dim):

    model = Sequential()

    model.add(Dense(256 * 7 * 7, input_dim=z_dim))
    model.add(Reshape((7, 7, 256)))

    model.add(Conv2DTranspose(128, kernel_size=3, strides=2, padding='same'))

    model.add(BatchNormalization())

    model.add(LeakyReLU(alpha=0.01))

    model.add(Conv2DTranspose(64, kernel_size=3, strides=1, padding='same'))

    model.add(BatchNormalization())

    model.add(LeakyReLU(alpha=0.01))

    model.add(Conv2DTranspose(1, kernel_size=3, strides=2, padding='same'))

    model.add(Activation('tanh'))

    return model
```

Transposed convolution layer, from 7 × 7 × 256 into 14 × 14 × 128 tensor

Reshapes input into 7 × 7 × 256 tensor via a fully connected layer

Leaky ReLU activation

Batch normalization

Transposed convolution layer, from 14 × 14 × 128 to 14 × 14 × 64 tensor

Batch normalization

Leaky ReLU activation

Output layer with tanh activation

Transposed convolution layer, from 14 × 14 × 64 to 28 × 28 × 1 tensor

4.4.3   *Implementing the Discriminator*

The Discriminator is a ConvNet of the familiar kind, one that takes in an image and outputs a prediction vector: in this case, a binary classification indicating whether the input image was deemed to be real rather than fake. Figure 4.5 depicts the Discriminator network we will implement.

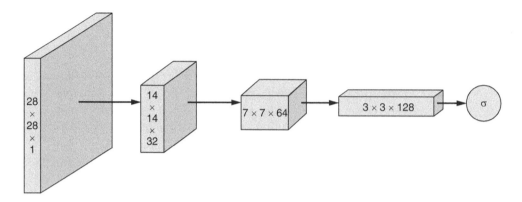

Figure 4.5   The Discriminator takes in a 28 × 28 × 1 image as input, applies several convolutional layers, and—using the *sigmoid* activation function σ—outputs a probability that the input image is real rather than fake. Between the convolutional layers, we apply batch normalization to stabilize the training process. (Image is not to scale.)

The input to the Discriminator is a 28 × 28 × 1 image. By applying convolutions, the image is transformed such that its base (width × height) gets progressively smaller and its depth gets progressively deeper. On all convolutional layers, we apply the *Leaky ReLU* activation function. Batch normalization is used on all convolutional layers except the first. For output, we use a fully connected layer and the *sigmoid* activation function.

Putting all the steps together, we do the following:

1 Use a convolutional layer to transform a 28 × 28 × 1 input image into a 14 × 14 × 32 tensor.
2 Apply the *Leaky ReLU* activation function.
3 Use a convolutional layer, transforming the 14 × 14 × 32 tensor into a 7 × 7 × 64 tensor.
4 Apply batch normalization and the *Leaky ReLU* activation function.
5 Use a convolutional layer, transforming the 7 × 7 × 64 tensor into a 3 × 3 × 128 tensor.
6 Apply batch normalization and the *Leaky ReLU* activation function.
7 Flatten the 3 × 3 × 128 tensor into a vector of size 3 × 3 × 128 = 1152.

8 Use a fully connected layer feeding into the *sigmoid* activation function to compute the probability of whether the input image is real.

The following listing is a Keras implementation of the Discriminator model.

Listing 4.4 DCGAN Discriminator

```
def build_discriminator(img_shape):

    model = Sequential()

    model.add(
        Conv2D(32,
               kernel_size=3,
               strides=2,
               input_shape=img_shape,
               padding='same'))

    model.add(LeakyReLU(alpha=0.01))

    model.add(
        Conv2D(64,
               kernel_size=3,
               strides=2,
               input_shape=img_shape,
               padding='same'))

    model.add(BatchNormalization())

    model.add(LeakyReLU(alpha=0.01))

    model.add(
        Conv2D(128,
               kernel_size=3,
               strides=2,
               input_shape=img_shape,
               padding='same'))

    model.add(BatchNormalization())

    model.add(LeakyReLU(alpha=0.01))

    model.add(Flatten())
    model.add(Dense(1, activation='sigmoid'))

    return model
```

Annotations:
- Convolutional layer, from $28 \times 28 \times 1$ into $14 \times 14 \times 32$ tensor
- Leaky ReLU activation
- Convolutional layer, from $14 \times 14 \times 32$ into $7 \times 7 \times 64$ tensor
- Batch normalization
- Leaky ReLU activation
- Convolutional layer, from $7 \times 7 \times 64$ tensor into $3 \times 3 \times 128$ tensor
- Batch normalization
- Leaky ReLU activation
- Output layer with sigmoid activation

4.4.4 *Building and running the DCGAN*

Aside from the network architectures used for the Generator and the Discriminator, the rest of the DCGAN network setup and implementation is the same as the one we used for the simple GAN in chapter 3. This underscores the versatility of the GAN architecture. Listing 4.5 code builds the model, and listing 4.6 trains the model.

Listing 4.5   Building and compiling the DCGAN

```
def build_gan(generator, discriminator):

    model = Sequential()

    model.add(generator)
    model.add(discriminator)

    return model


discriminator = build_discriminator(img_shape)
discriminator.compile(loss='binary_crossentropy',
                      optimizer=Adam(),
                      metrics=['accuracy'])

generator = build_generator(z_dim)

discriminator.trainable = False

gan = build_gan(generator, discriminator)
gan.compile(loss='binary_crossentropy', optimizer=Adam())
```

Combined Generator +
Discriminator model

Builds and compiles
the Discriminator

Builds the
Generator

Keeps Discriminator's
parameters constant
for Generator training

Builds and compiles
GAN model with fixed
Discriminator to train
the Generator

Listing 4.6   DCGAN training loop

```
losses = []
accuracies = []
iteration_checkpoints = []


def train(iterations, batch_size, sample_interval):

    (X_train, _), (_, _) = mnist.load_data()

    X_train = X_train / 127.5 - 1.0
    X_train = np.expand_dims(X_train, axis=3)

    real = np.ones((batch_size, 1))

    fake = np.zeros((batch_size, 1))

    for iteration in range(iterations):

        idx = np.random.randint(0, X_train.shape[0], batch_size)
        imgs = X_train[idx]

        z = np.random.normal(0, 1, (batch_size, 100))
        gen_imgs = generator.predict(z)

        d_loss_real = discriminator.train_on_batch(imgs, real)
        d_loss_fake = discriminator.train_on_batch(gen_imgs, fake)
```

Loads the
MNIST dataset

Rescales [0, 255]
grayscale pixel values
to [–1, 1]

Labels for real
images: all 1s

Labels for fake
images: all 0s

Gets a random
batch of real
images

Generates a batch
of fake images

Trains the
Discriminator

```
                    d_loss, accuracy = 0.5 * np.add(d_loss_real, d_loss_fake)

                    z = np.random.normal(0, 1, (batch_size, 100))
                    gen_imgs = generator.predict(z)

                    g_loss = gan.train_on_batch(z, real)

                    if (iteration + 1) % sample_interval == 0:

                        losses.append((d_loss, g_loss))
                        accuracies.append(100.0 * accuracy)
                        iteration_checkpoints.append(iteration + 1)

                        print("%d [D loss: %f, acc.: %.2f%%] [G loss: %f]" %
                              (iteration + 1, d_loss, 100.0 * accuracy, g_loss))

                        sample_images(generator)
```

Generates a batch of fake images ⟵ `z = np.random.normal(0, 1, (batch_size, 100))`

Trains the Generator ⟵ `g_loss = gan.train_on_batch(z, real)`

Saves losses and accuracies so they can be plotted after training

Outputs training progress ⟶ `print("%d [D loss: %f, acc.: %.2f%%] [G loss: %f]" %`

Outputs a sample generated image ⟵ `sample_images(generator)`

For completeness, we are also including the sample_images() function in the following listing. Recall from chapter 3 that this function outputs a 4 × 4 grid of images synthesized by the Generator in a given training iteration.

Listing 4.7 Displaying generated images

```
def sample_images(generator, image_grid_rows=4, image_grid_columns=4):

    z = np.random.normal(0, 1, (image_grid_rows * image_grid_columns, z_dim))

    gen_imgs = generator.predict(z)

    gen_imgs = 0.5 * gen_imgs + 0.5

    fig, axs = plt.subplots(image_grid_rows,
                            image_grid_columns,
                            figsize=(4, 4),
                            sharey=True,
                            sharex=True)

    cnt = 0
    for i in range(image_grid_rows):
        for j in range(image_grid_columns):
            axs[i, j].imshow(gen_imgs[cnt, :, :, 0], cmap='gray')
            axs[i, j].axis('off')
            cnt += 1
```

Sample random noise ⟶ `z = np.random.normal(...)`

Generates images from random noise ⟵ `gen_imgs = generator.predict(z)`

Rescales image pixel values to [0, 1] ⟶ `gen_imgs = 0.5 * gen_imgs + 0.5`

Sets image grid ⟵ `fig, axs = plt.subplots(...)`

Outputs a grid of images ⟶ `for i in range(image_grid_rows):`

Next, the following code is used to run the model.

```
iterations = 20000
batch_size = 128              ◁──┐   Sets
sample_interval = 1000           │   hyperparameters
                                           ┌  Trains the DCGAN for
                                           │  the specified number
train(iterations, batch_size, sample_interval)  ◁──┘  of iterations
```

4.4.5   Model output

Figure 4.6 shows a sample of handwritten digits produced by the Generator after the DCGAN is fully trained. For a side-by-side comparison, figure 4.7 shows a sample of digits produced by the GAN from chapter 3, and figure 4.8 shows a sample of real handwritten numerals from the MNIST dataset.

Figure 4.6   A sample of handwritten digits generated by a fully trained DCGAN

Figure 4.7   A sample of handwritten digits generated by the GAN implemented in chapter 3

Figure 4.8   A randomly generated grid of real handwritten digits from the MNIST dataset used to train our DCGAN. Unlike the images produced by the simple GAN we implemented in chapter 3, many of the handwritten digits produced by the fully trained DCGAN are essentially indistinguishable from the training data.

As evidenced by the preceding figures, all the extra work we put into implementing DCGAN paid off handsomely. Many of the images of handwritten digits that the network produces after being fully trained are virtually indistinguishable from the ones written by a human hand.

4.5   *Conclusion*

DCGAN demonstrates the versatility of the GAN framework. In theory, the Discriminator and Generator can be represented by any differentiable function, even one as complex as a multilayer convolutional network. However, DCGAN also demonstrates that there are significant hurdles to making more complex implementations work in practice. Without breakthroughs such as batch normalization, DCGAN would fail to train properly.

In the following chapter, we will explore some of the theoretical and practical limitations that make GAN training so challenging as well as the approaches to overcome them.

Summary

- Convolutional neural networks (ConvNets) use one or more convolutional filters that slide over the input volume. At each step as it slides over the input, a filter uses a single set of parameters to produce a single activation value. Together, all the activation values from all the filters produce the output layer.

- Batch normalization is a method that reduces the covariate shift (variations in input value distributions between layers during training) in neural networks by normalizing the output of each layer before it is passed as input to the next layer.

- Deep Convolutional GAN (DCGAN) is a Generative Adversarial Network with convolutional neural networks as its Generator and Discriminator. This architecture achieves superior performance in image-processing tasks, including handwritten digit generation, which we implemented in a code tutorial.

Part 2

Advanced topics in GANs

Part 2 explores a selection of advanced topics in GANs. Building on the foundational concepts from part 1, you will deepen your theoretical understanding of GANs and expand your practical toolkit of GAN implementations:

- Chapter 5 covers many of the theoretical and practical hurdles to training GANs and how to overcome them.
- Chapter 6 presents a groundbreaking training methodology called *Progressive GAN* that has enabled GANs to synthesize images with unprecedented resolution.
- Chapter 7 covers the use of GANs in semi-supervised learning (methods of training classifiers with only a small fraction of labeled examples), an area of immense practical importance.
- Chapter 8 introduces the Conditional GAN, a technique that enables targeted data generation by using labels (or other conditioning information) while training the Generator and Discriminator.
- Chapter 9 explores the CycleGAN, a general-purpose technique for image-to-image translation—turning one image (such as a photo of an apple) into another (such as a photo of an orange).

Training and common challenges: GANing for success

This chapter covers

- Meeting the challenges of evaluating GANs
- Min-Max, Non-Saturating, and Wasserstein GANs
- Using tips and tricks to best train a GAN

NOTE When reading this chapter, please remember that GANs are notoriously hard to both train and evaluate. As with any other cutting-edge field, opinions about what is the best approach are always evolving.

Papers such as "How to Train Your DRAGAN" are a testament to both the incredible capacity of machine learning researchers to make bad jokes and the difficulty of training Generative Adversarial Networks well. Dozens of arXiv papers preoccupy themselves solely with the aim of improving the training of GANs, and numerous workshops have been dedicated to various aspects of training at top academic conferences (including Neural Information Processing Systems, or NIPS, one of the prominent machine learning conferences[1]).

---

[1] NIPS 2016 featured a workshop on GAN training with many important researchers in the field, which this chapter was based on. NIPS has recently changed its abbreviation to NeurIPS.

But GAN training is an evolving challenge, and so a lot of resources—including those presented through papers and conferences—now need a certain amount of updating. This chapter provides a comprehensive yet up-to-date overview of training techniques. In this chapter, you also finally get to experience something no one has ever been known to hate—math. (But we promise not to use more than strictly necessary.)

Jokes aside, however, as the first chapter in the "Advanced Topics in GANs" section of this book, this is quite a dense chapter. We recommend that you go back and try some of the models with several parameters. Then you can return to this chapter, as you should be reading it with a strong understanding of not just what each part of a GAN does, but also the challenges in training them from your own experience.

Like the other chapters in this advanced section, this chapter is here to teach you as well as to provide a useful reference for at least a couple of years to come. Therefore, this chapter is a summary of the tips and tricks from people's experiences, blog posts, and most relevant papers. (If academia is not your cup of tea, now is the time to get out those doodling pens and scribble over the footnotes.) We look at this chapter as a short academic intermission that will give you a clear map indicating all the amazing present and future developments of GANs.

We also hope to thereby equip you with all the basic tools to understand the vast majority of new papers that may come out. In many books, this would be presented as pros and cons lists that would not give readers the full high-level understanding of the choices. But because GANs are such a new field, simple lists are not possible, as the literature has still not agreed on some aspects conclusively. GANs are also a fast-growing field, so we would much prefer to equip you with the ability to navigate it, rather than give you information that is likely to soon be outdated.

With the purpose of this chapter explained, let's clarify where GANs sit again. Figure 5.1 expands on the diagram from chapter 2 and shows the taxonomy of the models so you can understand what other generative techniques exist and how (dis)similar they are.

There are two key takeaways from this diagram:

- All of these generative models ultimately derive from Maximum Likelihood, at least implicitly.
- The variational autoencoder introduced in chapter 2 sits in the Explicit part of the tree. Remember that we had a clear loss function (the reconstruction loss)? Well, with GANs we do not have it anymore. Rather, we now have two competing loss functions that we will cover in lot more depth later. But as such, the system does not have a single analytical solution.

If you know any of the other techniques pictured, that's great. The key idea is that we are moving away from explicit and tractable, into the territory of implicit approaches toward training. However, by now you should be wondering: if we do not have an explicit loss function (even though we have the two separate losses encountered implicitly in the "Conflicting objectives" section of chapter 3), how do we evaluate a GAN? What if you're running parallel, large-scale experiments?

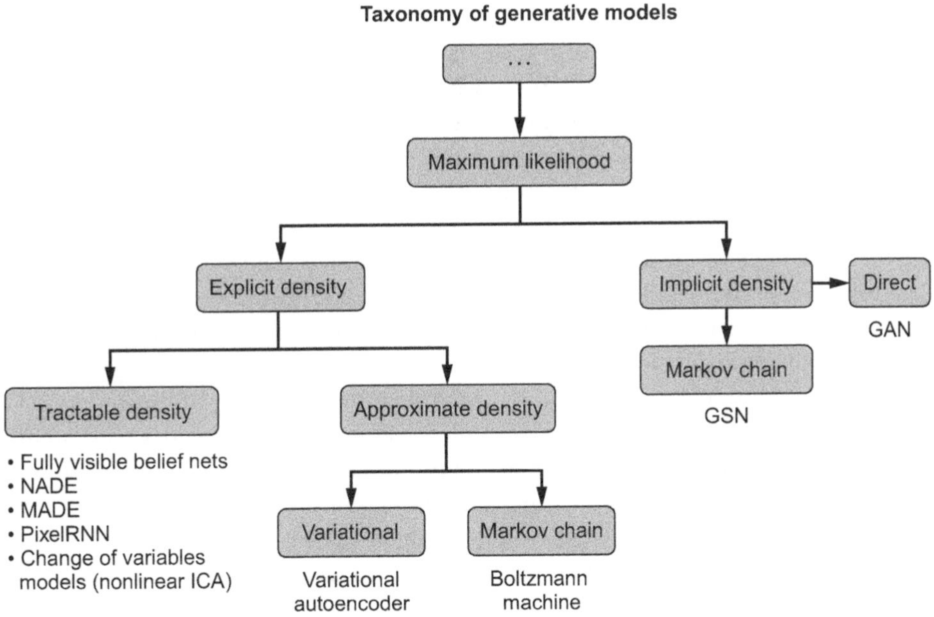

Taxonomy of generative models

Figure 5.1 Where do GANs fit in?
(Source: "Generative Adversarial Networks (GANs)," by Ian Goodfellow, NIPS 2016 tutorial, http://mng.bz/400V.)

To clear up potential confusion, not all the techniques in figure 5.1 come from deep learning, and we certainly do not need you to know any of them, other than VAEs and GANs!

5.1 Evaluation

Let's revisit the chapter 1 analogy about forging a da Vinci painting. Imagine that a forger (Generator) is trying to mimic da Vinci, to get the forged painting accepted at an exhibition. This forger is competing against an art critic (Discriminator) who is trying to accept only real work into the exhibition. In this circumstance, if you are the forger who is aiming to create a "lost piece" by this great artist in order to fool the critic with a flawless impersonation of da Vinci's style, how would you evaluate how well you're doing? How would each actor evaluate their performance?

GANs are trying to solve the problem of never-ending competition between the forger and the art critic. Indeed, given that typically the Generator is of greater interest than the Discriminator, we should think about its evaluation extra carefully. But how would we quantify the style of a great painter or how closely we imitate it? How would we quantify the overall quality of the generation?

5.1.1   Evaluation framework

The best solution would be to have da Vinci paint *all the paintings* that are possible to paint, using his style, and then see whether the image generated using a GAN would be somewhere in that collection. You can think of this process as a nonapproximate version of maximum likelihood maximization. In fact, we would know that the image either is or is not in this set, so no likelihood is involved. However, in practice, this solution is never really possible.

The next best thing would be to assess the image and point to instances of what to look for and then add up the number of errors or artifacts. But these will be highly localized and ultimately would always require a human critic to look at the art piece itself. It is a fundamentally nonscalable—although probably the second best—solution.

We want to have a statistical way of evaluating the quality of the generated samples, because that would scale and would allow us to evaluate as we are experimenting. If we do not have an easy metric to calculate, we also cannot monitor progress. This is a problem especially for evaluating different experiments—imagine measuring or even backpropagating with a human in the loop at each, for example, hyperparameter initialization. This is especially a problem, given that GANs tend to be quite sensitive to hyperparameters. So not having a statistical metric is difficult, because we'd have to check back with humans every time we want to evaluate the quality of training.

Why don't we just use something that we already understand, such as maximum likelihood? It is statistical and measures something vaguely desirable, and we implicitly derive from it anyway. Despite this, maximum likelihood is difficult to use because we need to have a good estimate of the underlying distribution and its likelihood—and that may mean more than billions of images.[2] There are also reasons to want to go beyond maximum likelihood, even if we just had a good sample—which is what we effectively have with the training set.

What else is wrong with maximum likelihood? After all, it is a well-established metric in much of the machine learning research. Generally, maximum likelihood has lots of desirable properties, but as we have touched on, using it is not tractable as an evaluation technique for GANs.

Furthermore, in practice, approximations of maximum likelihood tend to overgeneralize and therefore deliver samples that are too varied to be realistic.[3] Under maximum likelihood, we may find samples that would never occur in the real world, such as a dog with multiple heads or a giraffe with dozens of eyes but no body. But because we don't want GAN violence to give anyone nightmares, we should probably weed out samples that are "too general," using a loss function and/or the evaluation method.

Another way to think about overgeneralization is to start with a probability distribution of fake and real data (for example, images) and look at what the distance functions (a way to measure distance between real and fake images' distributions) would

---

[2] We give the problems of dimensionality better treatment in chapter 10.

[3] See "How (Not) to Train your Generative Model: Scheduled Sampling, Likelihood, Adversary?" by Ferenc Huszár, 2015, http://arxiv.org/abs/1511.05101.

do in cases where there should be zero probability mass. The additional loss due to these overgeneral samples could be tiny if they are not too different, for example, because these modes are close to real data in all but a few key problems such as multiple heads. An overgeneral metric would therefore allow creation of samples even when, according to the true data-generating process, there should not be any, such as a cow with multiple heads.

That is why researchers felt that we need different evaluation principles even though what we are effectively doing is always maximizing likelihood. We are just measuring it in different ways. For those curious, KL divergence and JS divergence—which we will visit in a bit—are also based on maximum likelihood, so here we can treat them as interchangeable.

Thus you now understand that we have to be able to evaluate a sample and that we cannot simply use maximum likelihood to do this. In the following pages, we will talk about the two most commonly used and accepted metrics for statistically evaluating the quality of the generated samples: the *inception score (IS)* and *Fréchet inception distance (FID)*. The advantage of those two metrics is that they have been extensively validated to be highly correlated with at least some desirable property such as visual appeal or realism of the image. The inception score was designed solely around the idea that the samples should be recognizable, but it has also been shown to correlate with human intuition about what constitutes a real image, as validated by Amazon Mechanical Turkers.[4]

5.1.2 Inception score

We clearly need a good statistical evaluation method. Let's start from a high-level wish list of what our ideal evaluation method would ensure:

- The generated samples look like some real, distinguishable thing—for example, buckets or cows. The samples look real, and we can generate samples of items in our dataset. Moreover, our classifier is confident that what it sees is an item it recognizes. Luckily, we already have computer vision classifiers that are able to classify an image as belonging to a particular class, with certain confidence. Indeed, the score itself is named after the Inception network, which is one of those classifiers.

- The generated samples are varied and contain, ideally, all the classes that were represented in the original dataset. This point is also highly desirable because our samples should be representative of the dataset we gave it; if our MNIST-generating GAN is always missing the number 8, we would not have a good generative model. We should have no *interclass* (between classes) mode collapse.[5]

---

[4] Amazon Mechanical Turk is a service that allows you to purchase people's time by the hour to work on a pre-specified task. It's something like on-demand freelancers or Task Rabbit, but only online.

[5] See "An Introduction to Image Synthesis with Generative Adversarial Nets," by He Huang et al., 2018, https://arxiv.org/pdf/1803.04469.pdf.

Although we might have further requirements of our generative model, this is a good start.

The *inception score (IS)* was first introduced in a 2016 paper that extensively validated this metric and confirmed that it indeed correlates with human perceptions of what constitutes a high-quality sample.[6] This metric has since become popular in the GAN research community.

We have explained why we want to have this metric. Now let's dive into the technical details. Computing the IS a simple process:

1 We take the Kullback–Leibler (KL) divergence between the real and the generated distribution.[7]
2 We exponentiate the result of step 1.

Let's look at an example: a failure mode in an Auxiliary Classifier GAN (ACGAN),[8] where we were trying to generate examples of daisies from the ImageNet dataset. When we ran the Inception network on the following ACGAN failure mode, we saw something like figure 5.2; your results may differ, depending on your OS, TensorFlow version, and implementation details.

Image	Category	Score
	daisy	0.05646
	book jacket, dust cover, dust jacket, dust wrapper	0.05086
	goldfish, Carassius auratus	0.04913
	hummingbird	0.02358
	panpipe, pandean pipe, syrinx	0.02029

Figure 5.2   ACGAN failure mode. Scores on the right indicate the softmax output.
(Source: Odena, 2017, https://arxiv.org/pdf/1610.09585.pdf.)

---

[6] See "Improved Techniques for Training GANS," by Tim Salimans et al., 2016, https://arxiv.org/pdf/1606.03498.pdf.

[7] We introduced KL divergence in chapter 2.

[8] See "Conditional Image Synthesis with Auxiliary Classifier GANs," by Augustus Odena et al., 2017, https://arxiv.org/pdf/1610.09585.pdf.

The important thing to note here is that the Inception classifier is not certain what it's looking at, especially among the first three categories. Humans would work out that it's probably a flower, but even we are not sure. Overall confidence in the predictions is also quite low (scores go up to 1.00). This is an example of something that would receive a low IS, which matches our two requirements from the start of the section. Thus, our metrics journey has been a success, as this matches our intuition.

5.1.3   *Fréchet inception distance*

The next problem to solve is the lack of variety of examples. Frequently, GANs learn only a handful of images for each class. In 2017, a new solution was proposed: the *Fréchet inception distance (FID)*.[9] The FID improves on the IS by making it more robust to noise and allowing the detection of *intraclass* (within class) sample omissions.

This is important, because if we accept the IS baseline, then producing only one type of a category technically satisfies the category-being-generated-sometimes requirement. But, for example, if we are trying to create a cat-generation algorithm, this is not actually what we want (say, if we had multiple breeds of cats represented). Furthermore, we want the GAN to output samples that present a cat from more than one angle and, generally, images that are distinct.

We equally do not want the GAN to simply memorize the images. Luckily, that is much easier to detect—we can look at the distance between images in pixel space. Figure 5.3 shows what that may look like. Technical implementation of the FID is again complex, but the high-level idea is that we are looking for a generated distribution of samples that minimizes the number of modifications we have to make to ensure that the generated distribution looks like the distribution of the true data.

The FID is calculated by running images through an Inception network. In practice, we compare the intermediate representations—feature maps or layers—rather than the final output (in other words, we *embed* them). More concretely, we evaluate the distance of the embedded means, the variances, and the covariances of the two distributions—the real and the generated one.

To abstract away from images, if we have a domain of well-understood classifiers, we can use their predictions as a measure of whether this particular sample looks realistic. To summarize, the FID is a way of abstracting away from a human evaluator and allows us to reason statistically, in terms of distributions, even about things as difficult to quantify as the realism of an image.

---

[9] See "GANs Trained by a Two Time-Scale Update Rule Converge to a Local Nash Equilibrium," by Martin Heusel et al., 2017, http://arxiv.org/abs/1706.08500.

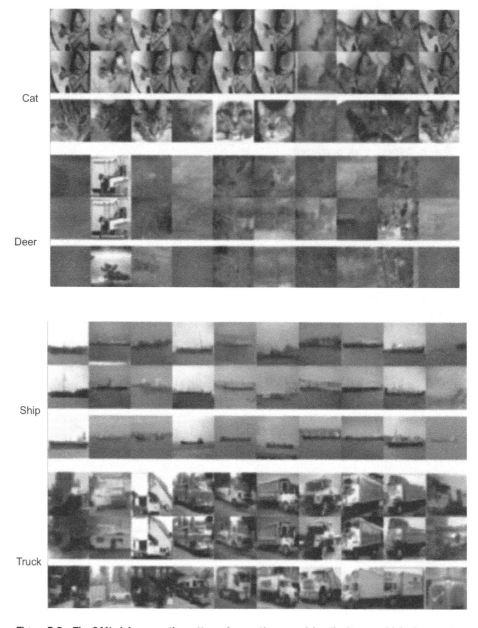

Figure 5.3   The GAN picks up on the patterns by mostly memorizing the items, which also creates an undesirable outcome indicating that the GAN has not learned much useful information and will most likely not generalize. The proof is in the images. The first two rows are pairs of duplicate samples; the last row is the nearest neighbor of the middle row in the training set. Note that these examples are very low resolution as they appear in the paper, due to a low-resolution GAN setup. (Source: "Do GANs Actually Learn the Distribution? An Empirical Study," by Sanjeev Arora and Yi Zhang, 2017, https://arxiv.org/pdf/1706.08224v2.pdf.)

Because this metric is so new, it is still worth waiting to see whether a flaw may be revealed in a later paper. But given the number of reputable authors who have already started using this metric, we decided to include it.[10]

5.2 Training challenges

Training a GAN can be complicated, and we will walk you through the best practices. But here we provide only a high-level, accessible set of explanations that do not deep dive into any of the mathematics that proves the theorems or shows the evidence, because the details are beyond the scope of this book. But we encourage you to go to the sources and decide for yourself. Frequently, the authors even provide code samples to help you get started.

Here is a list of the main problems:

- *Mode collapse*—In *mode collapse*, some of the modes (for example, classes) are not well represented in the generated samples. The mode collapses even though the real data distribution has support for the samples in this part of the distribution; for example, there will be no number 8 in the MNIST dataset. Note that mode collapse can happen even if the network has converged. We talked about *interclass* mode collapse during the explanation of the IS and *intraclass* mode collapse when discussing the FID.

- *Slow convergence*—This is a big problem with GANs and unsupervised settings, in which generally the speed of convergence and available compute are the main constraints—unlike with supervised learning, in which available labeled data is typically the first barrier. Moreover, some people believe that compute, not data, is going to be the determining factor in the AI race in the future. Plus, everyone wants fast models that do not take days to train.

- *Overgeneralization*—Here, we talk especially about cases in which modes (potential data samples) that should not have support (should not exist), do. For example, you might see a cow with multiple bodies but only one head, or vice versa. This happens when the GAN overgeneralizes and learns things that should not exist based on the real data.

Note that mode collapse and overgeneralization can sometimes most naively be resolved by reinitializing the algorithm, but such an algorithm is fragile, which is bad. This list gives us, broadly, two key metrics: speed and quality. But even these two metrics are similar, as much of training is ultimately focused on closing the gap between the real and the generated distribution faster.

---

[10] See "Is Generator Conditioning Causally Related to GAN Performance?" by Augustus Odena et al., 2018, http://arxiv.org/abs/1802.08768. See also S. Nowozin (Microsoft Research) talk at UCL, February 10, 2018.

So how do we resolve this? When it comes to GAN training, several techniques can help us improve the training process, just as you would with any other machine learning algorithm:

- Adding network depth
- Changing the game setup

    - Min-Max design and stopping criteria that were proposed by the original paper
    - Non-Saturating design and stopping criteria that were proposed by the original paper[11]
    - Wasserstein GAN as a recent improvement
- Number of training hacks with commentary
    - Normalizing the inputs
    - Penalizing the gradients
    - Training the Discriminator more
    - Avoiding sparse gradients
    - Changing to soft and noisy labels

5.2.1 *Adding network depth*

As with many machine learning algorithms, the easiest way to make learning more stable is to reduce the complexity. If you can start with a simple algorithm and iteratively add to it, you get more stability during training, faster convergence, and potentially other benefits. Chapter 6 explores this idea in more depth.

You could quickly achieve stability with both a simple Generator and Discriminator and then add complexity as you train, as explained in one of the most mind-blowing GAN papers.[12] Here, the authors from NVIDIA progressively grow the two networks so that at the end of each training cycle, we double the output size of the Generator and double the input of the Discriminator. We start with two simple networks and train until we achieve good performance.

This ensures that rather than starting with a massive parameter space, which is orders of magnitude larger than the initial input size, we start by generating an image of 4 × 4 pixels and navigating this parameter space before doubling the size of the output. We repeat this until we reach images of size 1024 × 1024.

See how impressive this is for yourself; both the pictures in figure 5.4 are generated. Now we are moving beyond the blurry 64 × 64 images that autoencoders can generate.

This approach has these advantages: stability, speed of training, and, most importantly, the quality of the samples produced as well as their scale. Although this paradigm is new, we expect more and more papers to use it. You should definitely

---

[11] See "Generative Adversarial Networks," by Ian Goodfellow et al., 2014, http://arxiv.org/abs/1406.2661.

[12] See "Progressive Growing of GANs for Improved Quality, Stability, and Variation," by Tero Karras et al., 2017, http://arxiv.org/abs/1710.10196.

Figure 5.4 Full HD images generated by GANs. You may consider this a teaser for the next chapter, where you will be rewarded for all your hard work in this one.
(Source: Karras et al., 2017, https://arxiv.org/abs/1710.10196.)

experiment with it also, because it is a technique that can be applied to virtually any type of GAN.

5.2.2 Game setups

One way to think about the two-player competitive nature of GANs is to imagine that you are playing the game of Go or any other board game that can end at any point, including chess. (Indeed, this borrows from DeepMind's approach to AlphaGo and its split into policy and value network.) As a player, you need to be able to not only know the game's objective and therefore what both players are trying to accomplish, but also understand how close you are to victory. So you have *rules* and you have a *distance (victory) metric*—for example, the number of pawns lost.

But just as not every board-game victory metric applies equally well to every game, some GAN victory metrics—distances or divergences—tend to be used with particular game setups and not with others. It is worth examining each loss function (victory metrics) and the player dynamics (game setup) separately.

Here, we start to introduce some of the mathematical notation that describes the GAN problem. The equations are important, and we promise we won't scare you with any more than necessary. The reason we introduce them is to give you a high-level understanding as well as equip you with the tools to understand what a lot of GAN researchers still do not seem to distinguish. (Maybe they should train the Discriminator in their head—oh, well.)

5.2.3 Min-Max GAN

As we explained earlier in this book, you can think of the GAN setup from a game-theoretical point of view, where you have two players trying to outplay each other. But even the original 2014 paper mentioned that there are two versions of the game. In principle, the more understandable and the more theoretically well-grounded approach is exactly the one we described: just consider the GAN problem a *min-max* game. Equation 5.1 describes the loss function for the Discriminator.

$$J^D = E_{x \sim p_r} \log[D(x)] + E_{z \sim p_g} \log[1 - D(G(z))] \qquad \text{Equation 5.1}$$

The *E*s stand for expectation over either *x* (true data distribution) or *z* (latent space), *D* stands for the Discriminator's function (mapping image to probability), and *G* stands for the Generator's function (mapping latent vector to an image). This first equation should be familiar from any binary classification problem. If we give ourselves some freedom and get rid of the complexity, we can rewrite this equation as follows:

$$J^D = D(x) - D(G(z)), \quad \text{for } D(x), D(G(z)) \in [0, 1]$$

This states that the Discriminator is trying to minimize the likelihood of mistaking a real sample for a fake one (first part) or a fake sample for a real one (the second part).

Now let's turn our attention to the Generator's loss function in equation 5.2.

$$J^G = -J^D \qquad \text{Equation 5.2}$$

Because we have only two agents and they are competing against each other, it makes sense that the Generator's loss would be a negative of the Discriminator's.

Putting it all together: we have two loss functions, and one is the negative value of the other. The adversarial nature is clear. The Generator is trying to outsmart the Discriminator. As for the Discriminator, remember that it is a binary classifier. The Discriminator also outputs only a single number—not the binary class—so it's punished for its confidence or lack thereof. The rest is just some fancy math to give us nice properties such as asymptotic consistency to the Jensen–Shannon divergence (which is a great phrase to memorize if you're trying to curse someone).

We previously explained why we typically don't use maximum likelihood. Instead, we use measures such as the KL divergence and the Jensen–Shannon divergence (JSD) and, more recently the earth mover's distance, also known as Wasserstein distance. But all these divergences help us understand the difference between the real and the generated distribution. For now, just think of the JSD as a symmetric version of the KL divergence, which we introduced in chapter 2.

DEFINITION *Jensen-Shannon divergence (JSD)* is a symmetric version of KL divergence. Whereas $KL(p,q)! = KL(q,p)$, it is the case that $JSD(p,q) == JSD(q,p)$.

For those of you who want more detail, KL divergence, as well as JSD, are generally regarded as what GANs are ultimately trying to minimize. These are both types of distance metrics that help us understand how different the two distributions are in a high-dimensional space. Some neat proofs connect those divergences and the min-max version of the GAN; however, these concerns are too academic for this book. If this paragraph makes little sense, you're not having a stroke; don't worry. It's just statistician things.

We typically do not use the Min-Max GAN (MM-GAN) beyond the nice theoretical guarantees it gives us. It serves as a neat theoretical framework to understand GANs: both as a game-theoretical concept—stemming from the competitive nature between the two networks/players—as well as an information-theoretical one. Beyond that, there are ordinarily no advantages to the MM-GAN. Typically, only the next two setups are used.

5.2.4 *Non-Saturating GAN*

In practice, it frequently turns out that the min-max approach creates more problems, such as slow convergence for the Discriminator. The original GAN paper proposes an alternative formulation: *Non-Saturating GAN* (NS-GAN). In this version of the problem, rather than trying to put the two loss functions as direct competitors of each other, we make the two loss functions independent, as shown in equation 5.3, but directionally consistent with the original formulation (equation 5.2).

Again, let's focus on a general understanding: the two loss functions are no longer set directly against each other. But in equation 5.3, you can see that the Generator is trying to minimize the opposite of the second term of the Discriminator in equation 5.4. Basically, it is trying not to get caught for the samples that it generates.

$$J^G = E_{z \sim p_g} \log[D(G(z))] \qquad \text{Equation 5.3}$$

$$J^D = E_{x \sim p_r} \log[D(x)] + E_{z \sim p_g} \log[1 - D(G(z))] \qquad \text{Equation 5.4}$$

The intuition for the Discriminator is the exact same as it was before—equation 5.1 and equation 5.4 are identical, but the equivalent of equation 5.2 has now changed. The main reason for the NS-GAN is that in the MM-GAN's case, the gradients can easily *saturate*—get close to 0, which leads to slow convergence, because the weight updates that are backpropagated are either 0 or tiny. Perhaps a picture would make this clearer; see figure 5.5.

You can see that around 0.0, the gradient of both maximum likelihood and MM-GAN is close to 0, which is where a lot of early training happens, whereas the NS-GAN has a lot higher gradient there, so training should happen much more quickly at the start.

We don't have a good theoretical understanding of why the NS variant should converge to the Nash equilibrium. In fact, because the NS-GAN is heuristically motivated, using this form no longer gives us any of the neat mathematical guarantees we used to get; see figure 5.6. Because of the complexity of the GAN problem, however, even in the NS-GAN's case, there is a chance that the training might not converge at all, although it has been empirically shown to perform better than the MM-GAN.

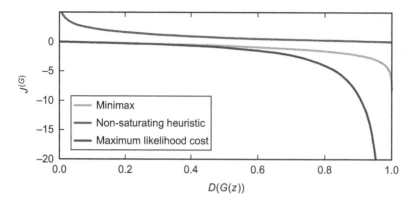

Figure 5.5 A sketch of what the hypothesized relationships are meant to look like in theory. The y-axis is the loss function for the Generator, whereas $D(G(z))$ is the Discriminator's "guess" for the likelihood of the generated sample. You can see that Minimax (MM) stays flat for too long, thereby giving the Generator too little information—the gradients vanish.
(Source: "Understanding Generative Adversarial Networks," by Daniel Seita, 2017, http://mng.bz/QQAj.)

But our dreadful sacrifice leads to significant improvement in performance. The neat thing about the NS approach is not only that the initial training is faster, but also, because the Generator learns faster, the Discriminator learns faster too. This is desirable, because (almost) all of us are on a tight computational and time budget, and the faster we can learn, the better. Some argue that the NS-GAN has not yet been surpassed on a fixed computational budget, and even Wasserstein GAN is not conclusively a better architecture.[13]

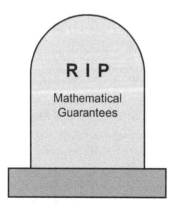

Figure 5.6 A moment of silence, please.

---

[13] See "Are GANs Created Equal? A Large-Scale Study," by Mario Lucic et al., 2017, http://arxiv.org/abs/1711.10337.

5.2.5 *When to stop training*

Strictly speaking, the NS-GAN

- Is no longer asymptotically consistent with the JSD
- Has an equilibrium state that theoretically is even more elusive

The first point is important, because the JSD is a meaningful tool in explaining why an implicitly generated distribution should even converge at all to the real data distribution. In principle, this gives us stopping criteria; but in practice, this is almost pointless, because we can never verify when the true distribution and the generated distribution have converged. People typically decide when to stop by looking at the generated samples every couple of iterations. More recently, some people have started looking at defining stopping criteria by FID, IS, or the less popular sliced Wasserstein distance.

The second point is also important because the instability obviously causes training problems. One of the more important questions is knowing when to stop. In the two original formulations of the GAN problem, we are never given a clear set of conditions under which the training has finished in practice. In principle, we are always told that once we reach Nash equilibrium, the training is done, but in practice this is again hard to verify, because the high dimensionality makes equilibrium difficult to prove.

If you want to plot the loss functions of the Generator and the Discriminator, they would typically jump all over the place. This makes sense because they're competing against each other, so if one gets better, the other one gets a larger loss. Just by looking at the two loss functions, it is unclear when we've actually finished training.

In the NS-GAN's defense, it should be said that it is still much faster than the Wasserstein GAN. As a result, the NS-GAN may get over these limitations by being able to run more quickly.

5.2.6 *Wasserstein GAN*

Recently, a new development in GAN training has emerged and quickly reached academic popularity: *Wasserstein GAN (WGAN)*.[14] It is now mentioned by virtually every major academic paper and many practitioners. Ultimately, the WGAN is important for three reasons:

- It significantly improves on the loss functions, which are now interpretable and provide clearer stopping criteria.
- Empirically, the WGAN tends to have better results.
- Unlike a lot of research into GANs, it has clear theoretical backing that starts from the loss and shows how the KL divergence that we are trying to approximate is ultimately not well justified theoretically or practically. Based on this theory, it then proposes a better loss function that mitigates this problem.

---

[14] See "Wasserstein GAN," by Martin Arjovsky et al., 2017, https://arxiv.org/pdf/1701.07875.pdf.

The importance of the first point should be fairly obvious from the previous section. Given the competitive nature between Generator and Discriminator, we don't have a clear point at which we want to stop training. The WGAN uses the earth mover's distance as a loss function that clearly correlates with the visual quality of the samples generated. The benefits of the second and third points are somewhat obvious—we want to have higher-quality samples and better theoretical grounding.

How is this magic achieved? Let's look at the Wasserstein loss for the Discriminator—or the *critic*, as the WGAN calls it—in more detail. Take a look at equation 5.5.

$$\max E_{x \sim P_r}[f_w(x)] - E_{z \sim p(z)}[f_w(g_\theta(z))] \qquad \text{Equation 5.5}$$

This equation is somewhat similar to what you have seen before (as a high-level simplification of equation 5.1), with some important differences. We now have the function f_w, which acts as a Discriminator. The critic is trying to estimate the earth mover's distance, and looks for the *maximum* difference between the real (first term) and the generated (second term) distribution under different (valid) parametrizations of the f_w function. And we are now simply measuring the difference. The critic is trying to make the Generator's life the hardest it could be by looking at different projections using f_w into shared space in order to maximize the amount of probability mass it has to move.

Equation 5.6 shows the Generator, as it now has to include the earth mover's distance.

$$\min E_{x \sim P_r}[f_w(x)] - E_{z \sim p(z)}[f_w(g_\theta(z))] \qquad \text{Equation 5.6}$$

On a high level, in this equation we are trying to *minimize* the distance between the expectation of the real distribution and the expectation of the generated distribution. The paper that introduced the WGAN itself is complex, but the gist is that f_w is a function satisfying a technical constraint.

> **NOTE** The technical constraint that f_w satisfies is $1 - $ Lipschitz: for all $x1$, $x2$: $|f(x1) - f(x2)| \leq |x1 - x2|$.

The problem that the Generator is trying to solve is similar to the one before, but let's go into more detail anyway:

1. We draw x from either the real distribution ($x \sim P_r$) or the generated distribution x^* ($g_\theta(z)$, where $z \sim p(z)$).
2. The generated samples are sampled from z (the latent space) and then transformed via g_θ to get the samples (x^*) in the same space and then evaluated using f_w.
3. We are trying to minimize our loss function—or distance function, in this case—the earth mover's distance. The actual numbers are calculated using the earth mover's distance, which we will explain later.

The setup is also great because we have a much more understandable loss (for example, no logarithms). We also have more tunable training, because in WGAN settings, we have to set a clipping constant, which acts a lot like a learning rate in standard machine learning. This gives us an extra parameter to tune, but that can be a double-edged sword, if your GAN architecture ends up being very sensitive to it. But without going into the mathematics too much, the WGAN has two practical implications:

- We now have clearer stopping criteria because this GAN has been validated by later papers that show a correlation between the Discriminator loss and the perceptual quality. We can simply measure the Wasserstein distance, and that helps inform when to stop.
- We can now train the WGAN to convergence. This is relevant because meta-review papers[15] showed that using the JS loss and the divergence between the Generator in the real distribution as a measure of training progress can often be meaningless.[16] To translate that into human terms, sometimes in chess, you need to lose a couple of rounds and therefore temporarily do worse in order to learn in a couple of iterations and ultimately do better.

This may sound like magic. But this is partially because the WGAN is using a different distance metric than anything you've encountered so far. It is called the *earth mover's distance*, or *Wasserstein distance*, and the idea behind it is clever. We will be nice for once and not torture you with more math, but let's talk about this idea.

You implicitly understand that there are two distributions that are both very high dimensional: the real data-producing one (that we never fully see) and the samples from the Generator (the fake one). Think about how vast the sample space for even a 32×32 RGB ($x3 \times 256$ pixel values) image is. Now imagine all of this probability mass for both of these distributions as being just two sets of hills. Chapter 10 revisits this in more detail. For reference, we include figure 5.7, but it builds largely on the same ideas as chapter 2.

Imagine having to move all the ground that represents probability mass from the fake distribution so that the distribution looks exactly like the real distribution, or at least what we have seen of it. That would be like your neighbor having a super cool sandcastle, and you having a lot of sand and trying to make the exact same sandcastle. How much work would that take, to move all of that mass into just the right places? Hey, it's okay, we've all been there; sometimes you just wish your sandcastle was a bit cooler and more sparkly.

Using an approximate version of the Wasserstein distance, we can evaluate how close we are to generating samples that look like they came from the real distribution. Why *approximate*? Well, for one because we never see the real data distribution, so it's difficult to evaluate the exact earth mover's distance.

---

[15] A *meta-review* is just a review of reviews. It helps researchers pool findings from across several papers.
[16] See "Many Paths to Equilibrium: GANs Do Not Need to Decrease a Divergence at Every Step," by William Fedus et al., 2018, https://openreview.net/forum?id=ByQpn1ZA-.

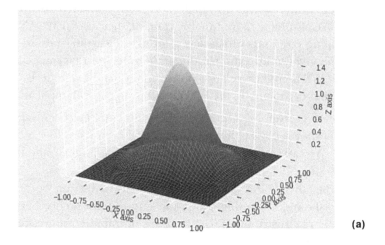

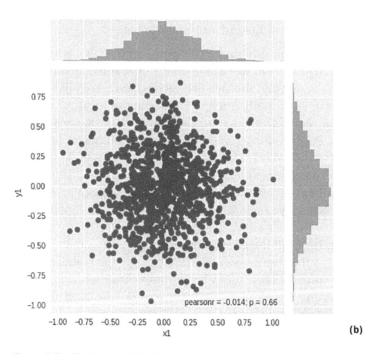

Figure 5.7   Plot (a) should be familiar from chapter 2. For extra clarity, we provide another view of a Gaussian distribution in plot (b) of the data drawn from the same distribution, but showing vertical slices of just the first distribution on the top and just the second distribution on the right. Plot (a) then is a probability density abstraction of this data, where the z-axis represents the probability of that point being sampled. Now, even though one of these is just an abstraction of the other, how would you compare the two? How would you make sure that they are the same even when we told you? What if this distribution had 3,072 possible dimensions? In this example, we have just two! We are building up to how we'd compare two heaps-of-sand-looking distributions as in (b), but remember that as our distributions get more complicated, properly matching like for like also gets harder.

In the end, all you need to know is that the earth mover's distance has nicer properties than either the JS or KL, and there are already important contributions building on the WGAN as well as validating its generally superior performance.[17] Although in some cases the WGAN does not completely outperform all the others, it is generally at least as good in every case (though it should be noted that some may disagree with this interpretation).[18]

Overall, the WGAN (or the gradient penalty version, *WGAN-GP*) is widely used and has become the de facto standard in much of GAN research and practice—though the NS-GAN should not be forgotten anytime soon. When you see a new paper that does not have the WGAN as one of the benchmarks being compared and does not have a good justification for not including it—be careful!

5.3 Summary of game setups

We have presented the three core versions of the GAN setup: min-max, non-saturating, and Wasserstein. One of these versions will be mentioned at the beginning of every paper, and now you'll have at least an idea of whether the paper is using the original formulation, which is more explainable but doesn't work as well in practice; or the non-saturating version, which loses a lot of the mathematical guarantees but works much better; or the newer Wasserstein version, which has both theoretical grounding and largely superior performance.

As a handy guide, table 5.1 presents a list of the NS-GAN, WGAN, and even the improved WGAN-GP formulations we use in this book. This is here so that you have the relevant versions in one place—sorry, MM-GAN. We have included the WGAN-GP here for completeness, because these three are the academic and industry go-tos.

Table 5.1 Summary of loss functions[a]

Name	Value function	Notes
NS-GAN	$L_D^{NS} = E[\log(D(x))] + E[\log(1 - D(G(z)))]$ $L_G^{NS} = E[\log(D(G(z)))]$	This is one of the original formulations. Typically not used in practice anymore, except as a foundational block or comparison. This is an equivalent formulation to the NS-GAN you have seen, just without the constants. But these are effectively equivalent.[b]

---

[17] See "Improved Training of Wasserstein GANs," by Ishaan Gulrajani et al., 2017, http://arxiv.org/abs/1704.00028.

[18] See Lucic et al., 2017, http://arxiv.org/abs/ 1711.10337.

Table 5.1 Summary of loss functions[a] (continued)

Name	Value function	Notes
WGAN	$L_D^{WGAN} = E[D(x)] - E[D(G(z))]$ $L_G^{WGAN} = E[D(G(z))]$	This is the WGAN with somewhat simplified loss. This seems to be creating a new paradigm for GANs. We explained this equation previously as equation 5.5 in greater detail.
WGAN -GP[c] (gradient penalties)	$L_D^{W-GP} = E[D(x)] - E[D(G(z))] + GPterm$ $L_G^{W-GP} = E[D(G(z))]$	This is an example of a GAN with a gradient penalty (GP). WGAN-GP typically shows the best results. We have not discussed the WGAN-GP in this chapter in great detail; we include it here for completeness.

a. Source: "Collection of Generative Models in TensorFlow," by Hwalsuk Lee, http://mng.bz/Xgv6.
b. We tend to use the constants in written code, and this cleaner mathematical formulation in papers.
c. This is a version of the WGAN with gradient penalty that is commonly used in new academic papers. See Gulrajani et al., 2017, http://arxiv.org/abs/1704.00028.

5.4 *Training hacks*

We are now departing from the well-grounded academic results into the areas that academics or practitioners just "figured out." These are simply hacks, and often you just have to try them to see if they work for you. The list in this section was inspired by Soumith Chintala's 2016 post, "How to Train a GAN: Tips and Tricks to Make GANs Work" (https://github.com/soumith/ganhacks), but some things have changed since then.

An example of what has changed is some of the architectural advice, such as the Deep Convolutional GAN (DCGAN) being a baseline for everything. Currently, most people start with the WGAN; in the future, the Self-Attention GAN (SAGAN is touched on in chapter 12) may be a focus. In addition, some things are still true, and we regard them as universally accepted, such as using the Adam optimizer instead of vanilla stochastic gradient descent.[19] We encourage you to check out the list, as its creation was a formative moment in GAN history.

5.4.1 *Normalizations of inputs*

Normalizing the images to be between –1 and 1 is still typically a good idea according to almost every machine learning resource, including Chintala's list. We generally normalize because of the easier tractability of computations, as is the case with the rest of

---

[19] Why is Adam better than vanilla stochastic gradient descent (SGD)? Because Adam is an extension of SGD that tends to work better in practice. Adam groups several training hacks along with SGD into one easy-to-use package.

machine learning. Given this restriction on the inputs, it is a good idea to restrict your Generator's final output with, for example, a *tanh* activation function.

5.4.2 Batch normalization

Batch normalization was discussed in detail in chapter 4. We include it here for completeness. As a note on how our perceptions of batch normalization have changed: originally batch norm was generally regarded as an extremely successful technique, but recently it has been shown to *sometimes* deliver bad results, especially in the Generator.[20] In the Discriminator, on the other hand, results have been almost universally positive.[21]

5.4.3 Gradient penalties

This training trick builds on point 10 in Chintala's list, which had the intuition that if the norms of the gradients are too high, something is wrong. Even today, networks such as BigGAN are innovating in this space, as we touch on in chapter 12.[22]

However, technical issues still remain: naive weighed clipping can produce vanishing or exploding gradients known from much of the rest of deep learning.[23] We can restrict the gradient norm of the Discriminator output with respect to its input. In other words, if you change your input a little bit, your updated weights should not change too much. Deep learning is full of magic like this. This is especially important in the WGAN setting, but can be applied elsewhere.[24] Generally, this trick has in some form been used by numerous papers.[25]

Here, we can simply use the native implementation of your favorite deep learning framework to penalize the gradient and not focus on the implementation detail beyond what we described. Smarter methods have recently been published by top researchers (including one good fellow) and presented at ICML 2018, but their widespread academic acceptance has not been proven yet.[26] A lot of work is being done to make GANs more stable—such as Jacobian clamping, which is also yet to be reproduced in any meta-study—so we will need to wait and see which methods will make it.

---

[20] See Gulrajani et al., 2017, http://arxiv.org/abs/ 1704.00028.

[21] See "Tutorial on Generative Adversarial Networks—GANs in the Wild," by Soumith Chintala, 2017, https://www.youtube.com/watch?v=Qc1F3-Rblbw.

[22] See "Large-Scale GAN Training for High-Fidelity Natural Image Synthesis," by Andrew Brock et al., 2019, https://arxiv.org/pdf/1809.11096.pdf.

[23] See Gulrajani et al., 2017, http://arxiv.org/abs/ 1704.00028.

[24] Though here the authors call the Discriminator *critic*, borrowing from reinforcement learning, as much of that paper is inspired by it.

[25] See "Least Squares Generative Adversarial Networks," by Xudong Mao et al., 2016, http://arxiv.org/abs/1611.04076. Also see "BEGAN: Boundary Equilibrium Generative Adversarial Networks," by David Berthelot et al., 2017, http://arxiv.org/abs/1703.10717.

[26] See Odena et al., 2018, http://arxiv.org/abs/1802.08768.

5.4.4 *Train the Discriminator more*

Training the Discriminator more is an approach that has recently gained a lot of success. In Chintala's original list, this is labeled as being uncertain, so use it with caution. There are two broad approaches:

- Pretraining the Discriminator before the Generator even gets the chance to produce anything.
- Having more updates for the Discriminator per training cycle. A common ratio is five Discriminator weight updates per one of the Generator's.

In the words of deep learning researcher and teacher Jeremy Howard, this works because it is "the blind leading the blind." You need to initially and continuously inject information about what the real-world data looks like.

5.4.5 *Avoid sparse gradients*

It intuitively makes sense that sparse gradients (such as the ones produced by ReLU or MaxPool) would make training harder. This is because of the following:

- The intuition, especially behind average pooling, can be confusing, but think of it this way: if we go with standard max pooling, we lose *all but the maximum* value for the entire receptive field of a convolution, and that makes it much harder to use the transposed convolutions—in DCGAN's case—to recover the information. With average pooling, we at least have a sense of what the *average* value is. It is still not perfect—we are still losing information—but at least less than before, because the average is more representative than the simple maximum.
- Another problem is information loss, if we are using, say, regular rectified linear unit (ReLU) activation. A way to look at this problem is to consider how much information is lost when applying this operation, because we might have to recover it later. Recall that $\text{ReLU}(x)$ is simply $\max(0,x)$, which means that for all the negative values, all this information is lost forever. If instead we ensure that we carry over the information from the negative regions and signify that this information is different, we can preserve all this information.

As we suggested, fortunately, a simple solution exists for both of these: we can use Leaky ReLU—which is something like $0.1 \times x$ for negative x, and $1 \times x$ for x that's at least 0—and average pooling to get around a lot of these problems. Other activation functions exist (such as *sigmoid*, ELU, and *tanh*), but people tend to use Leaky ReLU most commonly.

> **NOTE** The Leaky ReLU can be any real number, typically, $0 < x < 1$.

Overall, we are trying to minimize information loss and make the flow of information the most logical it can be, without asking the GAN to backpropagate the error in some strange way, where it also has to learn the mapping.

5.4.6 *Soft and noisy labels*

Researchers use several approaches to either add noise to labels or smooth them. Ian Goodfellow tends to recommend one-sided label smoothing (for example, using 0 and 0.9 as binary labels), but generally playing around with either adding noise or clipping seems to be a good idea.

Summary

- You have learned why evaluation is such a difficult topic for generative models and how we can train a GAN well with clear criteria indicating when to stop.
- Various evaluation techniques move beyond the naive statistical evaluation of distributions and provide us with something more useful that correlates with visual sample quality.
- Training is performed in three setups: the game-theoretical Min-Max GAN, the heuristically motivated Non-Saturating GAN, and the newest and theoretically well-founded Wasserstein-GAN.
- Training hacks that allow us to train faster include the following:
  - Normalizing inputs, which is standard in machine learning
  - Using gradient penalties that give us more stability in training
  - Helping to warm-start the Discriminator to ultimately give us a good Generator, because doing so sets a higher bar for the generated samples
  - Avoiding sparse gradients, because they lose too much information
  - Playing around with soft and noisy labels rather than the typical binary classification

Progressing with GANs

In this chapter, we provide a hands-on tutorial to build a Progressive GAN by using TensorFlow and the newly released TensorFlow Hub (TFHub). The *Progressive GAN* (aka *PGGAN*, or *ProGAN*) is a cutting-edge technique that has managed to generate full-HD photorealistic images. Presented at one of the top machine learning conferences, the International Conference on Learning Representations (ICLR) in 2018, this technique made such a splash that Google immediately integrated it as one of the few models to be part of the TensorFlow Hub. In fact, this technique was lauded by Yoshua Bengio—one of the grandfathers of deep learning—as "almost too good to be true." When it was released, it became an instant favorite of academic presentations and experimental projects.

We recommend that you go through this chapter with TensorFlow 1.7 or higher, but 1.8+ was the latest release at the time of writing, so that was the one we used.

For TensorFlow Hub, we suggest using a version no later than 0.4.0, because later versions have trouble importing due to compatibility issues with TensorFlow 1.x. After reading this chapter, you'll be able to implement all the key improvements of the Progressive GAN. These four innovations are as follows:

- Progressively growing and smoothly fading in higher-resolution layers
- Mini-batch standard deviation
- Equalized learning rate
- Pixel-wise feature normalization

This chapter features two main examples:

- Code for the crucial innovations of Progressive GANs—more specifically, the smoothly fading-in higher-resolution layers and the other three innovations as listed previously. The rest of the implementation of the Progressive GAN technique is too substantial to be included in this book.
- A pretrained, easily downloadable implementation as provided by Google on TFHub, which is a new centralized repository for machine learning models, similar to Docker Hub or Conda and PyPI repositories in the software package world. This implementation will allow us to do latent space interpolation to control the features of the generated examples. It will briefly touch on the seeding vectors in the latent space of the Generator so that we can get pictures that we want. You saw this idea in chapters 2 and 4.

The reasons we decided to implement the PGGAN using TFHub rather than from the ground up as we do in all the other chapters are threefold:

- Especially for practitioners, we want to make sure you are—at least in one chapter—exposed to the software engineering best practices that may speed up your workflow. Want to try a quick GAN on your problem? Just use one of the implementations on TFHub. There are now many more than when we were first writing this chapter, including many reference implementations (for example, for BigGAN in chapter 12 and NS-GAN in chapter 5). We want to give you access to easy-to-use, state-of-the-art examples, because this is the way that machine learning is going—automating as much of machine learning as possible so we can focus on what matters the most: delivering impact. Google's Cloud AutoML (https://cloud.google.com/automl/) and Amazon SageMaker (https://aws.amazon.com/sagemaker/) are prime examples of this trend. Even Facebook recently introduced PyTorch Hub, so both major frameworks now have one.
- The original implementation of PGGAN took the NVIDIA researchers *one to two months* to run, which we thought was impractical for any person to run on their own, especially if you want to experiment or get something wrong.[1] TFHub still

---

[1] See "Progressive Growing of GANs for Improved Quality, Stability, and Variation," by Tero Karras, 2018, https://github.com/tkarras/progressive_growing_of_gans.

gives you a fully trainable PGGAN, so if you want to repurpose the days of computation for something else, you can!

- We still want to show you PGGANs' most important innovations. But if we want to explain those well—including code—we can't fit all the implementation details into one chapter, even in Keras, as all the implementations tend to be pretty sizeable. TFHub allows us to skip over the boilerplate code and focus on the ideas that matter.

6.1   *Latent space interpolation*

Recall from chapter 2 that we have this lower-resolution space—called *latent space*—that seeds our output. As with the DCGAN from chapter 4 and indeed the Progressive GAN, the initial trained latent space has semantically meaningful properties. It means that we can find the vector offsets that, for example, introduce eyeglasses to an image of a face, and the same offset will introduce glasses in new images. We can also pick two random vectors and then move in equal increments between them and so gradually—smoothly—get an image that matches the second vector.

This is called *interpolation*, and you can see this process in figure 6.1. As the author of BigGAN said, meaningful transitions from one vector to another show that the GAN has learned some underlying structure.

Figure 6.1   We can perform latent space interpolation because the latent vector we send to the Generator produces consistent outcomes that are predictable in some ways; not only is the generative process predictable, but also the output is not jagged—or reacting sharply to small changes—considering the latent vector changes. If we, for example, want an image that is a blend of two faces, we just need to search somewhere around the average of the two vectors.

6.2   *They grow up so fast*

In previous chapters, you learned which results are easy to achieve with GANs and which are difficult. Moreover, things like *mode collapse* (showing only a few examples of the overall distribution) and lack of *convergence* (one of the causes of poor quality of the results) are no longer alien terms to us.

Recently, a Finnish NVIDIA team released a paper that has managed to blow many previous cutting-edge papers out of the water: "Progressive Growing of GANs for Improved Quality, Stability, and Variation," by Tero Karras et al. This paper features four fundamental innovations, so let's walk through them in order.

6.2.1 *Progressive growing and smoothing of higher-resolution layers*

Before we dive into what the Progressive GAN does, let's start with a simple analogy. Imagine looking at a mountain region from a bird's-eye view: you have lots of valleys, which have nice creeks and villages—generally quite habitable. Then you have many mountain tops that are rough and generally unpleasant to live on because of weather conditions. This sort of represents the loss function landscape, where we want to minimize the loss by going down the mountain slopes and into the valleys, which are much nicer.

We can imagine training as dropping a mountaineer into a random place in this mountain region and then following their path down the slope into a valley. This is what *stochastic gradient descent* does, and chapter 10 revisits this in a lot more detail. Now, unfortunately, if we start with a very complex mountain range, the mountaineer will not know which direction to travel. The space around our adventurer would be jagged and rough. It would be difficult to make out where the nicest, lowest valley is with lots of habitable lands. Instead, we zoom out and reduce the complexity of the mountain range to give the mountaineer a high-level picture of this particular area.

As our mountaineer gets closer to a valley, we can start increasing the complexity by zooming in on the terrain. Then we no longer see just the coarse/pixelated texture, but instead get to see the finer details. This approach has the advantage that as our mountaineer goes down the slope, they can easily make little optimizations to make the hiking easier. For example, they can take a path through a dried-up creek to make the descent into the valley even faster. That is *progressive growing*: increasing the resolution of the terrain as we go.

However, if you have ever seen an open world computer game or scrolled too quickly through Google Earth with 3D on, you know that quickly increasing the resolution of the terrain around you can be startling and unpleasant. Objects all of a sudden jump into existence. So instead, we progressively *smooth in* and slowly introduce more complexity as the mountaineer gets closer to the objective.

In technical terms, we are going from a few low-resolution convolutional layers to many high-resolution ones as we train. Thus, we first train the early layers and only then introduce a higher-resolution layer, where it is harder to navigate the loss space. We go from something simple—for example, 4×4 trained for several steps—to something more complex—for example, 1024×1024 trained for several epochs, as shown in figure 6.2.

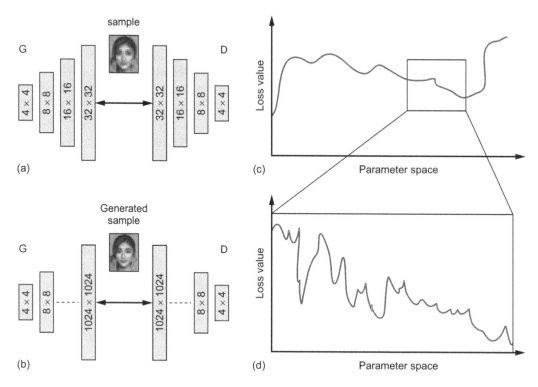

Figure 6.2 Can you see how we start with a smooth mountain range and gradually increase the complexity by zooming in? That is effectively what adding extra layers does to the loss function. This is handy, as our mountain region (loss function) is much easier to navigate when it is less jagged. You can think of it as follows: when we have a more complex structure (b), the loss function is jagged and hard to navigate (d), because there are so many parameters—especially in early layers—that can have a massive impact and generally increase the dimensionality of the problem. However, if we initially remove some part of the complexity (a), we can early on get a loss function that is much easier to navigate (c) and increases in complexity only as we gain confidence that we are at the approximately right part of the loss space. Only then do we move from (a) and (c) into (b) and (d) versions.

The problem in this scenario is that upon introducing even one more layer at a time (for example, from 4×4 to 8×8), we are still introducing a massive shock to the training. What the PGGAN authors do instead is smoothly fade in those layers, as in figure 6.3, in order to give the system time to adapt to the higher resolution.

However, rather than immediately jumping to this resolution, we smoothly fade in this new layer with higher resolution by a parameter alpha (α), which is between 0 and 1. Alpha affects how much we use either the old—but upscaled—layer or the natively larger one. On the side of the *D*, we simply shrink by $0.5x$ to allow for smoothly injecting the trained layer for discrimination. This is (b) in figure 6.3. When we are confident about this new layer, we keep the 32×32—(c) in the figure—and then we are getting ready to grow yet again after we have trained 32×32 properly.

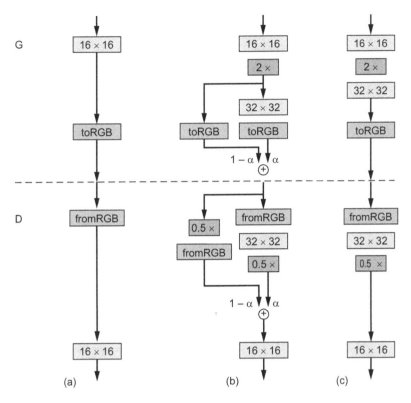

Figure 6.3 When we've trained for enough steps with, say, 16 × 16 resolution (a), we introduce another transposed convolution in the Generator (G) and another convolution in the Discriminator (D) to get the "interface" between G and D to be 32 × 32. But we also introduce two pathways: (1 – α) simple nearest neighbor upscaling, which does not have any trained parameters, but is also quite naïve; and (α) extra transposed convolution, which requires training but will ultimately perform much better.

6.2.2 Example implementation

For all the innovations we've detailed, in this section we'll give you working but isolated versions so that we can talk code. As an exercise, you may want to try implementing these things as one GAN network, maybe using the existing prior architectures. If you are ready, let's load up ye olde, trusty machine learning libraries and get cracking:

```
import tensorflow as tf
import keras as K
```

In the code, progressive smoothing in may look something like the following listing.

Listing 6.1 Progressive growing and smooth upscaling

```
def upscale_layer(layer, upscale_factor):
    '''
    Upscales layer (tensor) by the factor (int) where
    the tensor is [group, height, width, channels]
    '''
    height = layer.get_shape()[1]
    width = layer.get_shape()[2]
    size = (upscale_factor * height, upscale_factor * width)
    upscaled_layer = tf.image.resize_nearest_neighbor(layer, size)
    return upscaled_layer

def smoothly_merge_last_layer(list_of_layers, alpha):
    '''
    Smoothly merges in a layer based on a threshold value alpha.
    This function assumes: that all layers are already in RGB.
    This is the function for the Generator.
    :list_of_layers    :    items should be tensors ordered by resolution
    :alpha             :        float \in (0,1)
    '''
    last_fully_trained_layer = list_of_layers[-2]
    last_layer_upscaled = upscale_layer(last_fully_trained_layer, 2)

    larger_native_layer = list_of_layers[-1]

    assert larger_native_layer.get_shape() == last_layer_upscaled.get_shape()

    new_layer = (1-alpha) * upscaled_layer + larger_native_layer * alpha

    return new_layer
```

Hint! If you are using pure TensorFlow rather than Keras, always remember scope.

Now we have the originally trained layer.

The newly added layer not yet fully trained

This makes sure we can run the merging code.

This code block should take advantage of broadcasting.

Now that you have an understanding of the lower-level details of progressive growing and smoothing without unnecessary complexity, hopefully you can appreciate how general this idea is. Although Karras et al., were by no means the first to come up with some way of increasing model complexity during training, this seems like by far the most promising avenue and indeed the innovation that resonated the most. As of June 2019, this paper was cited over 730 times. With that context in mind, let's move on to the second big innovation.

6.2.3 *Mini-batch standard deviation*

The next innovation introduced by Karras et al. in their paper is *mini-batch standard deviation*. Before we dive into it, let's recall from chapter 5 the issue of mode collapse, which occurs when the GAN learns how to create a few good examples or only slight permutations on them. We generally want to produce the faces of all the people in the real dataset, maybe not just one picture of one woman.

Therefore, Karras et al. created a way for the Discriminator to tell whether the samples it is getting are varied enough. In essence, we calculate a single extra scalar statistic for the Discriminator. This statistic is the standard deviation of all the pixels in the mini-batch that are generated by the Generator or that come from the real data. That is an amazingly simple and elegant solution: now all the Discriminator needs to learn is that if the standard deviation is low in the images from the batch it is evaluating, the image is likely fake, because the real data has more variance.[2] The Generator has no choice but to increase the variance of the generated samples to have a chance to fool the Discriminator.

Moving beyond the intuition, the technical implementation is straightforward as it applies only to the Discriminator. Given that we also want to minimize the number of trainable parameters, we include only a single extra number, which seems to be enough. This number is appended as a feature map—think *dimension* or the last number in the `tf.shape` list.

The exact procedure is as follows and is depicted in listing 6.2:

1 [4D -> 3D] We compute the standard deviation across all the images in the batch, across all the remaining channels—height, width, and color. We then get a single image with standard deviations for each pixel and each channel.

2 [3D -> 2D] We average the standard deviations across all channels—to get a single feature map or matrix of standard deviations for that pixel, but with a collapsed color channel.

3 [2D -> Scalar/0D] We average the standard deviations for all pixels within the preceding matrix to get a single scalar value.

Listing 6.2 Mini-batch standard deviation

> **Hint! If you are using pure TensorFlow rather than Keras, always remember scope. A mini-batch group must be divisible by (or <=) group_size.**

```
def minibatch_std_layer(layer, group_size=4):
    '''
    Will calculate minibatch standard deviation for a layer.
    Will do so under a prespecified tf-scope with Keras.
    Assumes layer is a float32 data type. Else needs validation/casting.
    NOTE: there is a more efficient way to do this in Keras, but just for
    clarity and alignment with major implementations (for understanding)
    this was done more explicitly. Try this as an exercise.
    '''
    group_size = K.backend.minimum(group_size, tf.shape(layer)[0])    ⊲─┘

    shape = list(K.int_shape(input))        ◁─┐
    shape[0] = tf.shape(input)[0]
```

> **Just getting some shape information so that we can use it as shorthand as well as ensure defaults. We get the input from tf. shape, as the "pre-image" dimensions are typically cast as None before graph execution.**

---

2 Some may object that this can also happen when the sampled real data includes a lot of very similar pictures. Though this is technically true, in practice this is easy to fix, and remember that the similarity would have to be so high that a single pass of a simple nearest neighbor clustering would reveal it.

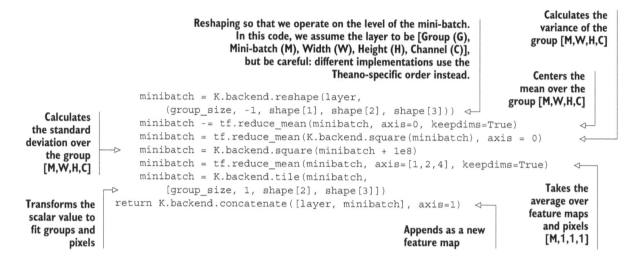

Reshaping so that we operate on the level of the mini-batch. In this code, we assume the layer to be [Group (G), Mini-batch (M), Width (W), Height (H), Channel (C)], but be careful: different implementations use the Theano-specific order instead.

Calculates the variance of the group [M,W,H,C]

Centers the mean over the group [M,W,H,C]

Calculates the standard deviation over the group [M,W,H,C]

Transforms the scalar value to fit groups and pixels

```
minibatch = K.backend.reshape(layer,
    (group_size, -1, shape[1], shape[2], shape[3]))
minibatch -= tf.reduce_mean(minibatch, axis=0, keepdims=True)
minibatch = tf.reduce_mean(K.backend.square(minibatch), axis = 0)
minibatch = K.backend.square(minibatch + 1e8)
minibatch = tf.reduce_mean(minibatch, axis=[1,2,4], keepdims=True)
minibatch = K.backend.tile(minibatch,
    [group_size, 1, shape[2], shape[3]])
return K.backend.concatenate([layer, minibatch], axis=1)
```

Appends as a new feature map

Takes the average over feature maps and pixels [M,1,1,1]

6.2.4   *Equalized learning rate*

Equalized learning rate is one of those deep learning dark art techniques that is probably not clear to anyone. Although the researchers do provide a short explanation in the PGGAN paper, they avoided the topic in oral presentations, suggesting that this is probably just a hack that seems to work. Frequently in deep learning this is the case.

Furthermore, many nuances about equalized learning rate require a solid understanding of the implementation of RMSProp or Adam—which is the used optimizer—and also of weights initialization. So don't worry if this does not make sense to you, because it probably does not really make sense to anyone.

But if you're curious, the explanation goes something as follows: we need to ensure that all the weights (w) are normalized (w') to be within a certain range such that $w' = w/c$ by a constant c that is different for each layer, depending on the shape of the weight matrix. This also ensures that if any parameters need to take bigger steps to reach optimum—because they tend to vary more—these relevant parameters can do that.

Karras et al. use a simple standard normal initialization and then scale the weights per layer at runtime. Some of you may be thinking that Adam already does that—yes, Adam allows learning rates to be different for different parameters, but there's a catch. Adam adjusts the backpropagated gradient by the estimated standard deviation of the parameter, which ensures that the scale of that parameter is independent of the update. Adam has different learning rates in different directions, but does not always take into account the *dynamic range*—how much a dimension or feature tends to vary over given mini-batches. As some point out, this seems to solve a similar problem as weights initialization.[3]

---

[3] See "Progressive Growing of GANs.md," by Alexander Jung, 2017, http://mng.bz/5A4B.

However, if this is not clear, do not worry; we highly recommend two excellent resources: Andrew Karpathy's 2016 computer science lecture for notes about weights initialization,[4] and a Distill article for details on how Adam works.[5] The following listing shows the equalized learning rate.

Listing 6.3 Equalized learning rate

```
def equalize_learning_rate(shape, gain, fan_in=None):
    '''
    This adjusts the weights of every layer by the constant from
    He's initializer so that we adjust for the variance in the dynamic
    range in different features
    shape   :  shape of tensor (layer): these are the dimensions
        of each layer.
    For example, [4,4,48,3]. In this case, [kernel_size, kernel_size,
        number_of_filters, feature_maps]. But this will depend
        slightly on your implementation.
    gain    :  typically sqrt(2)
    fan_in  :  adjustment for the number of incoming connections
        as per Xavier's / He's initialization
    '''
    if fan_in is None: fan_in = np.prod(shape[:-1])
    std = gain / K.sqrt(fan_in)
    wscale = K.constant(std, name='wscale', dtype=np.float32)
    adjusted_weights = K.get_value('layer', shape=shape,
        initializer=tf.initializers.random_normal()) * wscale
    return adjusted_weights
```

The default value is the product of all the shape dimensions minus the feature maps dimension; this gives us the number of incoming connections per neuron.

This uses He's initialization constant.[6]

Creates a constant out of the adjustment

Gets values for weights and then uses broadcasting to apply the adjustment

If you are still confused, rest assured that these initialization tricks and these complicated learning rate adjustments are rarely a point of differentiation in either academia or industry. Also, just because restricting weight values between –1 and 1 seems to work somewhat better in most reruns here, that does not mean this trick will generalize to other setups. So let's move to better-proven techniques.

6.2.5 *Pixel-wise feature normalization in the generator*

Let's begin with some motivation for why would we even want to normalize the features—stability of training. Empirically, the authors from NVIDIA have discovered that one of the early signs of divergent training was an explosion in feature magnitudes. A similar observation was made by the BigGAN authors in chapter 12. So Karras et al. introduced a technique to combat this. On a broader note, this is frequently how GAN training is done: we observe a particular problem with the training, so we introduce mechanisms to prevent that problem from happening.

---

[4] See "Lecture 5: Training Neural Networks, Part I," by Fei-Fei Li et al. 2016, http://mng.bz/6wOo.

[5] See "Why Momentum Really Works," by Gabriel Goh, 2017, Distill, https://distill.pub/2017/momentum/.

[6] See "Delving Deep into Rectifiers: Surpassing Human-Level Performance on ImageNet Classification," by Kaiming He et al., https://arxiv.org/pdf/1502.01852.pdf.

Note that most networks are using some form of normalization. Typically, they use either batch normalization or a virtual version of this technique. Table 6.1 presents an overview of normalization techniques used in the GANs presented in this book so far. You saw these in chapter 4 (DCGAN) and chapter 5—where we touched on the rest of the GANs and gradient penalties (GPs). Unfortunately, in order for batch normalization and its virtual equivalent to work, we must have large mini-batches so that the individual samples average themselves out.

Table 6.1   Use of normalization techniques in GANs

Method	Authors	G normalization	D normalization
DCGAN	(Radford et al., 2015, https://arxiv.org/abs/1511.06434)	Batch	Batch
Improved GAN	(Salimans et al., 2016, https://arxiv.org/pdf/1606.03498.pdf)	Virtual batch	Virtual batch
WGAN	(Arjovsky et al., 2017, https://arxiv.org/pdf/1701.07875.pdf)	—	Batch
WGAN-GP	(Gulrajani et al., 2017, http://arxiv.org/abs/1704.00028)	Batch	Layer norm

Based on the fact that all these major implementations use normalization, it is clearly important, but why not just used standard batch normalization? Unfortunately, batch normalization is too memory intensive at our resolution. We have to come up with something that allows us to work with a few examples—that fit into our GPU memory with the two network graphs—but still works well. Now we understand where the need for pixel-wise feature normalization comes from and why we use it.

If we jump into the algorithm, pixel normalization takes activation magnitude at each layer just before the input is fed into the next layer.

Pixel-wise feature normalization

For each feature map **do**

1. Take the pixel value of that feature map (fm) at a position (x, y).
2. Construct a vector for each (x, y), where
   a. $v_{0,0}$ = [(0,0) value for fm_1, (0,0) value for fm_2, ..., (0,0) value for fm_n]
   b. $v_{0,1}$ = [(0,1) value for fm_1, (0,1) value for fm_2, ..., (0,1) value for fm_n]
   ...
   c. $v_{n,n}$ = [(n,n) value for fm_1, (n,n) value for fm_2, ..., (n,n) value for fm_n]
3. Normalize each vector $v_{i,i}$ as defined in step 2 to have a unit norm; call it $n_{i,i}$.
4. Pass that in the original tensor shape to the next layer.

End for

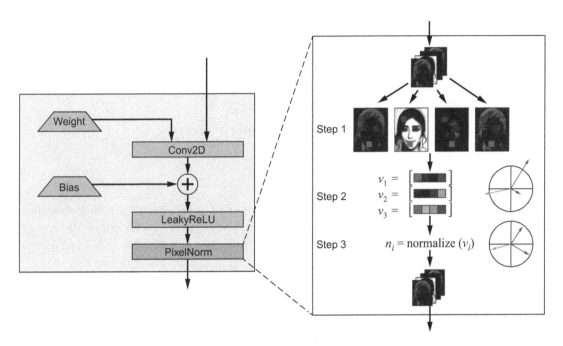

Figure 6.4 We map out all the points in an image (step 1) to a set of vectors (step 2), and then we normalize them so that they are all in the same range (typically between 0 and 1 in the high-dimensional space), which is step 3.

Figure 6.4 illustrates the process of pixel-wise feature normalization. The exact description of step 3 is shown in equation 6.1.

$$n_{(x, y)} = a_{(x, y)} / \sqrt{\frac{1}{N} \sum_{j=0}^{N-1} (a_{x, y}^{j})^2 + \varepsilon}$$

Equation 6.1

This formula *normalizes* (divides by the expression under the square root) each vector constructed in step 2 of figure 6.4. This expression is just an average of each squared value for that particular (x, y) pixel. One thing that may surprise you is the addition of a small noise term (ε). This is simply a way to ensure that we are not dividing by zero. The whole procedure is explained in greater detail in the 2012 paper "ImageNet Classification with Deep Convolutional Neural Networks," by Alex Krizhevsky et al. (http://mng.bz/om4d).

The last thing to note is that this term is applied only to the Generator, as the explosion in the activation magnitudes leads to an arms race only if *both* networks participate. The following listing shows the code.

Listing 6.4   Pixel-wise feature normalization

```
def pixelwise_feat_norm(inputs, **kwargs):
    '''
    Uses pixelwise feature normalization as proposed by
    Krizhevsky et at. 2012. Returns the input normalized
    :inputs      :    Keras / TF Layers
    '''
    normalization_constant = K.backend.sqrt(K.backend.mean(
        inputs**2, axis=-1, keepdims=True) + 1.0e-8)
    return inputs / normalization_constant
```

6.3   *Summary of key innovations*

We have gone through four clever ideas on how to improve GAN training; however, without grounding them in their effects on the training, it may be difficult to isolate those effects. Thankfully, the paper's authors provide a helpful table to help us understand just that; see figure 6.5.

Training configuration	CELEB-A						LSUN BEDROOM					
	Sliced Wasserstein distance ×10³					MS-SSIM	Sliced Wasserstein distance ×10³					MS-SSIM
	128	64	32	16	Avg		128	64	32	16	Avg	
(a) Gulrajani et al. (2017)	12.99	7.79	7.62	8.73	9.28	0.2854	11.97	10.51	8.03	14.48	11.25	**0.0587**
(b) + Progressive growing	4.62	**2.64**	3.78	6.06	4.28	**0.2838**	7.09	6.27	7.40	9.64	7.60	0.0615
(c) + Small minibatch	75.42	41.33	41.62	26.57	46.23	0.4065	72.73	40.16	42.75	42.46	49.52	0.1061
(d) + Revised training parameters	9.20	6.53	4.71	11.84	8.07	0.3027	7.39	5.51	3.65	9.63	6.54	0.0662
(e*) + Minibatch discrimination	10.76	6.28	6.04	16.29	9.84	0.3057	10.29	6.22	5.32	11.88	8.43	0.0648
(e) Minibatch stddev	13.94	5.67	2.82	5.71	7.04	0.2950	7.77	5.23	3.27	9.64	6.48	0.0671
(f) + Equalized learning rate	4.42	3.28	2.32	7.52	4.39	0.2902	**3.61**	3.32	**2.71**	6.44	4.02	0.0668
(g) + Pixelwise normalization	**4.06**	3.04	**2.02**	**5.13**	**3.56**	0.2845	3.89	**3.05**	3.24	**5.87**	**4.01**	0.0640
(h) Converged	2.95	2.38	1.98	5.16	3.12	0.2880	3.26	3.06	2.82	4.14	3.32	0.0633

Figure 6.5   Contributions of various techniques to score improvements. We can see that the introduction of equalized learning rate makes a big difference, and pixel-wise normalization adds to that, though what the authors do not tell us is how effective this technique would be if we had only pixel normalization and did not introduce equalized learning rate. We include this table only as an illustration of the rough magnitude of improvement we can expect from these changes—which is an interesting lesson on its own—but more detailed discussion follows.

The PGGAN paper's authors are using *sliced Wasserstein distance (SWD)*, where smaller is better. Recall from chapter 5 that a smaller Wasserstein—aka *earth mover's*—distance means better results as quantified by the amount of probability mass one has to move to make the two distributions similar. The SWD means that patches of both the real data and the generated samples minimize this distance. The nuances of this technique are explained in the paper, but as the authors said during their presentation at ICLR, better measures—such as the Fréchet inception distance (FID)—now exist. We covered the FID in greater depth in chapter 5.

One key takeaway from this table is that a mini-batch does not work well, because, at a megapixel resolution, we do not have enough virtual RAM to load many images into the GPU memory. We have to use a smaller mini-batch—which may, overall, perform worse—and we have to reduce the mini-batch sizes further, making our training difficult.

6.4 *TensorFlow Hub and hands-on*

Google has recently announced that as part of TensorFlow Extended and the general move toward implementing best practices from software engineering into the machine learning world, Google has created a central model and code repository called *TensorFlow Hub*, or *TFHub*. Working with TFHub is almost embarrassingly easy, especially with the models that Google has put there.

After importing the hub module and calling the right URL, TensorFlow downloads and imports the model all by itself, and you can start. These models are well-documented at the *same* URL that we use to download the model; just put them into your web browser. In fact, to get a pretrained Progressive GAN, all you need to type is an import statement and one line of code. That's it!

The following listing shows a complete example of code that should by itself generate a face—based on the random seed that you specify in latent_vector.[7] Figure 6.6 displays the output.

Listing 6.5 Getting started with TFHub

```
import matplotlib.pyplot as plt
import tensorflow as tf                              Imports the
import tensorflow_hub as hub                         Progressive GAN
                                                     from TFHub

with tf.Graph().as_default():                                    Latent
    module = hub.Module("https://tfhub.dev/google/progan-128/1")   dimension
    latent_dim = 512                                             that gets
                                                                 sampled at
    latent_vector = tf.random_normal([1, latent_dim], seed=1337)  runtime

    interpolated_images = module(latent_vector)         Uses the module to generate
                                                        images from the latent space.
                                                        Implementation details are
    with tf.Session() as session:                       online.
    session.run(tf.global_variables_initializer())
    image_out = session.run(interpolated_images)

plt.imshow(image_out.reshape(128,128,3))            Runs the TensorFlow session
plt.show()                                          and gets back the image in
                                                    shape (1,128,128,3)
```

Changes the seed to get different faces

Hopefully, this should be enough to get you started with Progressive GANs! Feel free to play around with the code and extend it. It should be noted here that the TFHub version of the Progressive GAN is not using the full 1024 × 1024, but rather just 128 × 128. This is probably because running the full version used to be computationally expensive, and the model size can grow huge quickly in the domain of computer vision problems.

---

[7] This example was generated with the use of TFHub and is based on the example Colab provided at http://mng.bz/nvEa.

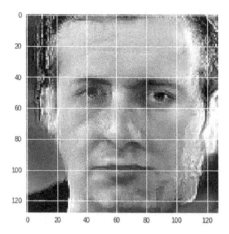

Figure 6.6   Output of listing 6.5. Try changing the seed in the `latent_vector` definition to get different outputs. A word of warning: even though this random seed argument should consistently define the output we are meant to get, we have found that on reruns we sometimes get different results, depending on the version of TensorFlow. This image is obtained using 1.9.0-rc1.

6.5   *Practical applications*

Understandably, people are curious about the practical applications and ability to generalize Progressive GANs. One great example we'll present is from our colleagues at Kheiron Medical Technologies, based in London, England. Recently, they released a paper that is a great testament to both the generalizability and practical applications of the PGGAN.[8]

Using a large dataset of medical mammograms,[9] these researchers managed to generate realistic 1280 × 1024 synthetic images of full-field digital mammography (FFDM), as shown in figure 6.7. This is a remarkable achievement on two levels:

- It shows the generalizability of this technique. Think about how different images of mammograms are from the images of human faces—especially structurally. The bar for whether a tissue structure makes sense is incredibly high, and yet their network manages to produce samples at the highest resolution to date that frequently fool medical professionals.

- It shows how these techniques can be applied to many fields and uses. For example, we can use this new dataset in a semi-supervised way, as you will discover in the next chapter. Or the synthetic dataset can be open sourced for medical research with arguably fewer worries from General Data Protection Regulation (GDPR) or other legal repercussions, as these do not belong to any one person.

---

[8] See "High-Resolution Mammogram Synthesis Using Progressive Generative Adversarial Networks," by Dimitrios Korkinof et al., 2018, https://arxiv.org/pdf/1807.03401.pdf.

[9] X-ray scans for the purposes of breast cancer screening.

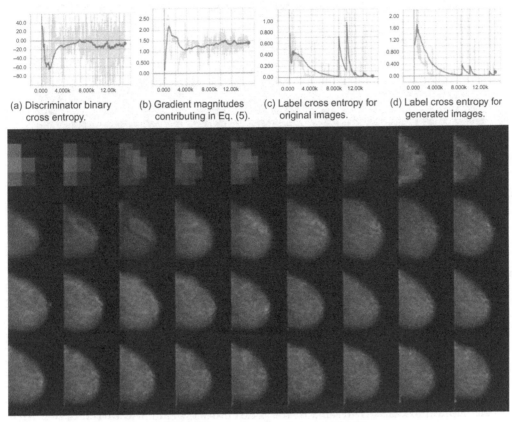

(a) Discriminator binary cross entropy.

(b) Gradient magnitudes contributing in Eq. (5).

(c) Label cross entropy for original images.

(d) Label cross entropy for generated images.

(e) The training progression of a successful run.

Figure 6.7 Progressive growing of FFDM. This is a great figure because it not only shows the progressively increasing resolution on these mammograms (e), but also some training statistics (a)–(d) to show you that training these GANs is messy for everyone, not just you.

Figure 6.8 shows how realistic these mammograms can look. These have been randomly sampled (so no cherry-picking) and then compared to one of the closest images in the dataset.

GANs may be used for many applications, not just fighting breast cancer or generating human faces, but also in 62 other medical GAN applications published through the end of July 2018.[10] We encourage you to look at them—but of course, not all of them use PGGANs. Generally, GANs are allowing massive leaps in many research fields, but are frequently applied nonintuitively. We hope to make these more accessible so that they can be used by more researchers. Make GANs, not war!

---

[10] See "GANs for Medical Image Analysis," by Salome Kazeminia et al., 2018, https://arxiv.org/pdf/1809 .06222.pdf.

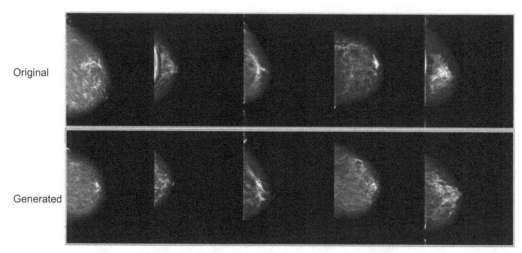

(a) Randomly sampled examples of real and generated CC views.

Figure 6.8   In comparing the real and the generated datasets, the data looks pretty realistic and generally close to an example in the training set. In their subsequent work, MammoGAN, Kheiron has shown that these images fool trained and certified radiologists.[11] That's generally a good sign, especially at this high resolution. Of course, in principle, we would love to have a statistical way of measuring the quality of the generation. But as we know from chapter 5, this is hard enough to do with standard images, let alone for any arbitrary GAN.

All of the techniques we presented in this chapter represent a general class of solving GAN problems—with a progressively more complex model. We expect this paradigm to pick up within GANs. The same is true for TensorFlow Hub: it is to TensorFlow what PyPI/Conda is to Python. Most Python programmers use them every week!

We hope that this new Progressive GAN technique opened your eyes to what GANs can do and why people are so excited about this paper. And hopefully not just for the cat meme vector that PGGAN can produce.[12] The next chapter will give you the tools so that you can start contributing to research yourself. See you then!

Summary

- We can achieve 1-megapixel synthetic images thanks to the state-of-the-art PGGAN technique.
- This technique has four key training innovations:
  - Progressive growing and smoothing in higher-resolution layers
  - Mini-batch standard deviation to enforce variation in the generated samples

---

[11] See "MammoGAN: High-Resolution Synthesis of Realistic Mammograms," by Dimitrios Korkinof et al., 2019, https://openreview.net/pdf?id=SJeichaN5E.

[12] See Gene Kogan's Twitter image, 2018, https://twitter.com/genekogan/status/1019943905318572033.

– Equalized learning rate that ensures we can take learning steps of appropriate sizes in each direction

– Pixel-wise vector normalization that ensures that the Generator and the Discriminator do not spiral out of control in an arms race

- You followed a hands-on tutorial using the newly released TensorFlow Hub and got to use their downsampled version of the Progressive GAN to generate images!

- You learned about how GANs are helping to fight cancer.

Semi-Supervised GAN

This chapter covers

- The booming field of innovations based on the original GAN model
- Semi-supervised learning and its immense practical importance
- Semi-Supervised GANs (SGANs)
- Implementation of an SGAN model

Congratulations—you have made it more than halfway through this book. By now, you not only have learned what GANs are and how they function, but also had an opportunity to implement two of the most canonical implementations: the original GAN that started it all and the DCGAN that laid the foundation for the bulk of the advanced GAN variants, including the Progressive GAN introduced in the previous chapter.

However, as with many fields, just when you think you are beginning to get a real hang of it, you uncover that the domain is much larger and more complex than initially thought. What might have seemed like a thorough understanding turns out to be no more than the tip of the iceberg.

GANs are no exception. Since their invention, they have remained an active area of research with countless variations added every year. An unofficial list—aptly named "The GAN Zoo" (https://github.com/hindupuravinash/the-gan-zoo)—which seeks to track all named GAN variants (GAN implementations with distinct names coined by the researchers who authored them) has grown to well over 300 at the time of this writing. However, judging from the fact that the original GAN paper has been cited more than 9,000 times to date (July 2019) and ranks among the most cited research papers in recent years in all of deep learning, the true number of GAN variations invented by the research community is likely even higher.[1] See figure 7.1.

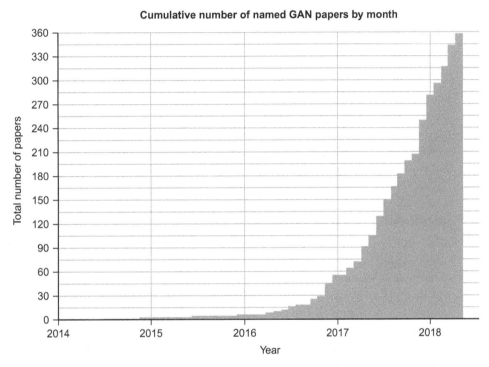

Cumulative number of named GAN papers by month

Figure 7.1 This graph approximates the monthly cumulative count of unique GAN implementations published by the research community, starting from GAN's invention in 2014 until the first few months of 2018. As the chart makes clear, the field of generative adversarial learning has been growing exponentially since its inception, and there is no end in sight to this growth in interest and popularity.
(Source: "The GAN Zoo," by Avinash Hindupur, 2017, https://github.com/hindupuravinash/the-gan-zoo.)

This, however, is no reason to despair. Although it is impossible to cover all these GAN variants in this book, or any book for that matter, we can cover a few of the key innovations that will give you a good idea of what's out there as well as the unique contributions each of these variations provides to the field of generative adversarial learning.

---

[1] According to a tracker from the Microsoft Academic (MA) search engine: http://mng.bz/qXXJ. See also "Top 20 Research Papers on Machine Learning and Deep Learning," by Thuy T. Pham, 2017, http://mng.bz/E1eq.

It is worth noting that not all of these named variants diverge drastically from the original GAN. Indeed, many of them are at a high level quite similar to the original model, such as the DCGAN in chapter 4. Even the many complex innovations such as the Wasserstein GAN (discussed in chapter 5) focus primarily on improving the performance and stability of the original GAN model or one similar to it.

In this and the following two chapters, we will focus on GAN variants that diverge from the original GAN not only in the architecture and underlying mathematics of their model implementations but also in their motivations and objectives. In particular, we will cover the following three GAN models:

- Semi-Supervised GAN (this chapter)
- Conditional GAN (chapter 8)
- CycleGAN (chapter 9)

For each of these GAN variants, you will learn about their objectives and what motivated them, their model architectures, and how their networks train and work. These topics will be covered both conceptually and through concrete examples. We will also provide tutorials with full working implementations of each of these models so that you can experience them firsthand.

So, without further ado, let's dive in!

7.1 Introducing the Semi-Supervised GAN

Semi-supervised learning is one of the most promising areas of practical application of GANs. Unlike supervised learning, in which we need a label for every example in our dataset, and unsupervised learning, in which no labels are used, semi-supervised learning has a class label for only a small subset of the training dataset. By internalizing hidden structures in the data, semi-supervised learning strives to generalize from the small subset of labeled data points to effectively classify new, previously unseen examples. Importantly, for semi-supervised learning to work, the labeled and unlabeled data must come from the same underlying distribution.

The lack of labeled datasets is one of the main bottlenecks in machine learning research and practical applications. Although unlabeled data is abundant (the internet is a virtually limitless source of unlabeled images, videos, and text), assigning class labels to them is often prohibitively expensive, impractical, and time-consuming. It took two and a half years to hand-annotate the original 3.2 million images in the ImageNet—a database of labeled images that helped enable many of the advances in image processing and computer vision in the last decade.[2]

Andrew Ng, a deep learning pioneer, Stanford professor, and former chief scientist of the Chinese internet giant Baidu, identified the enormous amounts of labeled data needed for training as the Achilles' heel of supervised learning, which is used for the

---

[2] See "The Data That Transformed AI Research—and Possibly the World," by Dave Gershgorn, 2017, http://mng.bz/DNVy.

vast majority of today's AI applications in industry.[3] One of the industries that suffers most from a lack of large labeled datasets is medicine, for which obtaining data (for example, outcomes from clinical trials) often requires great effort and expenditure, not to mention the even more important issues of ethics and privacy.[4] Accordingly, improving the ability of algorithms to learn from ever-smaller quantities of labeled examples has immense practical importance.

Interestingly, semi-supervised learning may also be one of the closest machine learning analogs to the way humans learn. When schoolchildren learn to read and write, the teacher does not have to take them on a road trip to see tens of thousands of examples of letters and numbers, ask them to identify these symbols, and correct them as needed—similarly to the way a supervised learning algorithm would operate. Instead, a single set of examples is all that is needed for children to learn letters and numerals and then be able to recognize them regardless of font, size, angle, lighting conditions, and many other factors. Semi-supervised learning aims to teach machines in a similarly efficient manner.

Serving as a source of additional information that can be used for training, generative models proved useful in improving the accuracy of semi-supervised models. Unsurprisingly, GANs have proven the most promising. In 2016, Tim Salimans, Ian Goodfellow, and their colleagues at OpenAI achieved almost 94% accuracy on the Street View House Numbers (SVHN) benchmark dataset using only 2,000 labeled examples.[5] For comparison, the best fully supervised algorithm at the time that used labels for all 73,257 images in the SVHN training set achieved an accuracy of around 98.40%.[6] In other words, the Semi-Supervised GAN achieved overall accuracy remarkably close to the fully supervised benchmark, while using fewer than 3% of the labels for training.

Let's find out how Salimans and his colleagues accomplished so much from so little.

7.1.1 What is a Semi-Supervised GAN?

Semi-Supervised GAN (SGAN) is a Generative Adversarial Network whose Discriminator is a multiclass classifier. Instead of distinguishing between only two classes (*real* and *fake*), it learns to distinguish between $N+1$ classes, where N is the number of classes in the training dataset, with one added for the fake examples produced by the Generator.

For example, the MNIST dataset of handwritten digits has 10 labels (one label for each numeral, 0 to 9), so the SGAN Discriminator trained on this dataset would predict between $10 + 1 = 11$ classes. In our implementation, the output of the SGAN

---

[3] See "What Artificial Intelligence Can and Can't Do Right Now," by Andrew Ng, 2016, http://mng.bz/lopj.

[4] See "What AI Can and Can't Do (Yet) for Your Business," by Michael Chui et al., 2018, http://mng.bz/BYDv.

[5] See "Improved Techniques for Training GANs," by Ian Goodfellow et al., 2016, https://arxiv.org/abs/1606.03498.

[6] See "Densely Connected Convolutional Networks," by Gao Huang et al., 2016, https://arxiv.org/abs/1608.06993.

Discriminator will be represented as a vector of 10 class probabilities (that sum up to 1.0) plus another probability that represents whether the image is real or fake.

Turning the Discriminator from a binary to a multiclass classifier may seem like a trivial change, but its implications are more far-reaching than may appear at first glance. Let's start with a diagram. Figure 7.2 shows the SGAN architecture.

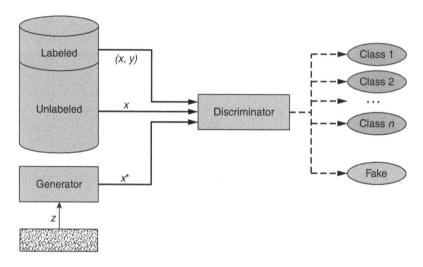

Figure 7.2   In this Semi-Supervised GAN, the Generator takes in a random noise vector z and produces a fake example x*. The Discriminator receives three kinds of data inputs: fake data from the Generator, real unlabeled examples x, and real labeled examples (x, y), where y is the label corresponding to the given example. The Discriminator then outputs a classification; its goal is to distinguish fake examples from the real ones and, for the real examples, identify the correct class. Notice that the portion of examples with labels is much smaller than the portion of the unlabeled data. In practice, the contrast is even starker than the one shown, with labeled data forming only a tiny fraction (often as little as 1–2%) of the training data.

As figure 7.2 indicates, the task of distinguishing between multiple classes not only impacts the Discriminator itself, but also adds complexity to the SGAN architecture, its training process, and its training objectives, as compared to the traditional GAN.

7.1.2   *Architecture*

The SGAN Generator's purpose is the same as in the original GAN: it takes in a vector of random numbers and produces fake examples whose goal is to be indistinguishable from the training dataset—no change here.

The SGAN Discriminator, however, diverges considerably from the original GAN implementation. Instead of two, it receives three kinds of inputs: fake examples produced by the Generator (x^*), real examples without labels from the training dataset (x), and real examples with labels from the training dataset (x, y), where y denotes the label for the given example x. Instead of binary classification, the SGAN Discriminator's goal is to correctly categorize the input example into its corresponding class if the example is real, or reject the example as fake (which can be thought of as a special additional class).

Table 7.1 summarizes the key takeaways about the two SGAN subnetworks.

Table 7.1 SGAN Generator and Discriminator networks

	Generator	**Discriminator**
Input	A vector of random numbers (z)	The Discriminator receives three kinds of inputs: ■ Unlabeled real examples (x) coming from the training dataset ■ Labeled real examples (x, y) coming from the training dataset ■ Fake examples (x*) produced by the Generator
Output	Fake examples (x*) that strive to be as convincing as possible	Probabilities, indicating the likelihood that the input example belongs either to one of the *N* real classes or to the *fake* class
Goal	Generate fake examples that are indistinguishable from members of the training dataset by fooling the Discriminator into classifying them as real	Learn to assign the correct class label to real examples while rejecting all examples coming from the Generator as fake

7.1.3 *Training process*

Recall that in a regular GAN, we train the Discriminator by computing the loss for $D(x)$ and $D(x^*)$ and backpropagating the total loss to update the Discriminator's trainable parameters to minimize the loss. The Generator is trained by backpropagating the Discriminator's loss for $D(x^*)$, seeking to maximize it, so that the fake examples it synthesizes are misclassified as real.

To train the SGAN, in addition to $D(x)$ and $D(x^*)$, we also have to compute the loss for the supervised training examples: $D((x, y))$. These losses correspond to the dual learning objective that the SGAN Discriminator has to grapple with: distinguishing real examples from the fake ones while also learning to classify real examples to their correct classes. Using the terminology from the original paper, these dual objectives correspond to two kinds of losses: the *supervised loss* and the *unsupervised loss.*[7]

7.1.4 *Training objective*

All the GAN variants you have seen so far are generative models. Their goal is to produce realistic-looking data samples; hence, the Generator network has been of primary interest. The main purpose of the Discriminator network has been to help the Generator improve the quality of images it produces. At the end of the training, we

---

[7] See "Improved Techniques for Training GANs," by Tim Salimans et al., 2016, https://arxiv.org/abs/1606.03498.

often disregard the Discriminator and use only the fully trained Generator to create realistic-looking synthetic data.

In contrast, in a SGAN, we care primarily about the Discriminator. The goal of the training process is to make this network into a semi-supervised classifier whose accuracy is as close as possible to a fully supervised classifier (one that has labels available for each example in the training dataset), while using only a small fraction of the labels. The Generator's goal is to aid this process by serving as a source of additional information (the fake data it produces) that helps the Generator learn the relevant patterns in the data, enhancing its classification accuracy. At the end of the training, the Generator gets discarded, and we use the trained Discriminator as a classifier.

Now that you've learned what motivated the creation of the SGAN and we've explained how the model works, it is time to see the model in action by implementing one.

7.2   Tutorial: Implementing a Semi-Supervised GAN

In this tutorial, we implement an SGAN model that learns to classify handwritten digits in the MNIST dataset by using only 100 training examples. At the end of the tutorial, we compare the model's classification accuracy to an equivalent fully supervised model to see for ourselves the improvement achieved by semi-supervised learning.

7.2.1   Architecture diagram

Figure 7.3 shows a high-level diagram of the SGAN model implemented in this tutorial. It is a bit more complex than the general, conceptual diagram we introduced at the beginning of this chapter. After all, the devil is in the (implementation) details.

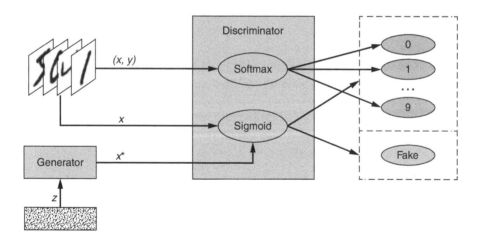

Figure 7.3   This SGAN diagram is a high-level illustration of the SGAN we implement in this chapter's tutorial. The Generator turns random noise into fake examples. The Discriminator receives real images with labels (x, y), real images without labels (x), and fake images produced by the Generator (x*). To distinguish real examples from fake ones, the Discriminator uses the *sigmoid* function. To distinguish between the real classes, the Discriminator uses the *softmax* function.

To solve the multiclass classification problem of distinguishing between the real labels, the Discriminator uses the *softmax* function, which gives probability distribution over a specified number of classes—in our case, 10. The higher the probability assigned to a given label, the more confident the Discriminator is that the example belongs to the given class. To compute the classification error, we use cross-entropy loss, which measures the difference between the output probabilities and the target, one-hot-encoded labels.

To output the real-versus-fake probability, the Discriminator uses the *sigmoid* activation function and trains its parameters by backpropagating the binary cross-entropy loss—the same as the GANs we implemented in chapters 3 and 4.

7.2.2 Implementation

As you may notice, much of our SGAN implementation is adapted from the DCGAN model from chapter 4. This is not out of laziness (well, maybe a little . . .), but rather so that you can better see the distinct modifications needed for SGAN without any distractions from implementation details in unrelated parts of the network.

A Jupyter notebook with the full implementation, including added visualizations of the training progress, is available in our GitHub repository (https://github.com/GANs-in-Action/gans-in-action), under the chapter-7 folder. The code was tested with Python 3.6.0, Keras 2.1.6, and TensorFlow 1.8.0. To speed up the training time, we recommend running the model on a GPU.

7.2.3 Setup

As usual, we start off by importing all the modules and libraries needed to run the model, as shown in the following listing.

Listing 7.1 Import statements

```
%matplotlib inline

import matplotlib.pyplot as plt
import numpy as np

from keras import backend as K

from keras.datasets import mnist
from keras.layers import (Activation, BatchNormalization, Concatenate, Dense,
                          Dropout, Flatten, Input, Lambda, Reshape)
from keras.layers.advanced_activations import LeakyReLU
from keras.layers.convolutional import Conv2D, Conv2DTranspose
from keras.models import Model, Sequential
from keras.optimizers import Adam
from keras.utils import to_categorical
```

We also specify the input image size, the size of the noise vector z, and the number of the real classes for the semi-supervised classification (one for each numeral our Discriminator will learn to identify), as shown in the following listing.

Listing 7.2   Model input dimensions

```
img_rows = 28
img_cols = 28
channels = 1

img_shape = (img_rows, img_cols, channels)        Input image
                                                   dimensions

z_dim = 100              Size of the noise vector, used
                         as input to the Generator

num_classes = 10        Number of classes
                        in the dataset
```

7.2.4   The dataset

Although the MNIST training dataset has 50,000 labeled training images, we will use only a small fraction of them (specified by the num_labeled parameter) for training and pretend that all the remaining ones are unlabeled. We accomplish this by sampling only from the first num_labeled images when generating batches of labeled data and from the remaining (50,000 – num_labeled) images when generating batches of unlabeled examples.

The Dataset object (shown in listing 7.3) also provides a function to return all the num_labeled training examples along with their labels as well as a function to return all 10,000 labeled test images in the MNIST dataset. After training, we will use the test set to evaluate how well the model's classifications generalize to previously unseen examples.

Listing 7.3   Dataset for training and testing

```
class Dataset:
    def __init__(self, num_labeled):         Number of labeled examples
                                             to use for training

        self.num_labeled = num_labeled

                                                          Loads the MNIST
                                                          dataset
        (self.x_train, self.y_train), (self.x_test,
                               self.y_test) = mnist.load_data()

        def preprocess_imgs(x):                        Rescales [0, 255]
            x = (x.astype(np.float32) - 127.5) / 127.5  grayscale pixel
            x = np.expand_dims(x, axis=3)               values to [–1, 1]
            return x
                                             Expands image dimensions to
                                             width × height × channels
        def preprocess_labels(y):
            return y.reshape(-1, 1)

        self.x_train = preprocess_imgs(self.x_train)      Training
        self.y_train = preprocess_labels(self.y_train)    data

        self.x_test = preprocess_imgs(self.x_test)        Testing
        self.y_test = preprocess_labels(self.y_test)      data
```

```
               def batch_labeled(self, batch_size):
Gets a random       idx = np.random.randint(0, self.num_labeled, batch_size)
   batch of         imgs = self.x_train[idx]
labeled images      labels = self.y_train[idx]
and their labels    return imgs, labels

               def batch_unlabeled(self, batch_size):
   Gets a          idx = np.random.randint(self.num_labeled, self.x_train.shape[0],
random batch                               batch_size)
 of unlabeled       imgs = self.x_train[idx]
   images           return imgs

               def training_set(self):
                   x_train = self.x_train[range(self.num_labeled)]
                   y_train = self.y_train[range(self.num_labeled)]
                   return x_train, y_train

               def test_set(self):
                   return self.x_test, self.y_test
```

In this tutorial, we will pretend that we have only 100 labeled MNIST images for training:

```
num_labeled = 100        Number of labeled examples to use
                         (the rest will be used as unlabeled)

dataset = Dataset(num_labeled)
```

7.2.5   *The Generator*

The Generator network is the same as the one we implemented for the DCGAN in chapter 4. Using transposed convolution layers, the Generator transforms the input random noise vector into $28 \times 28 \times 1$ image; see the following listing.

Listing 7.4   SGAN Generator

```
def build_generator(z_dim):
                                                 Reshapes input into a
    model = Sequential()                         7 × 7 × 256 tensor
                                                 via a fully connected
    model.add(Dense(256 * 7 * 7, input_dim=z_dim))    layer
Transposed  model.add(Reshape((7, 7, 256)))
convolution
layer, from model.add(Conv2DTranspose(128, kernel_size=3, strides=2, padding='same'))
7 × 7 × 256
to 14 × 14 × model.add(BatchNormalization())       Batch normalization
128 tensor
            model.add(LeakyReLU(alpha=0.01))        Leaky ReLU activation

Transposed  model.add(Conv2DTranspose(64, kernel_size=3, strides=1, padding='same'))
convolution
layer, from model.add(BatchNormalization())        Batch normalization
14 × 14 × 128
to 14 × 14 × model.add(LeakyReLU(alpha=0.01))       Leaky ReLU activation
64 tensor
```

```
model.add(Conv2DTranspose(1, kernel_size=3, strides=2, padding='same'))  ◁─┐
```

```
model.add(Activation('tanh'))  ◁─┐  Output layer        Transposed convolution
                                  │  with tanh          layer, from 14 × 14 ×
return model                      │  activation         64 to 28 × 28 × 1
                                                                    tensor
```

7.2.6 *The Discriminator*

The Discriminator is the most complex part of the SGAN model. Recall that the SGAN Discriminator has a dual objective:

- Distinguish real examples from fake ones. For this, the SGAN Discriminator uses the *sigmoid* function, outputting a single output probability for binary classification.

- For the real examples, accurately classify their label. For this, the SGAN Discriminator uses the *softmax* function, outputting a vector of probabilities, one for each of the target classes.

THE CORE DISCRIMINATOR NETWORK

We start by defining the core Discriminator network. As you may notice, the model in listing 7.5 is similar to the ConvNet-based Discriminator we implemented in chapter 4; in fact, it is exactly the same all the way until the $3 \times 3 \times 128$ convolutional layer, its batch normalization, and *Leaky ReLU* activation.

After that layer, we add a *dropout*, a regularization technique that helps prevent overfitting by randomly dropping neurons and their connections from the neural network during training.[8] This forces the remaining neurons to reduce their codependence and develop a more general representation of the underlying data. The fraction of the neurons to be randomly dropped is specified by the rate parameter, which is set to 0.5 in our implementation: model.add(Dropout(0.5)). We add dropout because of the increased complexity of the SGAN classification task and to improve the model's ability to generalize from only 100 labeled examples.

Listing 7.5   SGAN Discriminator

```
def build_discriminator_net(img_shape):

    model = Sequential()
                                  Convolutional layer,
    model.add(             ◁─┐    from 28 × 28 × 1 into
        Conv2D(32,              14 × 14 × 32 tensor
               kernel_size=3,
               strides=2,
               input_shape=img_shape,
               padding='same'))
```

---

[8] See "Improving Neural Networks by Preventing Co-Adaptation of Feature Detectors," by Geoffrey E. Hinton et al., 2012, https://arxiv.org/abs/1207.0580. See also "Dropout: A Simple Way to Prevent Neural Networks from Overfitting," by Nitish Srivastava et al., 2014, *Journal of Machine Learning Research* 15, 1929–1958.

```
model.add(LeakyReLU(alpha=0.01))
```
◁── **Leaky ReLU activation**

```
model.add(
    Conv2D(64,
           kernel_size=3,
           strides=2,
           input_shape=img_shape,
           padding='same'))
```
◁── **Convolutional layer, from 14 × 14 × 32 into 7 × 7 × 64 tensor**

```
model.add(BatchNormalization())
```
◁── **Batch normalization**

```
model.add(LeakyReLU(alpha=0.01))
```
◁── **Leaky ReLU activation**

```
model.add(
    Conv2D(128,
           kernel_size=3,
           strides=2,
           input_shape=img_shape,
           padding='same'))
```
◁── **Convolutional layer, from 7 × 7 × 64 tensor into 3 × 3 × 128 tensor**

```
model.add(BatchNormalization())
```
◁── **Batch normalization**

```
model.add(LeakyReLU(alpha=0.01))
```
◁── **Leaky ReLU activation**

```
model.add(Dropout(0.5))
```
◁── **Dropout**

```
model.add(Flatten())
```
◁── **Flattens the tensor**

```
model.add(Dense(num_classes))
```
◁── **Fully connected layer with num_classes neurons**

```
    return model
```

Note that the dropout layer is added after batch normalization and not the other way around; this has shown to have superior performance due to the interplay between the two techniques.[9]

Also, notice that the preceding network ends with a fully connected layer with 10 neurons. Next, we need to define the two Discriminator outputs computed from these neurons: one for the supervised, multiclass classification (using *softmax*) and the other for the unsupervised, binary classification (using *sigmoid*).

THE SUPERVISED DISCRIMINATOR

In the following listing, we take the core Discriminator network implemented previously and use it to build the supervised portion of the Discriminator model.

---

[9] See "Understanding the Disharmony between Dropout and Batch Normalization by Variance Shift," by Xiang Li et al., 2018, https://arxiv.org/abs/1801.05134.

Listing 7.6   SGAN Discriminator: supervised

```
def build_discriminator_supervised(discriminator_net):

    model = Sequential()

    model.add(discriminator_net)

    model.add(Activation('softmax'))

    return model
```

Softmax activation, outputs
predicted probability distribution
over the real classes

THE UNSUPERVISED DISCRIMINATOR

The following listing implements the unsupervised portion of the Discriminator model on top of the core Discriminator network. Notice the `predict(x)` function, in which we transform the output of the 10 neurons (from the core Discriminator network) into a binary, real-versus-fake prediction.

Listing 7.7   SGAN Discriminator: unsupervised

```
def build_discriminator_unsupervised(discriminator_net):

    model = Sequential()

    model.add(discriminator_net)

    def predict(x):
        prediction = 1.0 - (1.0 /
                          (K.sum(K.exp(x), axis=-1, keepdims=True) + 1.0))
        return prediction

    model.add(Lambda(predict))

    return model
```

Transforms distribution over
real classes into binary real-
versus-fake probability

Real-versus-fake output
neuron defined previously

7.2.7   *Building the model*

Next, we build and compile the Discriminator and Generator models. Notice the use of `categorical_crossentropy` and `binary_crossentropy` loss functions for the supervised loss and the unsupervised loss, respectively.

Listing 7.8   Building the models

```
def build_gan(generator, discriminator):

    model = Sequential()

    model.add(generator)
    model.add(discriminator)

    return model
```

Combined Generator +
Discriminator model

Core Discriminator network: these layers are shared during supervised and unsupervised training.

```
discriminator_net = build_discriminator_net(img_shape)

discriminator_supervised = build_discriminator_supervised(discriminator_net)
discriminator_supervised.compile(loss='categorical_crossentropy',
                                 metrics=['accuracy'],
                                 optimizer=Adam())

discriminator_unsupervised = build_discriminator_unsupervised(
                                 discriminator_net)
discriminator_unsupervised.compile(loss='binary_crossentropy',
                                   optimizer=Adam())

generator = build_generator(z_dim)
discriminator_unsupervised.trainable = False
gan = build_gan(generator, discriminator_unsupervised)
gan.compile(loss='binary_crossentropy', optimizer=Adam())
```

Builds and compiles the Discriminator for supervised training

Builds and compiles the Discriminator for unsupervised training

Builds the Generator

Keeps Discriminator's parameters constant for Generator training

Builds and compiles GAN model with fixed Discriminator to train the Generator. Note: uses Discriminator version with unsupervised output.

7.2.8   Training

The following pseudocode outlines the SGAN training algorithm.

SGAN training algorithm

For each training iteration *do*

1   Train the Discriminator (supervised):

   a   Take a random mini-batch of labeled real examples (x, y).

   b   Compute $D((x, y))$ for the given mini-batch and backpropagate the multi-class classification loss to update $\theta^{(D)}$ to minimize the loss.

2   Train the Discriminator (unsupervised):

   a   Take a random mini-batch of unlabeled real examples x.

   b   Compute $D(x)$ for the given mini-batch and backpropagate the binary classification loss to update $\theta^{(D)}$ to minimize the loss.

   c   Take a mini-batch of random noise vectors z and generate a mini-batch of fake examples: $G(z) = x*$.

   d   Compute $D(x*)$ for the given mini-batch and backpropagate the binary classification loss to update $\theta^{(D)}$ to minimize the loss.

3   Train the Generator:

   a   Take a mini-batch of random noise vectors z and generate a mini-batch of fake examples: $G(z) = x*$.

   b   Compute $D(x*)$ for the given mini-batch and backpropagate the binary classification loss to update $\theta^{(G)}$ to maximize the loss.

End for

The following listing implements the SGAN training algorithm.

Listing 7.9   SGAN training algorithm

```
supervised_losses = []
iteration_checkpoints = []


def train(iterations, batch_size, sample_interval):

    real = np.ones((batch_size, 1))

    fake = np.zeros((batch_size, 1))

    for iteration in range(iterations):

        imgs, labels = dataset.batch_labeled(batch_size)

        labels = to_categorical(labels, num_classes=num_classes)

        imgs_unlabeled = dataset.batch_unlabeled(batch_size)

        z = np.random.normal(0, 1, (batch_size, z_dim))
        gen_imgs = generator.predict(z)

        d_loss_supervised,
            accuracy = discriminator_supervised.train_on_batch(imgs, labels)

        d_loss_real = discriminator_unsupervised.train_on_batch(
            imgs_unlabeled, real)

        d_loss_fake = discriminator_unsupervised.train_on_batch(gen_imgs, fake)

        d_loss_unsupervised = 0.5 * np.add(d_loss_real, d_loss_fake)


        z = np.random.normal(0, 1, (batch_size, z_dim))
        gen_imgs = generator.predict(z)

        g_loss = gan.train_on_batch(z, np.ones((batch_size, 1)))

        if (iteration + 1) % sample_interval == 0:

            supervised_losses.append(d_loss_supervised)
            iteration_checkpoints.append(iteration + 1)

            print(
                "%d [D loss supervised: %.4f, acc.: %.2f%%] [D loss" +
                " unsupervised: %.4f] [G loss: %f]"
                % (iteration + 1, d_loss_supervised, 100 * accuracy,
                   (d_loss_unsupervised, g_loss))
```

Annotations:
- Labels for real images: all 1s
- Labels for fake images: all 0s
- Gets labeled examples
- One-hot-encoded labels
- Gets unlabeled examples
- Generates a batch of fake images
- Trains on real unlabeled examples
- Trains on real labeled examples
- Trains on fake examples
- Generates a batch of fake images
- Trains the Generator
- Saves the Discriminator's supervised classification loss to be plotted after training
- Outputs training progress

TRAINING THE MODEL

We use a smaller batch size because we have only 100 labeled examples for training. The number of iterations is determined by trial and error: we keep increasing the number until the Discriminator's supervised loss plateaus, but not too far past that point (to reduce the risk of overfitting):

Listing 7.10 Training the model

```
iterations = 8000
batch_size = 32
sample_interval = 800

train(iterations, batch_size, sample_interval)
```

Sets hyperparameters

Trains the SGAN for the specified number of iterations

MODEL TRAINING AND TEST ACCURACY

And now for the moment we have all been waiting for—let's find out how our SGAN performs as a classifier. During training, we see that we achieved supervised accuracy of 100%. Although this may seem impressive, remember that we have only 100 labeled examples from which to sample for supervised training. Perhaps our model just memorized the training dataset. What matters is how well our classifier can generalize to the previously unseen data in the training set, as shown in the following listing.

Listing 7.11 Checking the accuracy

```
x, y = dataset.test_set()
y = to_categorical(y, num_classes=num_classes)

_, accuracy = discriminator_supervised.evaluate(x, y)
print("Test Accuracy: %.2f%%" % (100 * accuracy))
```

Computes classification accuracy on the test set

Drum roll, please.

Our SGAN is able to accurately classify about 89% of the examples in the test set. To see how remarkable this is, let's compare its performance to a fully supervised classifier.

7.3 *Comparison to a fully supervised classifier*

To make the comparison as fair as possible, we use the same network architecture for the fully supervised classifier as the one used for the supervised Discriminator training, as shown in the following listing. The idea is that this will allow us to isolate the improvement to the classifier's ability to generalize that was achieved through the GAN-enabled semi-supervised learning.

Listing 7.12 Fully supervised classifier

```
mnist_classifier = build_discriminator_supervised(
                    build_discriminator_net(img_shape))
mnist_classifier.compile(loss='categorical_crossentropy',
                    metrics=['accuracy'],
                    optimizer=Adam())
```

Fully supervised classifier with the same network architecture as the SGAN Discriminator

We train the fully supervised classifier by using the same 100 training examples we used to train our SGAN. For brevity, the training code and the code outputting the training and test accuracy are not shown here. You can find the code in our GitHub repository, in the SGAN Jupyter notebook under the chapter-7 folder.

Like the SGAN Discriminator, the fully supervised classifier achieved 100% accuracy on the training dataset. On the test set, however, it was able to correctly classify only about 70% of the examples—about a whopping 20 percentage points worse than our SGAN. Put differently, the SGAN improved the training accuracy by almost 30%!

With a lot more training data, the fully supervised classifier's ability to generalize improves dramatically. Using the same setup and training, the fully supervised classifier with 10,000 labeled examples (100 times as many as we originally used), we achieve an accuracy of about 98%. But that would no longer be a *semi-supervised* setting.

7.4   Conclusion

In this chapter, we explored how GANs can be used for semi-supervised learning by teaching the Discriminator to output class labels for real examples. You saw that the SGAN-trained classifier's ability to generalize from a small number of training examples is significantly better than a comparable, fully supervised classifier.

From a GAN innovation perspective, a key distinguishing feature of the SGAN is the use of labels for Discriminator training. You may be wondering whether labels can be leveraged for Generator training as well. Funny you should ask—that is what the GAN variant in the next chapter (Conditional GAN) is all about.

Summary

- Semi-Supervised GAN (SGAN) is a Generative Adversarial Network whose Discriminator learns to do the following:
  - Distinguish fake examples from real ones
  - Assign the correct class label to the real examples
- The purpose of a SGAN is to train the Discriminator into a classifier that can achieve superior classification accuracy from as few labeled examples as possible, thereby reducing the dependency of classification tasks on enormous labeled datasets.
- In our implementation, we used *softmax* and multiclass cross-entropy loss for the supervised task of assigning real labels, and *sigmoid* and binary cross-entropy for the task of distinguishing between real and fake data.
- We demonstrated that SGAN's classification accuracy on the previously unseen data in the test set is far superior to a comparable fully supervised classifier trained on the same number of labeled training examples.

Conditional GAN

This chapter covers

- Using labels to train both the Generator and the Discriminator
- Teaching GANs to generate examples matching a specified label
- Implementing a Conditional GAN (CGAN) to generate handwritten digits of our choice

In the previous chapter, you learned about the SGAN, which introduced you to the idea of using labels in GAN training. SGANs use labels to train the Discriminator into a powerful semi-supervised classifier. In this chapter, you'll learn about the Conditional GAN (CGAN), which uses labels to train *both* the Generator and the Discriminator. Thanks to this innovation, a Conditional GAN allows us to direct the Generator to synthesize the kind of fake examples we want.

8.1 Motivation

As you have seen throughout this book, GANs are capable of producing examples ranging from simple handwritten digits to photorealistic images of human faces. However, although we could control the domain of examples our GAN learned to emulate by our selection of the training dataset, we could not specify any of the characteristics of the data samples the GAN would generate. For instance, the DCGAN we implemented in chapter 4 could synthesize realistic-looking handwritten digits, but we could not control whether it would produce, say, the number 7 rather than the number 9 at any given time.

On simple datasets like the MNIST, in which examples belong to only one of 10 classes, this concern may seem trivial. If, for instance, our goal is to produce the number 9, we can just keep generating examples until we get the number we want. On more complex data-generation tasks, however, the domain of possible answers gets too large for such a brute-force solution to be practical. Take, for example, the task of generating human faces. As impressive as the images produced by the Progressive GAN from chapter 6 are, we have no control over what face will get produced. There is no way to direct the Generator to synthesize, say, a male or a female face, let alone other features such as age or facial expression.

The ability to decide what kind of data will be generated opens the door to a vast array of applications. As a somewhat contrived example, imagine that we are detectives solving a murder mystery, and a witness describes the killer as a middle-aged woman with long red hair and green eyes. It would greatly expedite the process if instead of hiring a sketch artist (who can produce only one sketch at a time), we could enter the descriptive features into a computer program and have it output a range of faces matching the criteria. Our witness then could point us to the one that resembles the criminal most closely.

We are sure you can think of many other practical applications for which the ability to generate an image that matches the criteria of our choice would be a game-changer. In medical research, we could guide the creation of new drug compounds; in filmmaking and computer-generated imagery (CGI), we could create the exact scene we want with minimal input from human animators. The list goes on.

The CGAN is one of the first GAN innovations that made targeted data generation possible, and arguably the most influential one. In the remainder of this chapter, you will learn how CGANs work and implement a small-scale version by using (you guessed it!) the MNIST dataset.

8.2   *What is Conditional GAN?*

Introduced in 2014 by University of Montreal PhD student Mehdi Mirza and Flickr AI architect Simon Osindero, *Conditional GAN* is a generative adversarial network whose Generator and Discriminator are conditioned during training by using some additional information.[1] This auxiliary information could be, in theory, anything, such as a class label, a set of tags, or even a written description. For clarity and simplicity, we will use labels as the conditioning information as we explain how CGAN works.

During CGAN training, the Generator learns to produce realistic examples for each label in the training dataset, and the Discriminator learns to distinguish fake

---

[1] See "Conditional Generative Adversarial Nets," by Mehdi Mirza and Simon Osindero, 2014, https://arxiv.org/abs/1411.1784.

example-label pairs from real example-label pairs. In contrast to the Semi-Supervised GAN from the previous chapter, whose Discriminator learns to assign the correct label to each real example (in addition to distinguishing real examples from fake ones), the Discriminator in a CGAN does not learn to identify which class is which. It learns only to accept real, matching pairs while rejecting pairs that are mismatched and pairs in which the example is fake.

For example, the CGAN Discriminator should learn to reject the pair (**3**, 4), regardless of whether the example (handwritten numeral 3) is real or fake, because it does not match the label, 4. The CGAN Discriminator should also learn to reject all image-label pairs in which the image is fake, even if the label matches the image.

Accordingly, in order to fool the Discriminator, it is not enough for the CGAN Generator to produce realistic-looking data. The examples it generates also need to match their labels. After the Generator is fully trained, this then allows us to specify what example we want the CGAN to synthesize by passing it the desired label.

8.2.1 CGAN Generator

To formalize things a bit, let's call the conditioning label y. The Generator uses the noise vector z and the label y to synthesize a fake example $G(z, y) = x^*|y$ (read as "x^* given that, or conditioned on, y"). The goal of this fake example is to look (in the eyes of the Discriminator) as close as possible to a real example for the given label. Figure 8.1 illustrates the Generator.

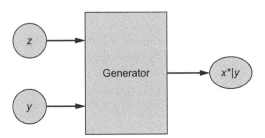

Figure 8.1 CGAN Generator: $G(z, y) = x^*|y$. Using random noise vector z and label y as inputs, the Generator produces a fake example $x^*|y$ that strives to be a realistic-looking match for the label.

8.2.2 CGAN Discriminator

The Discriminator receives real examples with labels (x, y), and fake examples with the label used to generate them, $(x^*|y, y)$. On the real example-label pairs, the Discriminator learns how to recognize real data *and* how to recognize matching pairs. On the Generator-produced examples, it learns to recognize fake image-label pairs, thereby learning to tell them apart from the real ones.

The Discriminator outputs a single probability indicating its conviction that the input is a real, matching pair. The Discriminator's goal is to learn to reject all fake examples and all examples that fail to match their label, while accepting all real example-label pairs, as shown in figure 8.2.

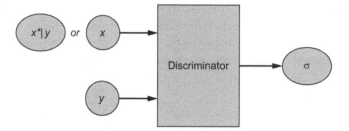

Figure 8.2   The CGAN Discriminator receives real examples along with their labels (*x*, *y*) and fake examples along with the label used to synthesize them (*x**|*y*, *y*). The Discriminator then outputs a probability (computed by the *sigmoid* activation function σ) indicating whether the input pair is real rather than fake.

8.2.3   *Summary table*

The two CGAN subnetworks, their inputs, outputs, and objectives are summarized in table 8.1.

Table 8.1   CGAN Generator and Discriminator networks

	Generator	Discriminator
Input	A vector of random numbers and a label: (z, y)	The Discriminator receives the following inputs: ■ Real examples with labels coming from the training dataset: (x, y) ■ Fake examples created by the Generator to match a given label, along with the label: $(x*|y, y)$
Output	Fake examples that strive to be as convincing as possible in matches for their labels: $G(z, y) = x*|y$	A single probability indicating whether the input example is a real, matching example-label pair
Goal	Generate realistic-looking fake data that match their labels	Distinguish between fake example-label pairs coming from the Generator and real example-label pairs coming from the training dataset

8.2.4   *Architecture diagram*

Putting it all together, figure 8.3 shows a high-level architecture diagram of a CGAN. Notice that for each fake example, the same label *y* is passed to both the Generator and the Discriminator. Also, note that the Discriminator is never explicitly trained to reject mismatched pairs by being trained on real examples with mismatching labels; its ability to identify mismatched pairs is a by-product of being trained to accept only real matching pairs.

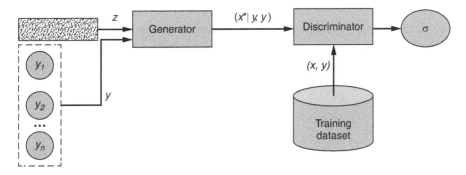

Figure 8.3 **The CGAN Generator uses a random noise vector z and a label y (one of the n possible labels) as inputs and produces a fake example x*|y that strives to be both realistic looking and a convincing match for the label y.**

> **NOTE** You may have noticed a pattern: for almost every GAN variant, we present you with a table summarizing the inputs, outputs, and objectives of the Discriminator and Generator networks, and with a network architecture diagram. This is not by accident; indeed, one of the main goals of these chapters is to give you a mental template—a reusable framework of sorts—for the kind of things to look for when you encounter GAN implementations that diverge from the original GAN. Analyzing the Generator and Discriminator networks and the overall model architecture are often the best first steps.

The CGAN Discriminator receives fake labeled examples $(x*|y, y)$ produced by the Generator and real labeled examples (x, y), and it learns to tell whether a given example-label is real or fake.

Enough for theory. It's time we put what you have learned into practice and implement our own CGAN model.

8.3 Tutorial: Implementing a Conditional GAN

In this tutorial, we will implement a CGAN model that learns to generate handwritten digits of our choice. At the end, we will generate a sample of images for each numeral to see how well the model learned to generate targeted data.

8.3.1 Implementation

Our implementation is inspired by the CGAN in the open source GitHub repository of GAN models in Keras (the same one we used in chapters 3 and 4).[2] In particular, we use the repository's approach of using `Embedding` layers to combine examples and labels into joint hidden representations (more on this later).

---

[2] See Erik Linder-Norén's Keras-GAN GitHub repository, 2017, https://github.com/eriklindernoren/Keras-GAN.

The rest of our CGAN model, however, diverges from the one found in the Keras-GAN repository. We refactored the embedding implementation to be more readable and added detailed explanatory comments. Crucially, we also adapted our CGAN to use convolutional neural networks, which yield significantly more realistic examples—recall the difference between the images produced by the GAN in chapter 3 and the DCGAN in chapter 4!

A Jupyter notebook with the full implementation, including added visualizations of the training progress, is available in our GitHub repository, under the chapter-8 folder: https://github.com/GANs-in-Action/gans-in-action. The code was tested with Python 3.6.0, Keras 2.1.6, and TensorFlow 1.8.0. To speed up the training time, we recommend running the model on a GPU.

8.3.2 *Setup*

You guessed it—the first step is to import all the modules and libraries needed for our model, as shown in the following listing.

Listing 8.1 Import statements

```
%matplotlib inline

import matplotlib.pyplot as plt
import numpy as np

from keras.datasets import mnist
from keras.layers import (
        Activation, BatchNormalization, Concatenate, Dense,
        Embedding, Flatten, Input, Multiply, Reshape)
from keras.layers.advanced_activations import LeakyReLU
from keras.layers.convolutional import Conv2D, Conv2DTranspose
from keras.models import Model, Sequential
from keras.optimizers import Adam
```

Just as before, we also specify the input image size, the size of the noise vector z, and the number of classes in our dataset, as shown here.

Listing 8.2 Model input dimensions

```
img_rows = 28
img_cols = 28
channels = 1

img_shape = (img_rows, img_cols, channels)    ◁──┐  Input image
                                                      dimensions

z_dim = 100        ◁──────────────────────
                                              Size of the noise
                                              vector, used as input
num_classes = 10   ◁──┐ Number of classes    to the Generator
                        in the dataset
```

8.3.3 CGAN Generator

In this section, we implement the CGAN Generator. By now, you should be familiar with much of this network from chapters 4 and 7. The modifications made for the CGAN center around input handling, where we use embedding and element-wise multiplication to combine the random noise vector z and the label y into a joint representation. Let's walk through what the code does:

1 Take label y (an integer from 0 to 9) and turn it into a dense vector of size z_dim (the length of the random noise vector) by using the Keras Embedding layer.

2 Combine the label embedding with the noise vector z into a joint representation by using the Keras Multiply layer. As its name suggests, this layer multiplies the corresponding entries of the two equal-length vectors and outputs a single vector of the resulting products.

3 Feed the resulting vector as input into the rest of the CGAN Generator network to synthesize an image.

Figure 8.4 illustrates the process, using the label 7 as an example.

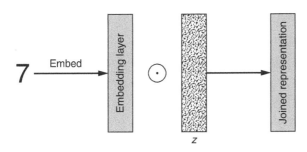

Figure 8.4   The steps used to combine the conditioning label (7 in this example) and the random noise vector z into a single joint representation

First, we embed the label into a vector of the same size as z. Second, we multiply the corresponding elements of the embedded label and z (the symbol ⊙ denotes element-wise multiplication). The resulting joined representation is then used as input into the CGAN Generator network.

And finally, the following listing shows what it all looks like in Python/Keras code.

Listing 8.3   CGAN Generator

```
def build_generator(z_dim):

    model = Sequential()

    model.add(Dense(256 * 7 * 7, input_dim=z_dim))
    model.add(Reshape((7, 7, 256)))

    model.add(Conv2DTranspose(128, kernel_size=3, strides=2, padding='same'))

    model.add(BatchNormalization())
```

Transposed convolution layer, from 7 × 7 × 256 into a 14 × 14 × 128 tensor

Reshapes input into a 7 × 7 × 256 tensor via a fully connected layer

Batch normalization

Transposed convolution layer, from 14 × 14 × 128 to a 14 × 14 × 64 tensor

```
model.add(LeakyReLU(alpha=0.01))        ←—— Leaky ReLU activation

model.add(Conv2DTranspose(64, kernel_size=3, strides=1, padding='same'))

model.add(BatchNormalization())         ←—— Batch normalization

model.add(LeakyReLU(alpha=0.01))        ←—— Leaky ReLU activation
```

Transposed convolution layer, from 14 × 14 × 64 to a 28 × 28 × 1 tensor

```
model.add(Conv2DTranspose(1, kernel_size=3, strides=2, padding='same'))

model.add(Activation('tanh'))     ←— Output layer with
                                       tanh activation

return model
```

```
def build_cgan_generator(z_dim):

    z = Input(shape=(z_dim, ))            ←— Random noise vector z

    label = Input(shape=(1, ), dtype='int32')   ←— Conditioning label: integer 0–9 specifying the number G should generate
```

Label embedding: turns labels into dense vectors of size z_dim; produces 3D tensor with shape (batch_size, 1, z_dim)

```
    label_embedding = Embedding(num_classes, z_dim, input_length=1)(label)

    label_embedding = Flatten()(label_embedding)    ←— Flattens the embedding 3D tensor into 2D tensor with shape (batch_size, z_dim)

    joined_representation = Multiply()([z, label_embedding])   ←— Element-wise product of the vectors z and the label embeddings

    generator = build_generator(z_dim)

    conditioned_img = generator(joined_representation)

    return Model([z, label], conditioned_img)    ←— Generates image for the given label
```

8.3.4   *CGAN Discriminator*

Next, we implement the CGAN Discriminator. Just as in the previous section, the network architecture should look familiar to you, except for the piece where we handle the input image and its label. Here, too, we use the Keras `Embedding` layer to turn input labels into dense vectors. However, unlike the Generator, where the model input is a flat vector, the Discriminator receives three-dimensional images. This necessitates customized handling, described in the following steps:

1 Take a label (an integer from 0 to 9) and—using the Keras `Embedding` layer—turn the label into a dense vector of size $28 \times 28 \times 1 = 784$ (the length of a flattened image).

2 Reshape the label embeddings into the image dimensions ($28 \times 28 \times 1$).

3 Concatenate the reshaped label embedding onto the corresponding image, creating a joint representation with the shape ($28 \times 28 \times 2$). You can think of it as an image with its embedded label "stamped" on top of it.

4   Feed the image-label joint representation as input into the CGAN Discriminator network. Note that in order for things to work, we have to adjust the model
input dimensions to $(28 \times 28 \times 2)$ to reflect the new input shape.

Again, to make it less abstract, let's see what the process looks like visually, using the
label 7 as an example; see figure 8.5.

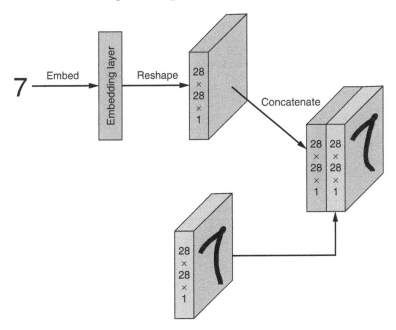

**Figure 8.5   The steps used to combine the label (7 in this case) and the input
image into a single joint representation**

First, we embed the label into a vector the size of a flattened image $(28 \times 28 \times 1 = 784)$.
Second, we reshape the embedded label into a tensor with the same shape as the
input image $(28 \times 28 \times 1)$. Third, we concatenate the reshaped label that is embedding onto the corresponding image. This joined representation is then passed as
input into the CGAN Discriminator network.

In addition to the preprocessing steps, we have to make a few additional adjustments to the Discriminator network compared to the one in chapter 4. (As in the previous chapter, basing the model on our DCGAN implementation should make it
easier to see the CGAN-specific changes without distractions from implementation
details in unrelated parts of the model.) First, we have to adjust the model input
dimensions to $(28 \times 28 \times 2)$ to reflect the new input shape.

Second, we increase the depth of the first convolutional layer from 32 to 64. The
reasoning behind this change is that there is more information to encode because of
the concatenated label embedding; this network architecture indeed yielded better
results experimentally.

At the output layer, we use the *sigmoid* activation function to produce a probability that the input image-label pair is real rather than fake—no change here. And finally, the following listing is our CGAN Discriminator implementation.

Listing 8.4   CGAN Discriminator

```
def build_discriminator(img_shape):

    model = Sequential()              Convolutional layer,
                                      from 28 × 28 × 2 into
    model.add(                        14 × 14 × 64 tensor
        Conv2D(64,
                kernel_size=3,
                strides=2,
                input_shape=(img_shape[0], img_shape[1], img_shape[2] + 1),
                padding='same'))
                                          Leaky ReLU
    model.add(LeakyReLU(alpha=0.01))      activation

    model.add(                        Convolutional layer,
        Conv2D(64,                    from 14 × 14 × 64 into
                kernel_size=3,        7 × 7 × 64 tensor
                strides=2,
                input_shape=img_shape,
                padding='same'))
                                      Batch
    model.add(BatchNormalization())   normalization

    model.add(LeakyReLU(alpha=0.01))     Leaky ReLU activation

    model.add(                        Convolutional layer,
        Conv2D(128,                   from 7 × 7 × 64 tensor
                kernel_size=3,        into 3 × 3 × 128 tensor
                strides=2,
                input_shape=img_shape,
                padding='same'))
                                      Batch
    model.add(BatchNormalization())   normalization

    model.add(LeakyReLU(alpha=0.01))     Leaky ReLU

    model.add(Flatten())
    model.add(Dense(1, activation='sigmoid'))    Output layer with
                                                 sigmoid activation
    return model


def build_cgan_discriminator(img_shape):
                                         Input image
    img = Input(shape=img_shape)
                                      Label for the
    label = Input(shape=(1, ), dtype='int32')    input image
```

**Label embedding:
turns labels into
dense vectors
of size z_dim;
produces 3D
tensor with shape
(batch_size, 1,
28 × 28 × 1)**

```
label_embedding = Embedding(num_classes,
                            np.prod(img_shape),
                            input_length=1)(label)

label_embedding = Flatten()(label_embedding)

label_embedding = Reshape(img_shape)(label_embedding)

concatenated = Concatenate(axis=-1)([img, label_embedding])

discriminator = build_discriminator(img_shape)

classification = discriminator(concatenated)

return Model([img, label], classification)
```

**Flattens the embedding
3D tensor into a 2D tensor
with shape (batch_size,
28 × 28 × 1)**

**Reshapes label
embeddings to
have the same
dimensions as
input images**

**Concatenates
images with
their label
embeddings**

**Classifies the
image-label pair**

8.3.5   Building the model

Next, we build and compile the CGAN Discriminator and Generator models, as shown
in the following listing. Notice that in the combined model used to train the Generator, the same input label is passed to the Generator (to generate a sample) and to the
Discriminator (to make a prediction).

Listing 8.5   Building and compiling the CGAN model

```
def build_cgan(generator, discriminator):

    z = Input(shape=(z_dim, ))

    label = Input(shape=(1, ))

    img = generator([z, label])

    classification = discriminator([img, label])

    model = Model([z, label], classification)

    return model


discriminator = build_cgan_discriminator(img_shape)
discriminator.compile(loss='binary_crossentropy',
                      optimizer=Adam(),
                      metrics=['accuracy'])

generator = build_cgan_generator(z_dim)

discriminator.trainable = False

cgan = build_cgan(generator, discriminator)
cgan.compile(loss='binary_crossentropy', optimizer=Adam())
```

**Random noise
vector z**

Image label

**Generated image
for that label**

**Combined Generator ->
Discriminator model
G([z, label]) = x*
D(x*) = classification**

**Builds and compiles
the Discriminator**

**Builds the
Generator**

**Builds and compiles CGAN
model with fixed Discriminator
to train the Generator**

**Keeps
Discriminator's
parameters
constant for
Generator
training**

8.3.6   *Training*

For the CGAN training algorithm, the details of each training iteration are as follows.

CGAN training algorithm

For each training iteration **do**

1 Train the Discriminator:

   a Take a random mini-batch of real examples and their labels (x, y).

   b Compute $D((x, y))$ for the mini-batch and backpropagate the binary classification loss to update $\theta^{(D)}$ to minimize the loss.

   c Take a mini-batch of random noise vectors and class labels (z, y) and generate a mini-batch of fake examples: $G(z, y) = x*|y$.

   d Compute $D(x*|y, y)$ for the mini-batch and backpropagate the binary classification loss to update $\theta^{(D)}$ to minimize the loss.

2 Train the Generator:

   a Take a mini-batch of random noise vectors and class labels (z, y) and generate a mini-batch of fake examples: $G(z, y) = x*|y$.

   b Compute $D(x*|y, y)$ for the given mini-batch and backpropagate the binary classification loss to update $\theta^{(G)}$ to maximize the loss.

End for

The following listing implements this CGAN training algorithm.

Listing 8.6   CGAN training loop

```
accuracies = []
losses = []


def train(iterations, batch_size, sample_interval):

    (X_train, y_train), (_, _) = mnist.load_data()          Loads the MNIST
                                                            dataset

    X_train = X_train / 127.5 - 1.                          Rescales [0, 255] grayscale
    X_train = np.expand_dims(X_train, axis=3)               pixel values to [−1, 1]

    real = np.ones((batch_size, 1))                         Labels for real
                                                            images: all 1s
    fake = np.zeros((batch_size, 1))

    for iteration in range(iterations):                    Gets a random batch
                                                           of real images and
                                                               their labels

        idx = np.random.randint(0, X_train.shape[0], batch_size)
        imgs, labels = X_train[idx], y_train[idx]
```

Labels for
fake images:
all 0s

```
z = np.random.normal(0, 1, (batch_size, z_dim))          Generates a batch
gen_imgs = generator.predict([z, labels])                of fake images
```

Trains the
Discriminator
```
d_loss_real = discriminator.train_on_batch([imgs, labels], real)
d_loss_fake = discriminator.train_on_batch([gen_imgs, labels], fake)
d_loss = 0.5 * np.add(d_loss_real, d_loss_fake)
```

```
                                                         Generates a batch
z = np.random.normal(0, 1, (batch_size, z_dim))          of noise vectors
```

Gets a batch
of random
labels
```
labels = np.random.randint(0, num_classes, batch_size).reshape(-1, 1)
```

```
g_loss = cgan.train_on_batch([z, labels], real)          Trains the
                                                         Generator
```

```
if (iteration + 1) % sample_interval == 0:
```

Outputs
training
progress
```
    print("%d [D loss: %f, acc.: %.2f%%] [G loss: %f]" %
          (iteration + 1, d_loss[0], 100 * d_loss[1], g_loss))
```

```
    losses.append((d_loss[0], g_loss))                   Saves losses and accuracies
    accuracies.append(100 * d_loss[1])                   so they can be plotted after
                                                         training
```

```
    sample_images()          Outputs sample of
                             generated images
```

8.3.7 Outputting sample images

You may recognize the next function from chapters 3 and 4. We used it to examine how the quality of the Generator-produced images improved as the training progressed. The function in listing 8.7 is indeed similar, but a few crucial differences exist.

First, instead of a 4 × 4 grid of random handwritten digits, we are generating a 2 × 5 grid of numbers, 1 through 5 in the first row, and 6 through 9 in the second row. This allows us to inspect how well the CGAN Generator is learning to produce specific numerals. Second, we are displaying the label for each example by using the set_title() method.

Listing 8.7 Displaying generated images

```
def sample_images(image_grid_rows=2, image_grid_columns=5):
```

Sample
random
noise
```
    z = np.random.normal(0, 1, (image_grid_rows * image_grid_columns, z_dim))
```

```
    labels = np.arange(0, 10).reshape(-1, 1)          Gets image labels 0–9
```

```
    gen_imgs = generator.predict([z, labels])          Generates images
                                                       from random noise
```

Rescales
image pixel
values to [0, I]
```
    gen_imgs = 0.5 * gen_imgs + 0.5
```

```
    fig, axs = plt.subplots(image_grid_rows,          Sets image grid
                            image_grid_columns,
                            figsize=(10, 4),
                            sharey=True,
                            sharex=True)
```

```
cnt = 0
for i in range(image_grid_rows):
    for j in range(image_grid_columns):
        axs[i, j].imshow(gen_imgs[cnt, :, :, 0], cmap='gray')
        axs[i, j].axis('off')
        axs[i, j].set_title("Digit: %d" % labels[cnt])
        cnt += 1
```

Outputs a grid of images ⊢→

Figure 8.6 shows sample output from this function and illustrates the improvement to the CGAN-produced numerals over the course of training.

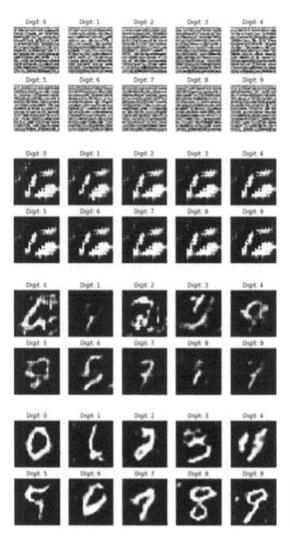

Figure 8.6 Starting from random noise, GCAN learns to produce realistic-looking numerals for each of the labels in the training dataset.

8.3.8 Training the model

And finally, let's run the model we just implemented:

```
iterations = 12000          ⟵┐  Sets
batch_size = 32              │  hyperparameters
sample_interval = 1000       ┘

train(iterations, batch_size, sample_interval)  ⟵  Trains the CGAN for
                                                    the specified number
                                                    of iterations
```

8.3.9 Inspecting the output: Targeted data generation

Figure 8.7 shows the images of digits produced by the CGAN Generator after it is fully trained. At each row, we instruct the Generator to synthesize a different numeral, from 0 to 9. Notice that each numeral is rendered in a different writing style, attesting

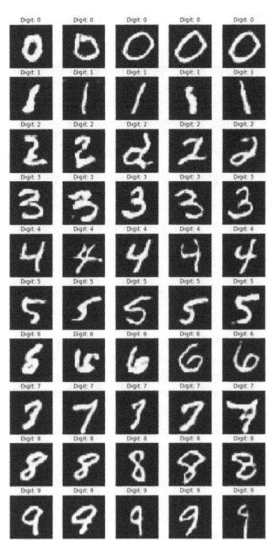

Figure 8.7 Each row shows a sample of images produced to match a given numeral, 0 through 9. As you can see, the CGAN Generator has successfully learned to produce every class represented in our dataset.

to CGAN's ability not only to learn to produce examples matching every label in the training dataset, but also to capture the full diversity of the training data.

8.4   *Conclusion*

In this chapter, you saw how labels could be used to guide the training of the Generator and the Discriminator to teach a GAN to produce fake examples of our choice. Along with the DCGAN, CGAN is one of the most influential early GAN variants that has inspired countless new research directions.

Perhaps the most impactful and promising of these is the use of conditional adversarial networks as a general-purpose solution to image-to-image translation problems. This is a class of problems that seeks to translate images from one modality into another. Applications of image-to-image translation range from colorizing black-and-white photos to turning a daytime scene into nighttime and synthesizing a satellite view from a map view.

One of the most successful early implementations based on the Conditional GAN paradigm is pix2pix, which uses pairs of images (one as the input and the other as the label) to learn to translate from one domain into another. Recall that, in theory as well as in practice, the conditioning information used to train a CGAN can be much more than just labels to provide for more complex use cases and scenarios. For example, for colorization tasks, an image pair would be a black-and-white photo (the input) and a colored version of the same photo (the label). You will see these illustrated in the following chapter.

We do not cover pix2pix in detail because only about a year after its publication, it was eclipsed by another GAN variant that not only outperformed pix2pix's performance on image-to-image translation tasks but also accomplished it without the need for paired images. The Cycle-Consistent Adversarial Network (or CycleGAN, as the technique came to be known) needs only two groups of images representing the two domains (for example, a group of black-and-white photos and a group of colored photos). You will learn all about this remarkable GAN variant in the following chapter.

Summary

- Conditional GAN (CGAN) is a GAN variant in which both the Generator and the Discriminator are conditioned on auxiliary data such as a class label during training.
- The additional information constrains the Generator to synthesize a certain type of output and the Discriminator to accept only real examples matching the given additional information.
- As a tutorial, we implemented a CGAN that generates realistic handwritten digits of our choice by using MNIST class labels as our conditioning information.
- Embedding maps an integer into a dense vector of the desired size. We used embedding to create a joint hidden representation from a random noise vector and a label (for CGAN Generator training) and from an input image and a label (for CGAN Discriminator training).

CycleGAN

This chapter covers

- Expanding on the idea of Conditional GANs by conditioning on an entire image
- Exploring one of the most powerful and complex GAN architectures: CycleGAN
- Presenting an object-oriented design of GANs and the architecture of its four main components
- Implementing a CycleGAN to run a conversion of apples to oranges

Finally, a technological breakthrough of almost universal appeal, seeing as everyone seems to love comparing apples to oranges. In this chapter, you will learn how! But this is no small feat, so we will need at least *two* sets of Discriminators and *two* Generators to achieve this. That obviously complicates the architecture, so we will have to spend more time discussing it, but at the very least, it is a great point to start thinking in a fully object-oriented programming (OOP) way.

143

9.1 *Image-to-image translation*

One fascinating area of GANs' application that we touched on at the end of the previous chapter is *image-to-image translation.* In this use, GANs have been massively successful—in video, static images, or even style transfer. Indeed, GANs have been at the forefront of many of these applications as they enable almost a new class of uses. Because of their visual nature, the more successful GAN variants typically make their rounds on YouTube and Twitter, so if you have not seen these videos, we encourage you to check them out by searching for *pix2pix, CycleGAN,* or *vid2vid.*

This type of translation in practice means that our input to the Generator is a picture, because we need our Generator (translator) to start from this image. In other words, we are mapping an image from one domain to another. Previously, the latent vector seeding the generation was typically a somewhat uninterpretable vector. Now we are swapping that for an input image.

A good way to think of image-to-image translation is as a special case of the Conditional GAN. However, in this case, we are conditioning on a complete image (rather than just a class)—typically of the same dimensionality as the output image—that is then provided to the network as a kind of a label (presented in chapter 8). One of the first famous examples in this space was an image-translation work coming out of the University of California, Berkeley, as shown in figure 9.1.

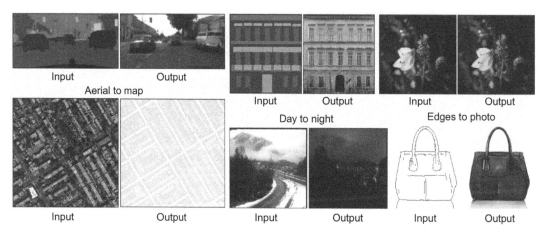

Figure 9.1 Conditional GANs provide a powerful framework for image translation that performs well across many domains.

(Source: "Image-to-Image Translation with Conditional Adversarial Networks," by Phillip Isola, https://github.com/phillipi/pix2pix.)

As you can see, we can map from any of the following:

- From semantic labels (for example, drawing blue where a car should be and purple where a road should be) to photorealistic images of streets
- From satellite images to a view like the one in Google Maps
- From day images to night images

- From black-and-white to color
- From outlines to synthesized fashion items

The idea is clearly powerful and versatile; however, the issue lies with the need for paired data. From chapter 8, you understand that we need labels for the Conditional GAN. Because in this case we are using another image as a label, the mapping does not make sense unless we're mapping to the corresponding image—the exact same image, except in the other domain.

So, the night image needs to be taken from exactly the same place as the day image. The fashion item's outline needs to have the exact match of a fully colored/synthesized item in the training set in the other domain. In other words, during training, the GAN needs to have access to corresponding labels of the items in the original domain.

This is typically done—for example, in the case of black-and-white images—by first taking loads of colored pictures, applying the B&W filter on all of them, and then using the unmodified image as one domain and the B&W-filtered images as the other. This ensures that we have the corresponding images in both domains. Then we can apply the trained GAN anywhere, but if we do not have an easy way of generating these "perfect" pairs, we are out of luck!

9.2 *Cycle-consistency loss: There and back aGAN*

The genius insight of this UC Berkeley group was that we do not, in fact, need perfect pairs.[1] Instead, we simply complete the cycle: we translate from one domain to another and then back again. For example, we go from summer picture (domain A) of a park to a winter one (domain B) and then back again to summer (domain A). Now we have essentially created a cycle, and, ideally, the original picture (a) and the reconstructed picture ($\hat{a}$) are the same. If they are not, we can measure their loss on a pixel level, thereby getting the first loss of our CycleGAN: *cycle-consistency loss*, which is depicted in figure 9.2.

A common analogy is thinking about the process of *back-translation*—a sentence in Chinese that is translated to English and then back again to Chinese should give back the same sentence. If not, we can measure the cycle-consistency loss by how much the first and the third sentences differ.

To be able to use the cycle-consistency loss, we need to have two Generators: one translating from A to B, called G_{AB}, sometimes referred to as simply G, and then another one translating from B to A, called G_{BA}, referred to as F for brevity. There are technically two losses—forward cycle-consistency loss and backward cycle-consistency loss—but because all they mean is that $\hat{a} = F(G(a)) \approx a$ as well as $\hat{b} = G(F(b)) \approx b$, you may think of these as essentially the same, but off by one.

---

[1] See "Unpaired Image-to-Image Translation Using Cycle-Consistent Adversarial Networks," by Jun-Yan Zhu et al., 2017, https://arxiv.org/pdf/1703.10593.pdf.

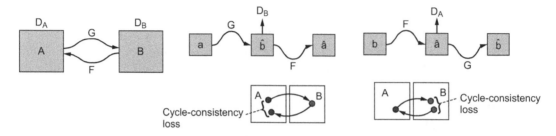

Figure 9.2   Because the loss works both ways, we can now reproduce not just images from summer to winter, but also from winter to summer. If G is our Generator from A to B, and F is our Generator from B to A, then

$$\hat{a} = F(G(a)) \approx a.$$

(Source: Jun-Yan Zhu et al., 2017, https://arxiv.org/pdf/1703.10593.pdf.)

9.3   *Adversarial loss*

In addition to the cycle-consistency loss, we still have the *adversarial loss*. Every translation with a Generator G_{AB} has a corresponding Discriminator D_B, and G_{BA} has Discriminator D_A. The way to think about it is that we are always testing, when translating *to* domain A, whether the picture looks real; hence we use D_A and vice versa.

This is the same idea as with simpler architectures, but now, because of the two losses, we have two Discriminators. We need to make sure that not only the translation from apple to orange looks real, but also that the translation from our estimated orange back to reconstructed apple looks real. Recall that the adversarial loss ensures that the images look real, and as a result, it is still key for the CycleGAN to work. Hence adversarial loss is presented as second. The first Discriminator in the cycle is especially important—otherwise, we'd simply get noise that would help the GAN memorize what it should reconstruct.[2]

9.4   *Identity loss*

The idea of *identity loss* is simple: we want to enforce that CycleGAN preserves the overall color structure (or *temperature*) of the picture. So we introduce a regularization term that helps us keep the tint of the picture consistent with the original image. Imagine this as a way of ensuring that even after applying many filters onto your image, you still can recover the original image.

This is done by feeding the images already in domain A to the Generator from B to A (G_{BA}), because the CycleGAN should understand that they are already in the correct domain. In other words, we penalize unnecessary changes to the image: if we feed in a zebra and are trying to "zebrafy" an image, we get the same zebra back, as there is nothing to do.[3] Figure 9.3 illustrates the effects of identity loss.

---

[2] In practice, this is a little bit more complicated and would depend on, for example, whether you include both forward and backward cyclical loss. But you may use this as a mental model for how to think of the importance of the adversarial loss—remembering that we have both mappings A-B-A and B-A-B, so both Discriminators get to be the first one at some point.

[3] Jun Yan Zhu et al., 2017, https://arxiv.org/pdf/1703.10593.pdf. More at http://mng.bz/loE8.

Input   Without identity loss   With identity loss

Figure 9.3 **A picture is worth a thousand words to clarify the effects of identity loss: there is a clear tint in the cases without identity loss, and since there seems to be no reason for it, so we try to penalize this behavior. Even in black and white, you should be able to see the difference. However, to see the full extent of it, check out the full-color version online.**

Even though identity loss is not, strictly speaking, required for the CycleGAN to work, we include it for completeness. Both our implementation and the CycleGAN authors' latest implementation contain it, because frequently this adjustment leads to empirically better results and enforces a constraint that seems reasonable. But even the CycleGAN paper itself mentions it only briefly as a seeming ex-post justification, so we do not cover it extensively.

Table 9.1 summarizes the losses you've learned about in this chapter.

Table 9.1   Losses

	Calculation	Measures	Ensures
Adversarial loss	$\mathcal{L}_{GAN}(G, D_B, B, A)$ $= E_{b \sim p(b)}[log D_B(b)]$ $+ E_{a \sim p(a)}[log(1 - D_B(G_{AB}(a)))]$ (This is just the good old NS-GAN presented in chapter 5.)	As in previous cases, the loss measures two terms: first is the likelihood of a given image being the real one rather than the translated image. Second is the part where the Generator may get to fool the Discriminator. Note that this formulation is only for D_B, with equivalent D_A that comes into the final loss.	That the translated images look real, sharp, and indistinguishable from the real ones.

Table 9.1   Losses *(continued)*

	Calculation	Measures	Ensures
Cycle-consistency loss: forward pass	Difference between a and $\hat{a}$ (denoted by $\|\hat{a} - a\|_1{}^a$)	The difference between the images from the original domain a and the twice-translated images $\hat{a}$.	That the original image and the twice-translated image are the same. If this fails, we may not have a coherent mapping A-B-A.
Cycle-consistency loss: backward pass	$\|\hat{b} - b\|_1$	The difference between the images from the original domain b and the twice-translated images $\hat{b}$.	That the original image and the twice-translated image are the same. If this fails, we may not have a coherent mapping B-A-B.
Overall loss	$\mathcal{L} = \mathcal{L}_{GAN}(G, D_B, A, B)$ $+ \mathcal{L}_{GAN}(F, D_A, B, A)$ $+ \lambda \mathcal{L}_{cyc}(G, F)$	All of the four losses combined (2× adversarial because of two Generators) plus cyclical loss: forward and backward in one term.	That the overall translation is photorealistic and makes sense (provides matching pictures).
Identity loss (outside the overall loss, for consistency with the CycleGAN paper notation)	$\mathcal{L}_{identity} =$ $= E_{a \sim p(a)}[\|\, G_{BA}(a) - a \,\|]$ $+ E_{b \sim p(b)}[\|\, G_{AB}(b) - b \,\|]$	The difference between the image in B and $G_{AB}(b)$ and vice versa.	That the CycleGAN changes parts of the image only when it needs to.

a. This notation may be unfamiliar to some, but it represents the L1 norm between the two items. For simplicity, you may think of this as for each pixel, an absolute difference between it and the corresponding pixel on the reconstructed image.

9.5   *Architecture*

The CycleGAN setup builds directly on the CGAN architecture and is, in essence, two CGANs joined together—or, as the CycleGAN authors themselves point out, an auto-encoder. Recall from chapter 2 that we had an input image x and the reconstructed image x^*, which was the result of reconstruction after being fed through the latent space z; see figure 9.4.

To translate this diagram into the CycleGAN's world, a is an image in the A domain, b is an image in B, and $\hat{a}$ is reconstructed A. In CycleGAN's case, however, we are dealing with a latent space—step 2—of equal dimensionality. It just happens to be another meaningful domain (B) that the CycleGAN has to find. Even with the autoencoder, the latent space was just another domain, though it was not as easily interpretable.

Compared to what we know from chapter 2, the main new concept is the introduction of the adversarial losses. These and many other mixtures of autoencoders and GANs are an active area of research in themselves! So that is also a good area for interested researchers. But for now, think of the two mappings as two autoencoders: $F(G(a))$

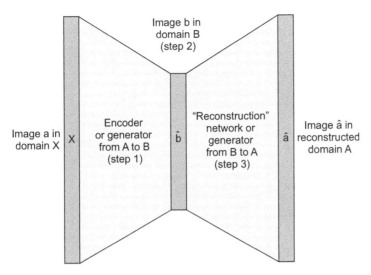

Figure 9.4 In this image of an autoencoder from chapter 2, we used the analogy of compressing (step 1) a human concept into a more compact written form in a letter (step 2) and then expanding this concept out to the (imperfect) idea of the same notion in someone else's head (step 3).

and $G(F(b))$. We take the basic idea of the autoencoder—including a kind of *explicit* loss function as substituted by the cycle-consistency loss—and add Discriminators to it. The two Discriminators, one at each step, ensure that both translations (including into the kind of *latent space*) look like real images in their respective domains.

9.5.1 CycleGAN architecture: building the network

Before we jump into the actual implementation of the CycleGAN, let's briefly look at the overall simplified implementation depicted in figure 9.5. There are two flows: in the top diagram, the flow A-B-A starts from an image in domain A, and in the bottom diagram, the flow B-A-B starts with an image in domain B.

The image then follows two paths: it is (1) fed to the Discriminator to get our decision as to whether it is real or not, and (2) (i) fed to the Generator to translate it to B, then (ii) evaluated by the Discriminator B to see if it looks real in domain B, and eventually (iii) translated back to A to allow us to measure the cyclic loss.

The bottom image is basically an *off-by-one* cycle of the top image and follows all the same fundamental steps. We'll use the apple2orange dataset, but many other datasets are available, including the famous horse2zebra dataset, which you can easily use by making a slight modification to the code and downloading the data by using the bash script provided.

To summarize figure 9.5 in another representation for further clarity, table 9.2 reviews all four major networks.

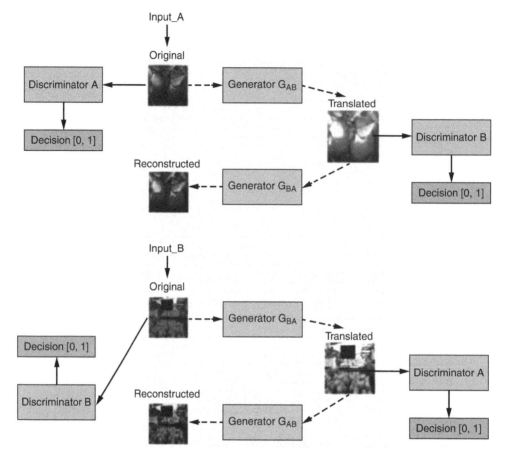

Figure 9.5   In this simplified architecture of the CycleGAN, we start with the input image, which either (1) goes to the Discriminator for evaluation or (2) is translated to one domain, evaluated by the other Discriminator, and then translated back.

(Source: "Understanding and Implementing CycleGAN in TensorFlow," by Hardik Bansal and Archit Rathore, 2017, https://hardikbansal.github.io/CycleGANBlog/.)

Table 9.2   Networks

	Input	Output	Goal
Generator: from A to B	We load either a real picture from A or a translation from B to A.	We translate it to domain B.	Try to create realistic-looking images in domain B.
Generator: from B to A	We load either a real picture from B or a translation from A to B.	We translate it to domain A.	Try to create realistic-looking images in domain A.
Discriminator A	We provide a picture in the A domain—either translated or real.	The probability that the picture is real.	Try to not get fooled by the Generator from B to A.
Discriminator B	We provide a picture in the B domain—either translated or real.	The probability that the picture is real.	Try to not get fooled by the Generator from A to B.

9.5.2 *Generator architecture*

Figure 9.6 shows the architecture of the Generator. We have re-created the diagram by using the variable names from our code and included the shapes for your benefit. This is an example of a *U-Net* architecture, because when you draw it in a way that each resolution gets its own level, the network looks like a U.

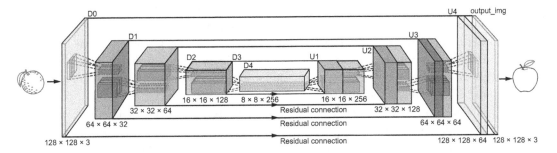

Figure 9.6   Architecture of the Generator. The generator itself has a *contraction path* (d0 to d3) and *expanding path* (u1 to u4). The contraction and expanding paths are sometimes referred to as *encoder* and *decoder*, respectively.

A couple of things to note here:

- We are using standard convolutional layers in the encoder.
- From those, we create *skip connections* so that the information has an easier time propagating through the network. In the figure, this is denoted by the outlines and color-coding between the d0 to d3 and u1 to u4, respectively. You can see that half of the blocks in the decoder are coming from those skip connections (notice double the number of feature maps!).[4]
- The decoder uses deconvolutional layers with one final convolutional layer to upscale the image into the equivalent size of the original image.

The autoencoder is a useful teaching tool for the architecture of the Generator alone as well, because the Generator has an encoder-decoder architecture:

- *Encoder*—Step 1 from figure 9.4: these are the convolutional layers that reduce the resolution of each feature map (*layer* or *slice*). This is the contraction path (d0 to d3).
- *Decoder*—Step 3 from figure 9.4: these are the *deconvolutional* layers (transposed convolutions) that upscale the image back to 128 × 128. This is the expansion path (u1 to u4).

---

[4] As you will see, this just means we concatenate the entire block/tensor to the equivalently colored tensor in the decoder part of the Generator.

To clarify, the autoencoder model here is useful in two ways. First, the overall Cycle-GAN architecture can be viewed as training two autoencoders.[5] Second, the U-Net itself has parts referred to as *encoder* and *decoder.*

You may also be a bit puzzled by the downscaling and the subsequent upscaling, but this is just so that we compress the image to the most meaningful representation, but at the same time are able to add back all the detail. It's the same reasoning as with the autoencoder, except now we also have a path to remember the nuances. This architecture—the *U-Net architecture*—has just been empirically shown in several domains as better performing on various segmentation tasks. The key idea is that although during downsampling we can focus on classification and understanding of large regions, including higher-resolution skip connections preserves the detail that can then be accurately segmented.

In our implementation of CycleGAN, we'll use the U-Net architecture with skip connections as shown in figure 9.6, which is more readable. However, many CycleGAN implementations use the ResNet architecture, which you can implement yourself with a bit more work.

NOTE The main advantage of ResNet is that it uses fewer parameters and introduces a step in the middle called *transformer,* which has residual connections in lieu of our encoder-decoder skip connections.

Based on our testing, at least on the dataset used, the apple2orange results remain the same. Instead of explicitly defining the transformer, we provide skip connections (as used in the diagram) from the convolutional to the deconvolutional layers. We will mention these similarities again in code. For now, just remember that.

9.5.3   *Discriminator architecture*

The CycleGAN's Discriminator is based on the PatchGAN architecture—we will dive into the technical details in the code section. One thing that may be confusing is that we do not get a single float as an output of this Discriminator, but rather a set of single-channel values that may be thought of as a set of mini-discriminators that we then average together.

Ultimately, this allows the design of the CycleGAN to be fully convolutional, meaning that it can scale relatively easily to higher resolutions. Indeed, in the examples of translating video games to reality or vice versa, the CycleGAN authors have used an upscaled version of the CycleGAN, with only minor modifications thanks to the fully convolutional design. Other than that, the Discriminator should be a relatively straightforward implementation of the Discriminators you have seen before, except there are now two of them.

---

[5] See Jun-Yan Zhu et al., 2017, https://arxiv.org/pdf/1703.10593.pdf.

9.6   *Object-oriented design of GANs*

We have always used objects in TensorFlow and object-oriented programming (OOP) in our code, but we have usually treated the architectures more functionally, because they were generally simple. In the CycleGAN's case, the architecture is complex, and as a result, we need a structure that allows us to keep accessing the original attributes and methods that we have defined. As a result, we will write out the CycleGAN as a Python class of its own with methods to build the Generator and Discriminator, and run the training.

9.7   *Tutorial: CycleGAN*

In this tutorial, we'll use the Keras-GAN implementation and use Keras with a TensorFlow backend.[6] Tested as late as Keras 2.2.4 and TensorFlow 1.12.0, `Keras_contrib` was installed from the hash 46fcdb9384b3bc9399c651b2b43640aa54098e64. This time, we have to use a different dataset (also to show you that despite our joke from chapter 2, we *do know* other datasets). But for educational purposes, we will keep using one of the simpler datasets—apple2orange. Let's jump right into it by doing all our usual imports, as shown in the following listing.

Listing 9.1   Import all the things

```
from __future__ import print_function, division
import scipy
from keras.datasets import mnist
from keras_contrib.layers.normalization import InstanceNormalization
from keras.layers import Input, Dense, Reshape, Flatten, Dropout, Concatenate
from keras.layers import BatchNormalization, Activation, ZeroPadding2D
from keras.layers.advanced_activations import LeakyReLU
from keras.layers.convolutional import UpSampling2D, Conv2D
from keras.models import Sequential, Model
from keras.optimizers import Adam
import datetime
import matplotlib.pyplot as plt
import sys
from data_loader import DataLoader
import numpy as np
import os
```

As promised, we'll use the object-oriented style of programming. In the following listing, we create a CycleGAN class with all the initializing parameters, including the data loader. The data loader is defined in the GitHub repository for our book. It simply loads the preprocessed data.

---

[6] See the Keras-GAN GitHub repository by Erik Linder-Norén, 2017, https://github.com/eriklindernoren/Keras-GAN.

Listing 9.2 Starting the CycleGAN class

```
class CycleGAN():
    def __init__(self):
        self.img_rows = 128
        self.img_cols = 128
        self.channels = 3
        self.img_shape = (self.img_rows, self.img_cols, self.channels)

        self.dataset_name = 'apple2orange'
        self.data_loader = DataLoader(dataset_name=self.dataset_name,
                                      img_res=(self.img_rows, self.img_cols))

        patch = int(self.img_rows / 2**4)
        self.disc_patch = (patch, patch, 1)

        self.gf = 32
        self.df = 64

        self.lambda_cycle = 10.0
        self.lambda_id = 0.9 * self.lambda_cycle

        optimizer = Adam(0.0002, 0.5)
```

Annotations:
- **Input shape** → (self.img_rows, self.img_cols, self.channels lines)
- **Configures data loader**
- **Uses the DataLoader object to import a preprocessed dataset**
- **Calculates output shape of D (PatchGAN)** → patch / self.disc_patch
- **Number of filters in the first layer of G** → self.gf = 32
- **Number of filters in the first layer of D** → self.df = 64
- **Cycle-consistency loss weight** → self.lambda_cycle = 10.0
- **Identity loss weight** → self.lambda_id

Two new terms are lambda_cycle and lambda_id. The second hyperparameter influences identity loss. The CycleGAN authors themselves note that this value influences how dramatic the changes are—especially early in the training process.[7] Setting a lower value leads to unnecessary changes: for example, completely inverting the colors early on. We have selected this value, based on rerunning the training process for apple2orange several times. Frequently, the process is theory-driven alchemy.

The first hyperparameter—lambda_cycle—controls how strictly the cycle-consistency loss is enforced. Setting this value higher will ensure that your original and reconstructed images are as close together as possible.

9.7.1 Building the network

So now that we have our basic parameters out of the way, we will build the basic network, as shown in listing 9.3. We will start from the high-level view and move down. This entails the following:

1. Creating the two Discriminators D_A and D_B and compiling them
2. Creating the two Generators:
   a. Instantiating G_{AB} and G_{BA}
   b. Creating placeholders for the image input for both directions
   c. Linking them both to an image in the other domain

---

[7] See "pytorch-CycleGAN-and-pix2pix Frequently Asked Questions," by Jun-Yan Zhu, April 2019, http://mng .bz/BY58.

d Creating placeholders for the reconstructed images back in the original domain

e Creating the identity loss constraint for both directions

f Not making the parameters of the Discriminators trainable for now

g Compiling the two Generators

Listing 9.3 Building the networks

```
self.d_A = self.build_discriminator()
self.d_B = self.build_discriminator()
self.d_A.compile(loss='mse',
                 optimizer=optimizer,
                 metrics=['accuracy'])
self.d_B.compile(loss='mse',
                 optimizer=optimizer,
                 metrics=['accuracy'])
```
Builds and compiles the Discriminators

```
self.g_AB = self.build_generator()
self.g_BA = self.build_generator()
```
Beginning here, we construct the computational graph of the Generators. These first two lines build the Generators.

```
img_A = Input(shape=self.img_shape)
img_B = Input(shape=self.img_shape)
```
Inputs images from both domains

```
fake_B = self.g_AB(img_A)
fake_A = self.g_BA(img_B)
```
Translates images to the other domain

```
reconstr_A = self.g_BA(fake_B)
reconstr_B = self.g_AB(fake_A)
```
Translates images back to original domain

```
img_A_id = self.g_BA(img_A)
img_B_id = self.g_AB(img_B)
```
Identity mapping of images

```
self.d_A.trainable = False
self.d_B.trainable = False
```
For the combined model, we will train only the Generators.

Discriminators determine validity of translated images
```
valid_A = self.d_A(fake_A)
valid_B = self.d_B(fake_B)

self.combined = Model(inputs=[img_A, img_B],
                outputs=[valid_A, valid_B,
                         reconstr_A, reconstr_B,
                         img_A_id, img_B_id])
```
Combined model trains Generators to fool Discriminators
```
self.combined.compile(loss=['mse', 'mse',
                            'mae', 'mae',
                            'mae', 'mae'],
                loss_weights=[1, 1,
                              self.lambda_cycle, self.lambda_cycle,
                              self.lambda_id, self.lambda_id],
                optimizer=optimizer)
```

One last thing to clarify from the preceding code: the outputs from the combined model come in lists of six. This is because we always get validities (from the Discriminator), reconstruction, and identity losses—one for A-B-A and one for the B-A-B cycle—hence six. The first two are squared errors, and the rest are mean absolute errors. The relative weights are influenced by the `lambda` factors described earlier.

9.7.2   *Building the Generator*

Next, we build the Generator code in listing 9.4, which uses the skip connections as we described in section 9.5.2. This is the U-Net architecture. This architecture is simpler to write than the ResNet architecture, which some implementations use. Within our Generator function we first define the helper functions:

1   Define the `conv2d()` function as follows:

   a   Standard 2D convolutional layer

   b   Leaky ReLU activation

   c   Instance normalization[8]

2   Define the `deconv2d()` function as a transposed[9] convolution (aka *deconvolution*) layer that does the following:

   a   Upsamples the `input_layer`

   b   Possibly applies dropout if we set the dropout rate

   c   Always applies `InstanceNormalization`

   d   More importantly, creates a skip connection between its output layer and the layer of corresponding dimensionality from the downsampling part from figure 9.4

   NOTE   In step 2d, we're using a simple `UpSampling2D`, which is not a learned parameter, but rather uses the nearest neighbors interpolation.

Then we create the actual Generator:

3   Take the input ($128 \times 128 \times 3$) and assign that to d0.

4   Run that through a convolutional layer d1, arriving at a $64 \times 64 \times 32$ layer.

5   Take d1 ($64 \times 64 \times 32$) and apply `conv2d` to get $32 \times 32 \times 64$ (d2).

6   Take d2 ($32 \times 32 \times 64$) and apply `conv2d` to get $16 \times 16 \times 128$ (d3).

7   Take d3 ($16 \times 16 \times 128$) and apply `conv2d` to get $8 \times 8 \times 256$ (d4).

8   u1: Upsample d4 and create a skip connection between d3 and u1.

9   u2: Upsample u1 and create a skip connection between d2 and u2.

10   u3: Upsample u2 and create a skip connection between d1 and u3.

11   u4: Use regular upsampling to arrive at a $128 \times 128 \times 64$ image.

---

[8]   Instance normalization is similar to the batch normalization in chapter 4, except that instead of normalizing based on information from the entire batch, we normalize each feature map within each channel separately. Instance normalization often results in better-quality images for tasks such as style transfer or image-to-image translation—just what we need for the CycleGAN!

[9]   Here, *transposed convolution* is—some argue—a more correct term. However, just think of it as the opposite of convolution, or deconvolution.

12 Use a regular 2D convolution to get rid of the extra feature maps and get only $128 \times 128 \times 3$ (height $\times$ width $\times$ color_channels)

Listing 9.4 Building the generator

```
def build_generator(self):
    """U-Net Generator"""

    def conv2d(layer_input, filters, f_size=4):
        """Layers used during downsampling"""
        d = Conv2D(filters, kernel_size=f_size,
                    strides=2, padding='same')(layer_input)
        d = LeakyReLU(alpha=0.2)(d)
        d = InstanceNormalization()(d)
        return d

    def deconv2d(layer_input, skip_input, filters, f_size=4,
        dropout_rate=0):
        """Layers used during upsampling"""
        u = UpSampling2D(size=2)(layer_input)
        u = Conv2D(filters, kernel_size=f_size, strides=1,
                    padding='same', activation='relu')(u)
        if dropout_rate:
            u = Dropout(dropout_rate)(u)
        u = InstanceNormalization()(u)
        u = Concatenate()([u, skip_input])
        return u

    d0 = Input(shape=self.img_shape)    ◁——— Image input

    d1 = conv2d(d0, self.gf)
    d2 = conv2d(d1, self.gf * 2)
    d3 = conv2d(d2, self.gf * 4)         Downsampling
    d4 = conv2d(d3, self.gf * 8)

    u1 = deconv2d(d4, d3, self.gf * 4)
    u2 = deconv2d(u1, d2, self.gf * 2)    Upsampling
    u3 = deconv2d(u2, d1, self.gf)

    u4 = UpSampling2D(size=2)(u3)
    output_img = Conv2D(self.channels, kernel_size=4,
                    strides=1, padding='same', activation='tanh')(u4)

    return Model(d0, output_img)
```

9.7.3 Building the Discriminator

Now for the Discriminator method, which uses a helper function that creates layers formed of 2D convolutions, LeakyReLU, and optionally, InstanceNormalization.

We apply these layers the following way, as shown in listing 9.5:

1 We take the input image ($128 \times 128 \times 3$) and assign that to d1 ($64 \times 64 \times 64$).
2 We take d1 ($64 \times 64 \times 64$) and assign that to d2 ($32 \times 32 \times 128$).

3　We take d2 ($32 \times 32 \times 128$) and assign that to d3 ($16 \times 16 \times 256$).

4　We take d3 ($16 \times 16 \times 256$) and assign that to d4 ($8 \times 8 \times 512$).

5　We take d4 ($8 \times 8 \times 512$) and flatten by conv2d to $8 \times 8 \times 1$.

Listing 9.5　Building the Discriminator

```
def build_discriminator(self):

    def d_layer(layer_input, filters, f_size=4, normalization=True):
        """Discriminator layer"""
        d = Conv2D(filters, kernel_size=f_size,
                    strides=2, padding='same')(layer_input)
        d = LeakyReLU(alpha=0.2)(d)
        if normalization:
            d = InstanceNormalization()(d)
        return d

    img = Input(shape=self.img_shape)

    d1 = d_layer(img, self.df, normalization=False)
    d2 = d_layer(d1, self.df * 2)
    d3 = d_layer(d2, self.df * 4)
    d4 = d_layer(d3, self.df * 8)

    validity = Conv2D(1, kernel_size=4, strides=1, padding='same')(d4)

    return Model(img, validity)
```

9.7.4　*Training the CycleGAN*

With all networks written, now we will implement the method that creates our training loop. For the CycleGAN training algorithm, the details of each training iteration are as follows.

CycleGAN training algorithm

For each training iteration *do*

1　Train the Discriminator:

　　a　Take a mini-batch of random images from each domain ($imgs_A$ and $imgs_B$).

　　b　Use the Generator G_{AB} to translate $imgs_A$ to domain B and vice versa with G_{BA}.

　　c　Compute $D_A(imgs_A, 1)$ and $D_A(G_{BA}(imgs_B), 0)$ to get the losses for real images in A and translated images from B, respectively. Then add these two losses together. The 1 and 0 in D_A serve as labels.

　　d　Compute $D_B(imgs_B, 1)$ and $D_B(G_{AB}(imgs_A), 0)$ to get the losses for real images in B and translated images from A, respectively. Then add these two losses together. The 1 and 0 in D_B serve as labels.

　　e　Add the losses from steps c and d together to get a total Discriminator loss.

2 Train the Generator:

  a We use the combined model to

   – Input the images from domain A (*imgs*$_A$) and B (*imgs*$_B$)
   – The outputs are

     1 Validity of A: $D_A(G_{BA}(imgs_B))$
     2 Validity of B: $D_B(G_{AB}(imgs_A))$
     3 Reconstructed A: $G_{BA}(G_{AB}(imgs_A))$
     4 Reconstructed B: $G_{AB}(G_{BA}(imgs_B))$
     5 Identity mapping of A: $G_{BA}(imgs_A))$
     6 Identity mapping of B: $G_{AB}(imgs_B))$

  b We then update the parameters of both Generators inline with the cycle-consistency loss, identity loss, and adversarial loss with

   – Mean squared error (MSE) for the scalars (discriminator probabilities)
   – Mean absolute error (MAE) for images (either reconstructed or identity-mapped)

End for

The following listing implements this CycleGAN training algorithm.

Listing 9.6   Training CycleGAN

```
def train(self, epochs, batch_size=1, sample_interval=50):

    start_time = datetime.datetime.now()

    valid = np.ones((batch_size,) + self.disc_patch)        ⟵  Adversarial loss
    fake = np.zeros((batch_size,) + self.disc_patch)            ground truths


    for epoch in range(epochs):
        for batch_i, (imgs_A, imgs_B) in enumerate(
            self.data_loader.load_batch(batch_size)):

                                                   Now we begin to train the
                                                   Discriminators. These
            fake_B = self.g_AB.predict(imgs_A)     lines translate images to
            fake_A = self.g_BA.predict(imgs_B)     the opposite domain.

            dA_loss_real = self.d_A.train_on_batch(imgs_A, valid)
            dA_loss_fake = self.d_A.train_on_batch(fake_A, fake)
            dA_loss = 0.5 * np.add(dA_loss_real, dA_loss_fake)

            dB_loss_real = self.d_B.train_on_batch(imgs_B, valid)
            dB_loss_fake = self.d_B.train_on_batch(fake_B, fake)
            dB_loss = 0.5 * np.add(dB_loss_real, dB_loss_fake)

            d_loss = 0.5 * np.add(dA_loss, dB_loss)
```

Trains the Discriminators (original images = real / translated = Fake)

Total Discriminator loss

Trains the
Generators ⌐⇢

```
g_loss = self.combined.train_on_batch([imgs_A, imgs_B],
                                       [valid, valid,
                                        imgs_A, imgs_B,
                                        imgs_A, imgs_B])
```

If at save interval ⌐⇢
=> save generated
image samples

```
if batch_i % sample_interval == 0:
    self.sample_images(epoch, batch_i)    ⟵
```

This function is similar to what you
have encountered and is made
explicit in the GitHub repository.

9.7.5   *Running CycleGAN*

We have written all of this complicated code and are now ready to instantiate a Cycle-GAN object and look at some results, from the sampled images:

```
gan = CycleGAN()
gan.train(epochs=100, batch_size=64, sample_interval=10)
```

Figure 9.7 shows some results of our hard work.

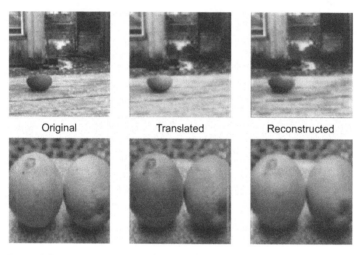

Original   Translated   Reconstructed

Figure 9.7   Apples translated into oranges, and oranges into apples. These
are results as they appear verbatim in our Jupyter notebook. (Results may
vary slightly based on random seeds, implementation of TensorFlow and
Keras, and hyperparameters.)

9.8   *Expansions, augmentations, and applications*

When you run these results, we hope you will be as impressed as we were. Because of the absolutely astonishing results, lots of researchers flocked to improve on the technique. This section details a CycleGAN extension and then discusses some CycleGAN applications.

9.8.1 Augmented CycleGAN

"Augmented CycleGAN: Learning Many-to-Many Mappings from Unpaired Data" is a really neat extension to standard CycleGAN that injects latent space information during both translations. Presented at ICML 2018 in Stockholm, Augmented Cycle-GAN gives us extra variables that drive the generative process.[10] In the same way that we have used latent space in Conditional GANs' case, we can use it in the CycleGAN setting over and above what CycleGAN already does.

For example, if we have an outline of a shoe in the A domain, we can generate a sample in the B domain, where the same type of shoe is blue. In traditional Cycle-GAN's case, it would always be blue. But now, with the latent variables at our disposal, it can be orange, yellow, or whatever we choose.

This is also a useful framework to think about the limitations of the original Cycle-GAN: because we are not given any extra seeding parameters (such as an extra latent vector z), we cannot control or alter what comes out the other end. If from a particular handbag outline we get an image that is orange, it will always be orange. Augmented CycleGAN gives us more control over the outcomes, as shown in figure 9.8.

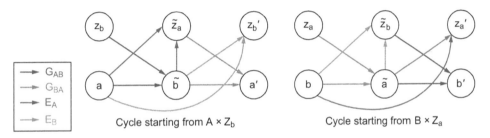

Figure 9.8   In this information flow of the augmented CycleGAN, we have latent vectors z_a and z_b that seed the Generator along with the image input, effectively reducing the problem to two CGANs joined together. This allows us to control the generation.
(Source: "Augmented CycleGAN: Learning Many-to-Many Mappings from Unpaired Data," by Amjad Almahairi et al., 2018, http://arxiv.org/abs/1802.10151.)

9.8.2 Applications

Many CycleGAN (or CycleGAN-inspired) applications have been proposed in the short time it has been around. They usually revolve around creating simulated virtual environments and subsequently making them photorealistic. For example, imagine you need more training data for a self-driving car company: just simulate it in Unity or a GTA 5 graphics engine and then use CycleGAN to translate the data.

This works especially well if you need to have particular risk situations that are expensive or time-consuming to re-create (for example, car crashes, or fire trucks speeding to reach a destination), but you need them in your dataset. For a self-driving

---

[10] See "Augmented Cyclic Adversarial Learning for Low Resource Domain Adaptation," by Ehsan Hosseini-Asl, 2019, https://arxiv.org/pdf/1807.00374.pdf.

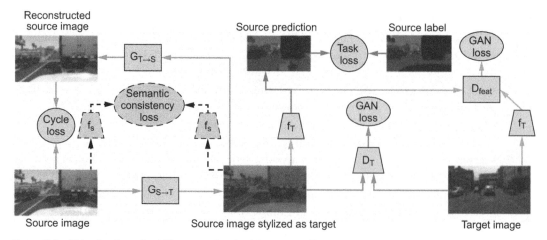

Figure 9.9   **This structure should be somewhat familiar from earlier, so hopefully this chapter has at least given you a head start. One extra thing to point out: we now have an extra step with labels and semantic understanding that gives us the so-called *task loss*. This allows us to also check the produced image for semantic meaning.**

car company, this could be extremely useful to balance the dataset with at-risk situations, which are rare, but correct behavior is all the more important.

One example of this kind of framework is Cycle Consistent Adversarial Domain Adaptation (CyCADA).[11] Unfortunately, a full explanation of the way it works is beyond the scope of this chapter. This is because there are many more such frameworks: some even experiment with CycleGAN in language, music, or other forms of domain adaptation. To give you a sense of the complexity, figure 9.9 shows the architecture and design of CyCADA.

Summary

- Image-to-image translation frameworks are frequently difficult to train because of the need for perfect pairs; the CycleGAN solves this by making this an unpaired domain translation.
- The CycleGAN has three losses:
  - Cycle-consistent, which measures the difference between the original image and an image translated into a different domain and back again
  - Adversarial, which ensures realistic images
  - Identity, which preserves the color space of the image
- The two Generators use the U-Net architecture, and the two Discriminators use the PatchGAN-based architecture.
- We implemented an object-oriented design of the CycleGAN and used it to convert apples to oranges.
- Practical applications of the CycleGAN include self-driving car training and extensions that allow us to create different styles of images during the translation process.

---

[11] See "CyCADA: Cycle-Consistent Adversarial Domain Adaptation," by Judy Hoffman et al., 2017, https://arxiv.org/pdf/1711.03213.pdf.

Part 3

Where to go from here

Part 3 explores a selection of practical use cases and other areas where you can apply what you've learned about GANs and their implementations in Parts 1 and 2:

- Chapter 10 discusses adversarial examples (means of intentionally deceiving classifiers into making mistakes), an area with great practical and theoretical importance.
- Chapter 11 explores practical applications of GANs in medicine and fashion, whose implementations use the GAN variants covered in this book.
- Chapter 12 outlines the ethical considerations of GANs and their applications. We also mention emerging GAN techniques for those interested in continuing to explore this field beyond this book.

Adversarial examples

This chapter covers

- A fascinating research area that precedes GANs and has an interwoven history
- Deep learning approaches in a computer vision setting
- Our own adversarial examples with real images and noise

Over the course of this book, you have come to understand GANs as an intuitive concept. However, in 2014, GANs seemed like a massive leap of faith, especially for those unfamiliar with the emerging field of adversarial examples, including Ian Goodfellow's and others' work in this field.[1] This chapter dives into *adversarial examples*—specially constructed examples that make other classification algorithms fail catastrophically.

We also talk about their connections to GANs and how and why adversarial learning is still largely an unsolved problem in ML—an important but rarely discussed flaw

---

[1] See "Intriguing Properties of Neural Networks," by Christian Szegedy et al., 2014, https://arxiv.org/pdf/1312.6199.pdf.

of the current approaches. That is true even though adversarial examples have an important role to play in ML robustness, fairness, and (cyber)security.

There is no denying we have made substantial progress in machine learning's capacity to match and surpass human-level performance over the last five years—for example, in computer vision (CV) classification tasks or the ability to play games.[2] However, looking only at metrics and ROC curves[3] is insufficient for us to understand (a) why neural networks make the decisions they do (how they work) and (b) what errors they are prone to making. This chapter touches on the first and dives into the second. Before we begin, it should be said that although this chapter deals almost exclusively with CV problems, adversarial examples have been identified in diverse areas such as text or even in humans.[4]

First of all, when we speak about neural networks' performance, we frequently read that their error rate is lower than that of humans on the large ImageNet dataset. This often-cited statistic—which started more as an academic joke than anything else—belies the performance differences hidden underneath this average. While humans' error rate tends to be driven mostly by their inability to distinguish between different breeds of dogs that appear prominently in this dataset, the machine learning failures are much more ominous. Upon further investigation, adversarial examples were born.

Unlike humans, CV algorithms struggle with problems that are very different in nature and can be close to the training data. Because the algorithm has to make predictions for every picture possible, it has to extrapolate between the isolated and far-apart individual instances it has seen in the training data, even if we have lots of them.

When we have trained networks such as Inception V3 and VGG-19, we have found an amazing way of making image classification work on a thin manifold around the training data. But when people tried to poke holes in the classification ability of these algorithms, they discovered a cosmic crater—current machine learning algorithms get easily fooled by even minor distortions. Virtually all major successful machine learning algorithms to date suffer from this flaw to some extent, and, indeed, some speculate that is why machine learning works at all.

NOTE In supervised settings, think of our training set. We have a training manifold—just a fancy word describing a high-dimensional distribution in which our examples live. For example, our 300 × 300 pixel images live in a 270,000 dimensional space (300 × 300 × 3 colors). That makes training very complicated.

---

[2] What constitutes human-level performance in vision-classification tasks is a complicated topic. However, at least in, for example, Dota 2 and Go, AI has beat human experts by a substantial margin.

[3] A *receiver operating characteristic (ROC) curve* explains the trade-offs between false positives and negatives. We also encountered them in chapter 2. For more details, Wikipedia has an excellent explanation.

[4] See "Adversarial Attacks on Deep Learning Models in Natural Language Processing: A Survey," by Wei Emma Zhang et al., 2019, http://arxiv.org/abs/1901.06796. See also "Adversarial Examples That Fool Both Computer Vision and Time-Limited Humans," by Gamaleldin F. Elsayed et al., 2018, http://arxiv.org/abs/1802.08195.

10.1　Context of adversarial examples

To start, we want to quickly touch on why we included this chapter toward the end of the book:

- With adversarial examples, we are typically trying to generate new examples that fool our existing systems to misclassify the input. We do this usually either as evil attackers or perhaps just as researchers to see how robustly our system will behave. Adversarial examples are about as closely a related topic to GANs as it gets, though important differences exist.
- This will give you a sense of why GANs can be so hard to train and why our existing systems are so fragile.
- Adversarial examples allow for a different set of applications from GANs, and we hope to give you at least the basics of their capabilities.

In terms of applications, adversarial examples are interesting for several reasons:

- As discussed, adversarial examples can be used for malicious purposes, so it is important to test for robustness in critical systems. What if an attacker could easily fool a facial-recognition system to gain access to your phone?
- They help us understand machine learning fairness—which is a topic of growing importance. We can use adversarially learned representations that are useful for classifications but do not allow an attacker to recover protected facts, as probably one of the best ways of ensuring that our ML is not discriminating against anyone.
- In a similar vein, we can use adversarial learning to protect the privacy of sensitive—perhaps medical or financial—information about individuals. In this case, we are simply focusing on information about individuals not being recoverable.

As current research stands, learning about adversarial examples is the only way to start to understand adversarial defenses, as most papers begin with a description of the types of attacks they defend against and only then try to solve them. At the time of writing this book, no universal defenses work against all types of attack. But whether this is a good reason to study them depends on your view on adversarial examples. We decided not to cover defenses in detail—above the high-level ideas toward the end of this chapter—because anything beyond that is beyond the scope of this book.

10.2　Lies, damned lies, and distributions

To truly understand adversarial examples, we must come back to the domain of CV classification tasks—partially to understand how difficult a task it is. Recall that to go from raw pixels to ultimately being able to classify sets of images is challenging.

This is in part because, in order to have a truly generalizable algorithm, we have to make sensible predictions on data nowhere near anything that we have seen in the training set. Moreover, the pixel-level differences between the image at hand and the closest image in the training set of the same class are large, even when we slightly change the angle at which the picture was taken.

When we have our training set of 100,000 examples of 300 × 300 images in RGB space, we have to somehow deal with 270,000 dimensions. When we consider all *possible* images (not the ones that we actually observe, but the ones that *could* happen), the pixel value of each dimension is independent of the other dimensions, because we can always generate a valid picture by rolling a hypothetical 256-sided dice 270,000 times. Therefore, we theoretically have $256^{270,000}$ examples (a number that is 650,225 digits long) at 8-bit color space.

We would need a lot of examples to cover even 1% of this space. Of course, most of these images would not make any sense. Frequently, our training set is a lot sparser than that, so we need our algorithms to train using this relatively limited data to extrapolate even into regions they have not seen at all yet. This is because the algorithm most likely has seen nothing near what we have in the training set.

NOTE Having 100,000 examples is frequently cited as a minimum at which deep learning algorithms should really start to shine.

We understand that algorithms have to meaningfully generalize; they have to be able to meaningfully fill in the huge part of space where they have not seen any example. Computer vision algorithms work mostly because they can come up with good guesses for the vast swaths of missing probability, but their strength is also their greatest weakness.

10.3 Use and abuse of training

In this section, we introduce two ways of thinking about adversarial examples—one from first principles and the other by analogy. The first way to think about adversarial examples is to start from the way machine learning classification is trained. Remember that these are networks with tens of millions of parameters. Throughout training, we update some of them so that the class matches the label as provided in the training set. We need to find just the right parameter updates, which is what the stochastic gradient descent (SGD) allows us to do.

Now think back to the simple classifier days, before you knew a lot about GANs. Here we have some sort of learnable classification function $f_\theta(x)$ (for example, a deep neural network, or DNN), which is parametrized by θ (parameters of the DNN) and takes x (for example, an image) as input and produces a classification $\hat{y}$. At training time, we then take $\hat{y}$ and compare it with the true y, which is how we get our loss (L). We then update the parameters of $f_\theta(x)$ such that the loss is minimized. Equations 10.1, 10.2, and 10.3 summarize.[5]

---

[5] Please remember, this is just a quick summary, and we have to skip over some details, so if you can point them out—great. If not, we suggest picking up a book such as *Deep Learning with Python* by François Chollet (Manning, 2017) to brush up on the specifics.

$$\hat{y} = f_\theta(x) \qquad \text{Equation 10.1}$$

$$L = \| y - \hat{y} \| \qquad \text{Equation 10.2}$$

$$\min_\theta \| y - \hat{y} \| \text{ s.t. } \hat{y} = f_\theta(x) \qquad \text{Equation 10.3}$$

In essence, we have defined *prediction* as the output of the neural net after being fed an example (equation 10.1). *Loss* is some form of the difference between the true and predicted label (equation 10.2). The overall problem is then phrased as trying to minimize the difference between the true and predicted labels over the parameters of the DNN, which then constitute the prediction given an example (equation 10.3).

This is all working great, but how do we actually minimize our classification loss? How do we solve the optimization problem as phrased in equation 10.3? We usually use an SGD-based method to take batches of x; then we take the derivative of the loss function with respect to the current parameters (θ_t) multiplied by our learning rate (α), which constitutes our new parameters (θ_{t+1}). See equation 10.4.

$$\theta_{t+1} = \theta_t - \alpha * \frac{\partial L}{\partial \theta} \qquad \text{Equation 10.4}$$

This was the quickest introduction to deep learning you will ever find. But now that you have this context, think about whether this powerful tool (SGD) could be used for other purposes as well. For instance, what happens when we take a step *up* the loss space rather than *down*? Turns out, maximizing the error rather than minimizing it is much easier, but also important. And like many great discoveries, it started as a seeming bug that turned into a hack: what if we start updating the pixels rather than the weights? If we update them maliciously, adversarial examples happen.

Some of you may be confused, about this quick recap of SGD, so let's remind ourselves what a typical loss space could look like in figure 10.1.

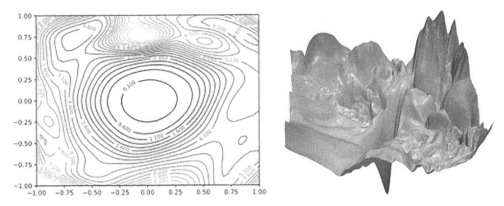

Figure 10.1 In this typical loss space, remember, this is the type of loss value we can feasibly get with our deep learning algorithms. On the left, you have 2D contour lines of equal loss, and on the right, you have a 3D rendering of what a loss space may look like. Remember the mountaineering analogy from chapter 6? (Source: "Visualizing the Loss Landscape of Neural Nets," by Tom Goldstein et al., 2018, https://github.com/tomgoldstein/loss-landscape.)

The second useful (though imperfect) mental model to think about adversarial examples is by analogy. You may think of adversarial examples as Conditional GANs like those we encountered in the preceding two chapters. With adversarial examples, we are conditioning on an entire image and trying to produce a *domain transferred* or similar image, except in a domain that fools the classifier. The "generator" can be a simple stochastic gradient ascent that simply adjusts the image to fool some other classifier.

Whichever of the two ways makes sense to you, let's now dive straight into adversarial examples and what they look like. They were discovered with an observation of how easy it is to misclassify these altered images. One of the first methods to achieve this is the *fast sign gradient method (FSGM)*, which is as simple as our previous description.

You start with the gradient update (equation 10.4), look at the sign, and then make a small step in the opposite direction. In fact, frequently the images come out looking (almost) identical! A picture is worth a thousand words to show you how little noise is needed; see figure 10.2.

Figure 10.2 A bit of noise makes a lot of difference. The picture in the middle has the noise (difference) applied to it (the picture to the right). Of course, the right picture is heavily amplified—approximately 300 times—and shifted so that it can create a meaningful image.

Now we run a ResNet-50 pretrained classifier on this unmodified vacation image and check the top three predictions, shown in table 10.1; drumroll, please.

Table 10.1 Original image predictions

Order	Class	Confidence
First	mountain_tent	0.6873
Second	promontory	0.0736
Third	valley	0.0717

The top three are all sensible, with mountain_tent taking the top spot, as it should. Table 10.2 shows the adversarial image predictions. The top three miss mountain_tent completely, with some suggestions that at least match the outdoors, but even the modi-fied image is clearly not a suspension bridge.

Table 10.2 Adversarial image predictions

Order	Class	Confidence
First	volcano	0.5914
Second	suspension_bridge	0.1685
Third	valley	0.0869

This is how much we can distort the prediction, with a budget of only approximately 200 pixel values—the equivalent of taking a *single* almost-black pixel and turning it into an almost-white pixel—spread across the whole image.

A somewhat scary thing is how little code it takes to create this whole example. In this chapter, we'll use an amazing library called foolbox, which provides many great convenience methods to create adversarial examples. Without further ado, let's dive into it. We start with our well-known imports, plus foolbox, which is a library designed specifically to make adversarial attacks easier.

Listing 10.1 Our trusty imports

```
import numpy as np
from keras.applications.resnet50 import ResNet50
from foolbox.criteria import Misclassification, ConfidentMisclassification
from keras.preprocessing import image as img
from keras.applications.resnet50 import preprocess_input, decode_predictions
import matplotlib.pyplot as plt
import foolbox
import pprint as pp
Import keras
%matplotlib inline
```

Next, we define a convenience function to load in more images.

Listing 10.2 Helper function

```
def load_image(img_path: str):
  image = img.load_img(img_path, target_size=(224, 224))
  plt.imshow(image)
  x = img.img_to_array(image)
  return x

image = load_image('DSC_0897.jpg')
```

Next, we have to set Keras to register our model and download ResNet-50 from the Keras convenience function.

Listing 10.3   Creating tables 10.1 and 10.2

We make the image (1, 224, 224, 3) so that it fits ResNet-50, which expects images for predictions to be in batches.

Instantiates model

```
keras.backend.set_learning_phase(0)          ⟵
kmodel = ResNet50(weights='imagenet')
preprocessing = (np.array([104, 116, 123]), 1)
```

Creates the foolbox model object from the Keras model

```
fmodel = foolbox.models.KerasModel(kmodel, bounds=(0, 255),
    preprocessing=preprocessing)
```

```
to_classify = np.expand_dims(image, axis=0)
preds = kmodel.predict(to_classify)          ⟵
print('Predicted:', pp.pprint(decode_predictions(preds, top=20)[0]))
label = np.argmax(preds)
```

We call predict and print the results.

Gets the index of the highest number, as a label to be used later

```
image = image[:, :, ::-1]                                    ⟵
attack = foolbox.attacks.FGSM(fmodel, threshold=.9,
    criterion=ConfidentMisclassification(.9))
adversarial = attack(image, label)           ⟵
```

::-1 reverses the color channels, because Keras ResNet-50 expects BGR instead of RGB.

Applies attack on source image

```
new_preds = kmodel.predict(np.expand_dims(adversarial, axis=0))    ⟵
print('Predicted:', pp.pprint(decode_predictions(new_preds, top=20)[0]))
```

Creates the attack object, setting high misclassification criteria

Gets the new predictions on the adversarial image

That's how easy it is to use these examples! Now you may be thinking, maybe that's just ResNet-50 that suffers from these examples. Well, we have some bad news for you. ResNet not only proved to be the hardest classifier to break as we were testing various code setups for this chapter, but also is an uncontested winner on DAWNBench in every ImageNet category (which is the most challenging task in the CV category on DAWNBench), as shown in figure 10.3.[6]

But the biggest problem of adversarial examples is their pervasiveness. Adversarial examples generalize beyond deep learning and transfer to different ML techniques. If we generate an adversarial example against one technique, there is a reasonable chance it will work even on another model we are trying to attack, as illustrated in figure 10.4.

---

[6] See "Image Classification on ImageNet," at DAWNBench, https://dawn.cs.stanford.edu/benchmark/#imagenet.

Image Classification on ImageNet

Training Time 𝒮

All Submissions

Objective: Time taken to train an image classification model to a top-5 validation accuracy of 93% or greater on ImageNet.

Rank	Time to 93% Accuracy	Model	Hardware	Framework
1 Dec 2018	0:09:22	ResNet-50 *ModelArts Service of Huawei Cloud* source	16 * 8 * Tesla-V100(ModelArts Service)	Huawei Optimized MXNet
2 Nov 2018	0:10:28	ResNet-50 *ModelArts Service of Huawei Cloud* source	16 nodes with RDMA (8*V100 for each node)	TensorFlow v1.8.0
3 Sep 2018	0:18:06	ResNet-50 *fast.ai/DIUx (Yaroslav Bulatov, Andrew Shaw, Jeremy Howard)* source	16 p3.16xlarge (AWS)	PyTorch 0.4.1

Figure 10.3   DAWNBench is a great place to see the current state-of-the-art models and ResNet-50 dominance, at least as of early July 2019.

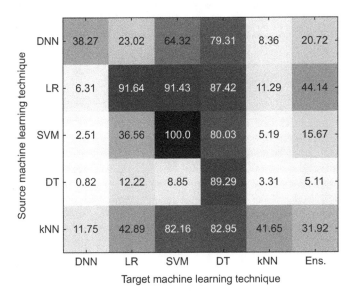

Figure 10.4   The numbers here denote the percentage of adversarial examples crafted to fool the classifier in that row that also fooled that column's classifier. The methods are deep neural networks (DNNs), logistic regression (LR), support-vector machine (SVM), decision trees (DT), nearest neighbors (kNN), and ensembles (Ens.).

(Source: "Transferability in Machine Learning: from Phenomena to Black-Box Attacks Using Adversarial Samples," by Nicolas Papernot et al., 2016, https://arxiv.org/pdf/1605.07277.pdf.)

10.4   Signal and the noise

Worse yet, many of the adversarial examples are so easy to construct that we can just as easily fool the classifier by Gaussian noise that we can sample from `np.random.normal`. On the other hand—and to support our earlier point of ResNet-50 being a fairly robust architecture—we will show you that other architectures suffer from this issue much more.

Figure 10.5 shows the result of running ResNet-50 on pure Gaussian noise. However, we can use an adversarial attack on the noise itself to see how misclassified our image can get—rather quickly.

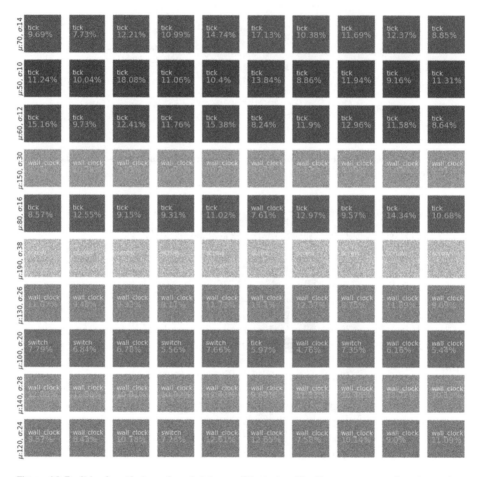

Figure 10.5   It is clear that we do not get a confident classification as a wrong class in most cases on just naively sampled noise. So that is plus points to ResNet-50. On the left, we include the mean and variance we used so that you can see their impact.

In listing 10.4, we'll use a *projected gradient descent (PGD) attack*, illustrated in figure 10.6. Although this is still a simple attack, it warrants a high-level explanation. Unlike with the previous attacks, we are now taking a step regardless of where it may lead us—even

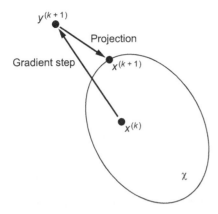

Figure 10.6 Projected gradient descent takes a step in the optimal direction, wherever it may be, and then uses projection to find the nearest equivalent point in the set of points. In this case, we are trying to ensure that we still end up with a valid picture: we take an example $x(k)$ and take the optimal step to $y^{(k+1)}$ to then project it to a valid set of images as $x^{(k+1)}$.

"invalid" pixel values—and then projecting back onto the feasible space. Now let's apply the PGD attack onto our Gaussian noise in figure 10.7 and run ResNet-50 to see how we do.

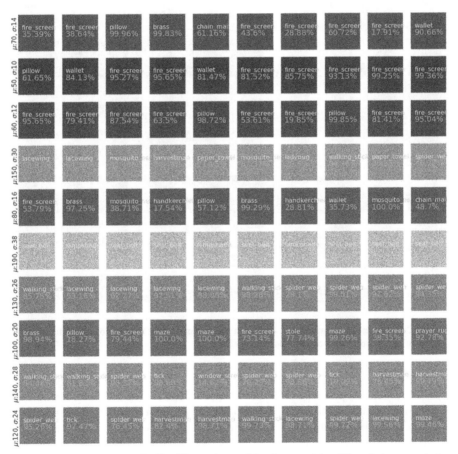

Figure 10.7 When we run ResNet-50 on adversarial noise, we get a different story: most of the items are misclassified after applying a PGD attack—still a simple attack.

To demonstrate that most architectures are even worse, we'll look into Inception V3—an architecture that has earned fame in the CV community. Indeed, this network has been deemed so reliable that we touched on it in chapter 5. In figure 10.8, you can see that even something that gave birth to the inception score still fails on trivial examples. To dispel any doubts, Inception V3 is still one of the better pretrained networks out there and does have superhuman accuracy.

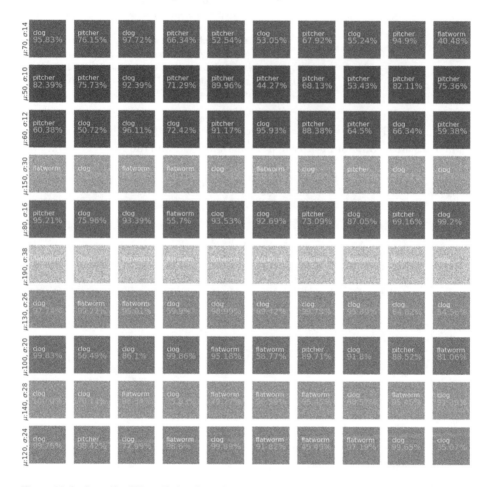

Figure 10.8   Inception V3 applied to Gaussian noise. Notice that we are not using any attacks; this noise is just sampled from the distribution.

NOTE   This was just regular Gaussian noise. You can see in the code for yourself that no adversarial step was applied. Sure, you could argue that the noise could have been preprocessed better. But even that is a massive adversarial weakness.

If you are anything like us, you are thinking, no way, I want to see for myself. Well, now we give you the code to reproduce those figures. Because the code for each is similar, we go through it only once and for next time promise DRYer code.

> **NOTE** For an explanation of *don't repeat yourself (DRY)* code, see Wikipedia at https://en.wikipedia.org/wiki/Don%27t_repeat_yourself.

Listing 10.4 Gaussian noise

Sample noise for each mean and variance

```
fig = plt.figure(figsize=(20,20))
sigma_list = list(max_vals.sigma)          Lists of means and
mu_list = list(max_vals.mu)                variances as floats
conf_list = []
                                                         Only 0–255
                                           The core function   pixel values
                                           that renders        permitted
def make_subplot(x, y, z, new_row=False):  figure 10.8
    rand_noise = np.random.normal(loc=mu, scale=sigma, size=(224,224, 3))
    rand_noise = np.clip(rand_noise, 0, 255.)
    noise_preds = kmodel.predict(np.expand_dims(rand_noise, axis=0))
    prediction, num = decode_predictions(noise_preds, top=20)[0][0][1:3]
    num = round(num * 100, 2)
    conf_list.append(num)                       Gets the predicted
    ax = fig.add_subplot(x,y,z)                 class and confidence,
    ax.annotate(prediction, xy=(0.1, 0.6),      respectively
            xycoords=ax.transAxes, fontsize=16, color='yellow')
    ax.annotate(f'{num}%' , xy=(0.1, 0.4),
            xycoords=ax.transAxes, fontsize=20, color='orange')
    if new_row:
        ax.annotate(f'$\mu$:{mu}, $\sigma$:{sigma}' ,
                xy=(-.2, 0.8), xycoords=ax.transAxes,
                rotation=90, fontsize=16, color='black')
    ax.imshow(rand_noise / 255)
    ax.axis('off')                      Division by 255 to
                                        convert [0, 255] to [0, 1]

for i in range(1,101):                  The main for loop that
    if (i-1) % 10==0:                   allows us to insert
        mu = mu_list.pop(0)             subplots into the figure
        sigma = sigma_list.pop(0)
        make_subplot(10,10, i, new_row=True)
    else:
        make_subplot(10,10, i)

plt.show()
```

Gets our first prediction

Sets up annotating code for figure 10.8 and then adds the annotations and text

10.5 *Not all hope is lost*

Some people now start to worry about the security implications of adversarial examples. However, it is important to keep this in a meaningful perspective of a hypothetical attacker. If the attacker can change every pixel slightly, why not change the whole image?[7] Why not just feed in another one that is completely different? Why does the passed-in example have to be imperceptibly—rather than visibly—different?

Some people give the example of self-driving cars and adversarially perturbing stop signs. But if we can do that, why wouldn't the attackers completely spray-paint over the stop signs or simply physically obscure the stop sign with a high speed-limit sign for a little while? Because these "traditional attacks," unlike adversarial examples, will work 100% of the time, whereas an adversarial attack works only when it transfers well and manages to not get distorted by the preprocessing.

This does not mean that when you have a mission-critical ML application, you can just ignore this problem. However, it most cases, adversarial attacks require far more effort than more commonplace vectors of attack, so bearing that in mind is worthwhile.

Yet, as with most security implications, adversarial attacks also have adversarial defenses that attempt to defend against the many types of attacks. The attacks covered in this chapter have been some of the easier ones, but even simpler ones exist—such as drawing a single line through MNIST. Even that is sufficient to fool most classifiers.

Adversarial defenses are an ever-evolving game, in which many good defenses are available against some types of attacks, but not all. The turnaround can be so quick that just three days after the submission deadline for ICLR 2018, seven of the eight proposed and examined defenses were broken.[8]

10.6 *Adversaries to GANs*

To make the connection with GANs even clearer, imagine a system generating adversarial examples, and another one saying how good that example is—depending on whether the example managed to fool the system or not. Doesn't that remind you of a Generator (adversary) and a Discriminator (classification algorithm)? These two algorithms are again competing: the adversary is trying to fool the classifier with slight perturbations of the image, and the classifier is trying to not get fooled. Indeed, a way to think of GANs is almost as ML-in-the-loop adversarial examples that eventually come up with images.

On the other hand, you can think of iterated adversarial attacks as if you took a GAN and, rather than specifying that the objective is to generate the most realistic examples, you specify that the objective is to generate examples that will fool the classifier. Of course, you have to always remember that important differences exist, and typically you have a fixed classifier in deployed systems. But that does not preclude us from using this idea in *adversarial training* in which some implementations even include a repeated retraining of the classifier based on the adversarial examples that fooled it. These techniques are then moving closer to a typical GANs setup.

---

[7] See "Motivating the Rules of the Game for Adversarial Example Research," by Justin Gilmer et al., 2018, http://arxiv.org/abs/1807.06732.

[8] *ICLR* is the *International Conference on Learning Representations*, one of the smaller but excellent machine learning conferences. See Anish Athalye on Twitter in 2018, http://mng.bz/ad77. It should be noted that there were three more defenses unexamined by the author.

To give you an example, let's take a look at one technique that has held its ground for a while as a viable defense. In the *Robust Manifold Defense*, we take the following steps to defend against the adversarial examples:[9]

1 We take an image x (adversarial or regular) and
   a Project it back to the latent space z.
   b Use the generator G to generate a similar example to x, called $x*$ by $G(z)$.
2 We use the classifier C to classify this example $C(x*)$, which generally already tends to misclassify way less than running the classification directly on x.

However, the authors of this defense find out that there are still *some* ambiguous cases in which the classifier does get fooled by minor perturbations. Still, we encourage you to check out their paper, as these cases tend to be unclear to humans as well, which is a sign of a robust model. To fix this, we apply *adversarial training* on the manifold: we get some of these adversarial cases into the training set so the classifier learns to distinguish those from the real training data.

This paper demonstrates that using GANs can give us classifiers that do not completely break down after minor perturbations, even against some of the most sophisticated methods. Performance of the downstream classifier does drop as with most of these defenses, because our classifier now has to be trained to implicitly deal with these adversarial cases. But even despite this setback, it is not a universal defense.

Adversarial training, of course, has some interesting applications. For example, for a while, the best results—state of the art—in semi-supervised learning were achieved by using adversarial training.[10] This was subsequently challenged by GANs (remember chapter 7?) and other approaches, but that does not mean that by the time you are reading these lines, adversarial training will not be the state of the art again.

Hopefully, this gave you another reason to study GANs and adversarial examples—partially because in mission-critical classification tasks, GANs may be the best defense going forward or because of other applications beyond the scope of this book.[11] That is best left for a hypothetical *Adversarial Examples in Action*.

To sum up, we have laid out the notion of adversarial examples and made the connection to GANs even more specific. This is an underappreciated connection, but one that can solidify your understanding of this challenging subject. Furthermore, one of the defenses against adversarial examples are GANs themselves![12] So GANs also have the potential to solve this gap that likely led to their existence in the first place.

---

[9] See "The Robust Manifold Defense: Adversarial Training Using Generative Models," by Ajil Jalal et al., 2019, https://arxiv.org/pdf/1712.09196.pdf.

[10] See "Virtual Adversarial Training: A Regularization Method for Supervised and Semi-Supervised Learning," by Takeru Miyato et al., 2018, https://arxiv.org/pdf/1704.03976.pdf.

[11] This was a hotly debated topic at ICLR 2019. Though most of these conversations were informal, using (pseudo) invertible generative models as a way to classify "out-of-sample"ness of an image seems like a fruitful avenue.

[12] See Jalal et al., 2019, https://arxiv.org/pdf/1712.09196.pdf.

10.7 Conclusion

Adversarial examples are an important field, because even commercial computer vision products suffered from this shortcoming and can still be easily fooled by academics.[13] Beyond security and machine learning explainability applications, many practical uses remain in fairness and robustness.

Furthermore, adversarial examples are an excellent way of solidifying your own understanding of deep learning and GANs. Adversarial examples take advantage of the difficulty in training classifiers in general and the relative ease of fooling the classifier in *one particular case*. The classifier has to make predictions for many images, and crafting a special offset to fool the classifier exactly right is easy because of the many degrees of freedom. As a result, we can easily get adversarial noise that completely changes the label of a picture without changing the image perceptibly.

Adversarial examples can be found in many domains and many areas of AI, not just deep learning or computer vision. But as you saw in the code, creating the ones in computer vision is not challenging. Defenses against these examples exist, and you saw one using GANs, but adversarial examples are far from being solved completely.

Summary

- Adversarial examples, which come from abusing the dimensionality of the problem space, are an important aspect of machine learning because they show us why GANs work and why some classifiers can be easily broken.
- We can easily generate our own adversarial examples with real images and noise.
- Few meaningful attack vectors can be used with adversarial examples.
- Applications of adversarial examples include cybersecurity and machine learning fairness, and we can defend against them by using GANs.

---

[13] See "Black-Box Adversarial Attacks with Limited Queries and Information," by Andrew Ilyas et al., 2018, https://arxiv.org/abs/1804.08598.

Practical applications
of GANs

11

This chapter covers

- Use of GANs in medicine
- Use of GANs in fashion

As captivating as generating handwritten digits and turning apples into oranges may be, GANs can be used for a lot more. This chapter explores some of the practical applications of GANs. It is only fitting that this chapter focuses on areas where GANs have been harnessed for practical use. After all, one of our main goals with this book is to give you the knowledge and tools necessary to not only understand what has been accomplished with GANs to date, but also to empower you to find new applications of your choosing. There is no better place to start that journey than taking a look at several successful examples of just that.

You have already seen several innovative use cases of GANs. Chapter 6 showed how Progressive GANs can create not only photorealistic renditions of human faces, but also samples of, arguably, much greater practical importance: medical mammograms. Chapter 9 showed how the CycleGAN can create realistic simulated virtual environments by translating clips from a video game into movie-like scenes, which can then be used to train self-driving cars.

This chapter reviews GAN applications in greater detail. We will walk through what motivated these applications, what makes them uniquely suited to benefit from the advances made possible by GANs, and how their creators went about implementing them. Specifically, we will look at GAN applications in medicine and fashion. We chose these two fields based on the following criteria:

- They showcase not only academic but also, and primarily, the business value of GANs. They represent how the academic advances achieved by GAN researchers can be applied to solve real-world problems.
- They use GAN models that are understandable with the tools and techniques discussed in this book. Instead of introducing new concepts, we will look at how the models we implemented can be applied to uses other than the MNIST.
- They are understandable without the need for specialized domain expertise. For example, GAN applications in chemistry and physics tend to be hard to comprehend for anyone without a strong background in the given field.

Moreover, the chosen fields and the examples we selected serve to illustrate the versatility of GANs. In medicine, we show how GANs can be useful in situations with limited data. In fashion, we present the other extreme and explore GAN applications in scenarios where extensive datasets are available. Even if you have no interest in medicine or fashion, the tools and approaches that you will learn about in this chapter are applicable to countless other use cases.

Sadly, as is all too often the case, the practical applications we will review are virtually impossible to reproduce in a coding tutorial because of the proprietary or otherwise hard-to-obtain nature of the training data. Instead of a full coding tutorial like the ones throughout this book, we can provide only a detailed explanation of the GAN models and the implementation choices behind them. Accordingly, by the end of this chapter, you should be fully equipped to implement any of the applications in this chapter by making only small modifications to the GAN models we implemented earlier and feeding them a dataset for the given use case or one similar to it. With that, let's dive in.

11.1 GANs in medicine

This section presents applications of GANs in medicine. Namely, we look at how to use GAN-produced synthetic data to enlarge a training dataset to help improve diagnostic accuracy.

11.1.1 Using GANs to improve diagnostic accuracy

Machine learning applications in medicine face a range of challenges that lend the field well to benefiting from GANs. Perhaps most important, it is challenging to procure training datasets large enough for supervised machine learning algorithms because of difficulties involved in collecting medical data.[1] Obtaining samples of medical conditions tends to be prohibitively expensive and impractical.

---

[1] See "Synthetic Data Augmentation Using GAN for Improved Liver Lesion Classification," by Maayan Frid-Adar et al., 2018, http://mng.bz/rPBg.

Unlike datasets of handwritten letters for optical character recognition (OCR) or footage of roads for self-driving cars, which anyone can procure, examples of medical conditions are harder to come by, and they often require specialized equipment to collect. Not to mention the all-important considerations of patient privacy that limit how medical data can be collected and used.

In addition to difficulties in obtaining medical datasets, it is also challenging to properly label this data, a process that often requires annotations by people with expert knowledge of a given condition.[2] As a result, many medical applications have been unable to benefit from advances in deep learning and AI.

Many techniques have been developed to help address the problem of small labeled datasets. In chapter 7, you learned how GANs can be used to enhance the performance of classification algorithms in a semi-supervised setting. You saw how the SGAN achieved superior accuracy while using only a tiny subset of labels for training. This, however, addresses only half of the problem medical researchers face. Semi-supervised learning helps in situations in which we have a large dataset, but only a small portion of it is labeled. In many medical applications, having labels for a tiny portion of the dataset is only part of the problem—this small portion is often the only data we have! In other words, we do not have the luxury of thousands of additional samples from the same domain just waiting to be labeled or used in a semi-supervised setting.

Medical researchers strive to overcome the challenge of insufficient datasets by using data-augmentation techniques. For images, these include small tweaks and transformations such as scaling (zooming in and out), translations (moving left/right and up/down), and rotations.[3] These strategies allow a single example to be used to create many others, thereby expanding the dataset size. Figure 11.1 shows examples of data augmentations commonly used in computer vision.

As you may imagine, standard data augmentation has many limitations. For one, small modifications yield examples that do not diverge far from the original image. As a result, the additional examples do not add much variety to help the algorithm learn to generalize.[4] In the case of handwritten digits, for example, we want to see the number 6 rendered in different writing styles, not just permutations of the same underlying image.

In the case of medical diagnostics, we want different examples of the same underlying pathology. Enriching a dataset with synthetic examples, such as those produced by GANs, has the potential to further enrich the available data beyond traditional augmentation techniques. That is precisely what the Israeli researchers Maayan Frid-Adar, Eyal Klang, Michal Amitai, Jacob Goldberger, and Hayit Greenspan set out to investigate.

---

[2] Ibid.

[3] Ibid.

[4] Ibid.

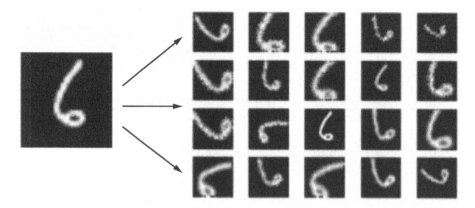

Figure 11.1   Techniques used to enlarge a dataset by altering existing data include scaling (zooming in and out), translations (moving left/right and up/down), and rotations. Although effective at increasing dataset sizes, classic data augmentation techniques bring only limited additional data diversity.
(Source: "Data Augmentation: How to Use Deep Learning When You Have Limited Data," by Bharath Raj, 2018, http://mng.bz/dxPD.)

Encouraged by GANs' ability to synthesize high-quality images in virtually any domain, Frid-Adar and his colleagues decided to explore the use of GANs for medical data augmentation. They chose to focus on improving the classification of liver lesions. One of their primary motivations for focusing on the liver is that this organ is one of the three most common sites for metastatic cancer, with over 745,000 deaths caused by liver cancer in 2012 alone.[5] Accordingly, tools and machine learning models that would help doctors diagnose at-risk patients have the potential to save lives and improve outcomes for countless patients.

11.1.2   *Methodology*

Frid-Adar and his team found themselves in a catch-22 situation: their goal was to train a GAN to augment a small dataset, but GANs themselves need a lot of data to train. In other words, they wanted to use GANs to create a large dataset, but they needed a large dataset to train the GAN in the first place.

Their solution was ingenious. First, they used standard data-augmentation techniques to create a larger dataset. Second, they used this dataset to train a GAN to create synthetic examples. Third, they used the augmented dataset from step 1 along with the GAN-produced synthetic examples from step 2 to train a liver lesion classifier.

The GAN model the researchers used was a variation on the Deep Convolutional GAN (DCGAN) covered in chapter 4. Attesting to the applicability of GANs across a

---

[5]   See "Cancer Incidence and Mortality Worldwide: Sources, Methods, and Major Patterns in GLOBOCAN 2012," by J. Ferlay et al., 2015, *International Journal of Cancer*, https://www.ncbi.nlm.nih.gov/pubmed/25220842.

wide array of datasets and scenarios, Frid-Adar et al. had to make only minor tweaks and customizations to make the DCGAN work for their use case. As evidenced by figure 11.2, the only parts of the model that needed adjustment were the dimensions of the hidden layers and the dimensions of the output from the Generator and input into the Discriminator network.

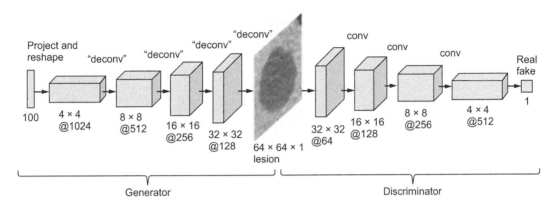

Figure 11.2   The DCGAN model architecture employed by Frid-Adar et al. to generate synthetic images of liver lesions to augment their dataset, aiming to improve classification accuracy. The model architecture is similar to the DCGAN in chapter 4, underscoring the applicability of GANs across a wide array of datasets and use cases. (Note that the figure shows only the GAN flow for fake examples.)
(Source: Frid-Adar et al., 2018, http://mng.bz/rPBg)

Instead of 28 × 28 × 1-sized images like those in the MNIST dataset, this GAN deals with images that are 64 × 64 × 1. As noted in their paper, Frid-Adar et al. also used 5 × 5 convolutional kernels—but then again, that is also only a small change to the network hyperparameters. Except for the image size, which is given by the training data, all these adjustments were in all likelihood determined by trial and error. The researchers kept tweaking the parameters until the model produced satisfactory images.

Before we review how well the approach devised by Frid-Adar and his team worked, let's pause for a moment and appreciate how far your understanding of GANs has progressed. As early as chapter 4 in this book, you had already learned enough about GANs to apply them to a real-world scenario, discussed in a paper presented at the 2018 International Symposium on Biomedical Imaging.[6]

---

[6]   See Frid-Adar et al., 2018, http://mng.bz/rPBg.

11.1.3 *Results*

Using DCGAN for data augmentation, Frid-Adar and his team achieved a significant improvement in classification accuracy compared to the baseline (standard data augmentation only).[7] Their results are summarized in figure 11.3, which shows the classification accuracy (y-axis) as the number of training examples (x-axis) increases.

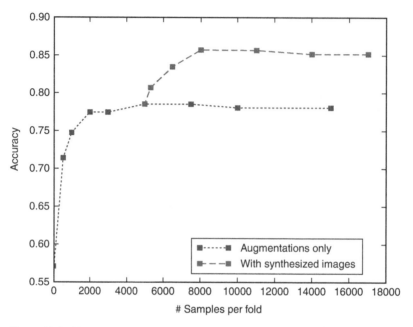

Figure 11.3   This chart shows classification accuracy as new examples are added using two dataset augmentation strategies: standard/classic data augmentation; and augmentation using synthetic examples produced by DCGAN. Using standard augmentation (dotted line), the classification performance peaks at around 80%. Using GAN-created examples (dashed line) boosts the accuracy to over 85%.
(Source: Frid-Adar et al., 2018, http://mng.bz/rPBg.)

The dotted line depicts classification performance for classic data augmentation. The performance improves as the quantity of new (augmented) training examples increases; however, the improvement plateaus around the accuracy of 80%, beyond which additional examples fail to yield improvement.

The dashed line shows the additional increase in accuracy achieved by augmenting the dataset using GAN-produced synthetic examples. Starting from the point beyond which additional classically augmented examples stopped improving accuracy, Frid-Adar et al. added synthetic data produced by their DCGAN. The classification

---

[7] Ibid.

performance improved from around 80% to over 85%, demonstrating the usefulness of GANs.

Improved classification of liver lesions is only one of many data-constrained use cases in medicine that can benefit from data augmentation through GAN-produced synthetic examples. For example, a team of British researchers led by Christopher Bowles from the Imperial College London harnessed GANs (in particular, the Progressive GANs discussed in chapter 6) to boost performance on brain segmentation tasks.[8] Crucially, an improvement in performance can unlock a model's usability in practice, especially in fields like medicine, where accuracy may mean the difference between life and death.

Let's switch gears and explore applications of GANs in a field with much lower stakes and a whole different set of considerations and challenges: fashion.

11.2 GANs in fashion

Unlike medicine, for which data is hard to obtain, researchers in fashion are fortunate to have huge datasets at their disposal. Sites like Instagram and Pinterest have countless images of outfits and clothing items, and retail giants like Amazon and eBay have data on millions of purchases of everything from socks to dresses.

In addition to data availability, many other characteristics make fashion well-suited to AI applications. Fashion tastes vary greatly from customer to customer, and the ability to personalize content has the potential to unlock significant business benefits. In addition, fashion trends change frequently, and it is vital for brands and retailers to react quickly and adapt to customers' shifting preferences.

In this section, we explore some of the innovative uses of GANs in fashion.

11.2.1 Using GANs to design fashion

From drone deliveries to cashier-less grocery stores, Amazon is no stranger to headline news about its futuristic endeavors. In 2017, Amazon earned another one, this time about the company's ambition to develop an AI fashion designer by using no other technique than GANs.[9] The story, published in *MIT Technology Review*, is unfortunately short on details besides the mention of using GANs to design new products matching a particular style.

Luckily, researchers from Adobe and the University of California, San Diego, published a paper in which they set out to accomplish the same goal.[10] Their approach can give us a hint about what goes on behind the secretive veil of Amazon's AI research labs seeking to reinvent fashion. Using a dataset of hundreds of thousands of

---

[8] See "GAN Augmentation: Augmenting Training Data Using Generative Adversarial Networks," by Christopher Bowles et al., 2018, https://arxiv.org/abs/1810.10863.

[9] See "Amazon Has Developed an AI Fashion Designer," by Will Knight, 2017, *MIT Technology Review*, http://mng.bz/VPqX.

[10] See "This AI Learns Your Fashion Sense and Invents Your Next Outfit," by Jackie Snow, 2017, *MIT Technology Review*, http://mng.bz/xlJ8.

users, items, and reviews scraped from Amazon, lead author Wang-Cheng Kang and his collaborators trained two separate models: one that recommends fashion and the other that creates it.[11]

For our purposes, we can treat the recommendation model as a black box. The only thing we need to know about the model is what it does: for any person-item pair, it returns a preference score; the greater the score, the better match the item is for the person's tastes. Nothing too unusual.

The latter model is a lot more novel and interesting—not only because it uses GANs, but also thanks to the two creative applications Kang and his colleagues devised:

- Creating new fashion items matching the fashion taste of a given individual
- Suggesting personalized alterations to existing items based on an individual's fashion preferences.

In this section, we explore how Kang and his team achieved these goals.

11.2.2 *Methodology*

Let's start with the model. Kang and his colleagues use a Conditional GAN (CGAN), with a product's category as the conditioning label. Their dataset has six categories: tops (men's and women's), bottoms (men's and women's), and shoes (men's and women's).

Recall that in chapter 8, we used MNIST labels to teach a CGAN to produce any handwritten digit we wanted. In a similar fashion (pun intended), Kang et al. use the category labels to train their CGAN to generate fashion items belonging to a specified category. Even though we are now dealing with shirts and pants instead of threes and fours, the CGAN model setup is almost identical to the one we implemented in chapter 8. The Generator uses random noise z and conditioning information (label/category c) to synthesize an image, and the Discriminator outputs a probability that a particular image-category pair is real rather than fake. Figure 11.4 details the network architecture Kang et al. used.

Each box represents a layer; *fc* stands for *fully connected layer*; *st* denotes *strides* for the convolutional kernel whose dimensions (width × height) are given as the first two numbers in the conv/deconv layers; and *deconv* and *conv* denote what kind of layer is used: a regular convolution or a transposed convolution, respectively. The number directly after the *conv* or *deconv* sets the depth of the layer or, equivalently, the number of convolutional filters used. *BN* tells us that batch normalization was used on the output of the given layer. Also, notice that Kang et al. chose to use least squares loss instead of cross-entropy loss.

Equipped with a CGAN capable of producing realistic clothing items for each of the top-level categories in their dataset, Kang and his colleagues tested it on two

---

[11] See "Visually-Aware Fashion Recommendation and Design with Generative Image Models," by Wang-Cheng Kang et al., 2017, https://arxiv.org/abs/1711.02231.

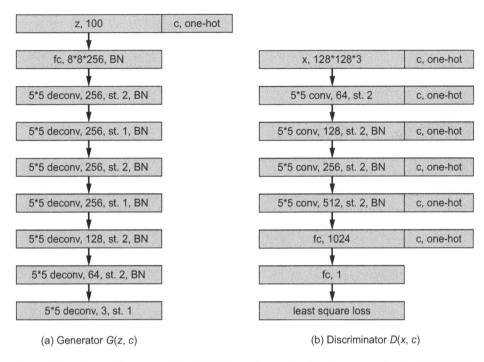

(a) Generator $G(z, c)$ (b) Discriminator $D(x, c)$

Figure 11.4 The architectures of the CGAN Generator and the Discriminator networks that Kang et al. use in their study. The label c represents the category of clothing. The researchers use it as the conditioning label to guide the Generator to synthesize an image matching the given category, and the Discriminator to identify real image-category pairs.
(Source: Kang et al., 2017, https://arxiv.org/abs/1711.02231.)

applications with significant practical potential: creating new personalized items and making personalized alterations to existing items.

11.2.3 Creating new items matching individual preferences

To ensure that the produced images are customized to an individual's fashion taste, Kang and his colleagues came up with an ingenious approach. They started off with the following insight: given that their recommendation model assigns scores to *existing* items based on how much a person would like the given item, the ability to generate *new* items maximizing this preference score would likely yield items matching the person's style and taste.[12]

Borrowing a term from economics and choice theory,[13] Kang et al. call this process *preference maximization*. What is unique about Kang et al.'s approach is that their universe of possible items is not limited to the corpus of training data or even the entire

---

[12] Ibid.
[13] See "Introduction to Choice Theory," by Jonathan Levin and Paul Milgrom, 2004, http://mng.bz/AN2p.

Amazon catalog. Thanks to their CGAN, they can fine-tune the generation of new items to virtually infinite granularity.

The next problem Kang and his colleagues had to solve was ensuring that the CGAN Generator would produce a fashion item maximizing individual preference. After all, their CGAN was trained to produce realistic-looking images for only a given category, *not* a given person. One possible option would be to keep generating images and check their preference score until we happen upon one whose score is sufficiently high. However, given the virtually infinite variations of the images that can be generated, this approach would be extremely inefficient and time-consuming.

Instead, Kang and his team solved the issue by framing it as an optimization problem: in particular, constraint maximization. The constraint (the boundary within which their algorithm had to operate) is the size of the latent space, given by the size of the vector z. Kang et al. used the standard size (100-dimensional vector) with each number in $[-1, 1]$ range. To make the values differentiable so that they can be used in an optimization algorithm, the authors set each element in the vector z to the *tanh* function, initialized randomly.[14]

The researchers then employed gradient ascent. *Gradient ascent* is just like gradient descent, except that instead of *minimizing* a cost function by iteratively moving in the direction of the steepest *decrease*, we are *maximizing* a reward function (in this case, the score given by the recommendation model) by iteratively moving in the direction of the steepest *increase*.

Kang et al.'s results are shown in figure 11.5, which compares the top three images from the dataset with the top three generated images for six different individuals. Attesting to the ingenuity of Kang et al.'s solution, the examples they produced have higher preference scores, suggesting that they are a better match for the shoppers' style and preferences.

The three columns on the left show the items from the dataset with the highest scores; the three columns on the right show generated items with the highest scores. Based on the preference score, the generated images are a better match for the shoppers' preferences.

Kang and his team didn't stop there. In addition to creating new items, they explored whether the model they developed could be used to make changes to existing items, tailored to an individual's style. Given the highly subjective nature of fashion shopping, having the ability to alter a garment until it is "just right" has significant potential business benefits. Let's see how Kang et al. went about solving this challenge.

---

[14] See Kang et al., 2017, https://arxiv.org/abs/1711.02231.

(a) Top-3 results from dataset (b) Top-3 results from GAN

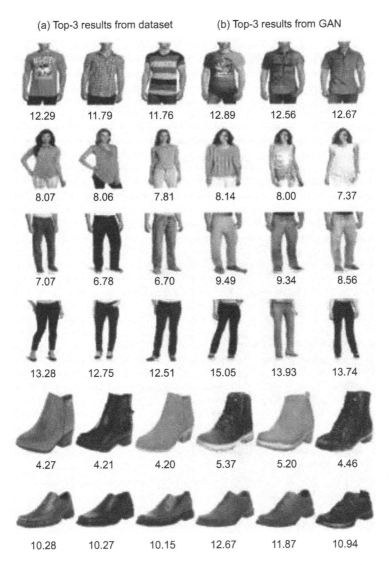

| 12.29 | 11.79 | 11.76 | 12.89 | 12.56 | 12.67 |

| 8.07 | 8.06 | 7.81 | 8.14 | 8.00 | 7.37 |

| 7.07 | 6.78 | 6.70 | 9.49 | 9.34 | 8.56 |

| 13.28 | 12.75 | 12.51 | 15.05 | 13.93 | 13.74 |

| 4.27 | 4.21 | 4.20 | 5.37 | 5.20 | 4.46 |

| 10.28 | 10.27 | 10.15 | 12.67 | 11.87 | 10.94 |

Figure 11.5 In the results Kang et al. present in their paper, every image is annotated with its preference score. Each row shows results for a different shopper and product category (men's and women's tops, men's and women's bottoms, and men's and women's shoes).
(Source: Kang et al., 2017, https://arxiv.org/abs/1711.02231.)

11.2.4 *Adjusting existing items to better match individual preferences*

Recall that the numbers in the latent space (represented by the input vector z) have real-world meaning, and that vectors that are mathematically close to one another (as measured by their distance in the high-dimensional space they occupy) tend to produce images that are similar in terms of content and style. Accordingly, as Kang et al. point out, in order to generate variations of some image *A*, all we need to do is to find the latent vector *zA* that the Generator would use to create the image. Then, we could produce images from neighboring vectors to generate similar images.

To make it a little less abstract, let's look at a concrete example using our favorite dataset, the MNIST. Consider an input vector z' that, when fed into the Generator, produces an image of the number 9. If we then feed the vector z'' that is, mathematically speaking, very close to z' in the 100-dimensional latent space the vectors occupy, then z'' will produce another, slightly different, image of the number 8. This is illustrated in figure 11.6. You saw a little bit of this back in chapter 2. In the context of variational autoencoders, the intermediate/compressed representation works just like *z* does in the world of GANs.

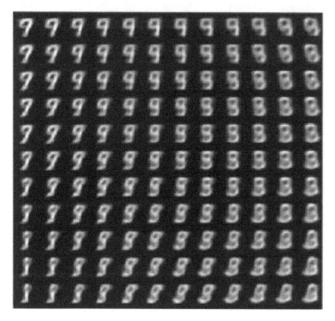

Figure 11.6 Variations on the digit 9 obtained by moving around in the latent space (image reproduced from chapter 2). Nearby vectors produce variations on the same digit. For example, notice that as we move from left to right in the first row, the numeral 9 starts off being slightly right-slanted but eventually turns fully upright. Also notice that as we move far enough away, the number 9 morphs into another, visually similar digit. Progressive variations like these apply equally to more complex datasets, where the variations tend to be more nuanced.

Of course, in fashion, things are more nuanced. After all, a photo of a dress is incomparably more complex than a grayscale image of a numeral. Moving in the latent space around a vector producing, say, a T-shirt, can produce a T-shirt in different colors, patterns, and styles (V-neck as opposed to crew-neck, for example). It all depends on the types of encodings and meanings the Generator has internalized during training. The best way to find out is to try.

This brings us to the next challenge Kang and his team had to overcome. In order for the preceding approach to work, we need the vector *z* for the image we want to alter. This would be straightforward if we wanted to modify a synthetic image: we can just record the vector *z* each time we generate an image so that we can refer to it later. What complicates the situation in our scenario is that we want to modify a *real* image.

By definition, a real image cannot have been produced by the Generator, so there is no vector *z*. The best we can do is to find latent space representation of a generated image as close as possible to the one we seek to modify. Put differently, we have to find a vector *z* that the Generator uses to synthesize an image similar to the real image, and use it as a proxy for the hypothetical *z* that would have produced the real image.

That is precisely what Kang et al. did. Just as before, they start by formulating the scenario as an optimization problem. They define a loss function in terms of the so-called *reconstruction loss* (a measure of the difference between two images; the greater the loss, the more different a given pair of images is from one another).[15] Having formulated the problem in this way, Kang et al. then iteratively find the closest possible generated image for any real image by using gradient descent (minimizing the reconstruction loss). Once we have a fake image that is similar to the real image (and hence also the vector *z* used to produce it), we can modify it through the latent space manipulations.

This is where the approach Kang and his colleagues devised shows its full potential. We can move around the latent space to points that generate images similar to the one we want to modify, while also optimizing for the preferences of the given user. We can see this process in figure 11.7: as we move from left to right in each row, the shirts and pants get progressively more personalized.

For instance, the person of the first row was looking for a more colorful option and, as Kang et al. observed, the person in row 5 seems to prefer brighter colors and a more distressed look; and the last person, it appears, prefers skirts over jeans. This is hyperpersonalization at its finest. No wonder Amazon took notice.

The leftmost photo shows the real product from the training dataset; the second photo from the left shows a generated image closest to the real photo that was used as a starting point for the personalization process. Each image is annotated with its preference score. As we move from left to right, the item is progressively optimized for the given individual. As evidenced by the increasing scores, the personalization process improves the likelihood that the item matches the given shopper's style and taste.

---

[15] Ibid.

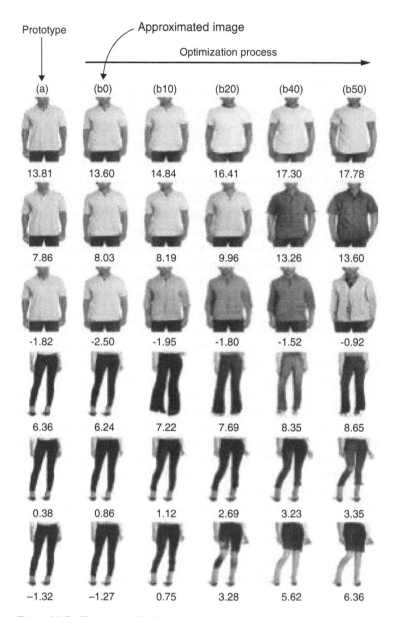

Figure 11.7   The personalization process for six shoppers (three male and three female) using the same starting image: polo shirt for males and a pair of pants for women.

(Source: Kang et al., 2017, https://arxiv.org/abs/1711.02231.)

11.3   Conclusion

The applications covered in this chapter only scratch the surface of what is possible with GANs. Countless other use cases exist in medicine and fashion alone, not to mention other fields. What is certain is that GANs have expanded far beyond academia, with myriad applications leveraging their ability to synthesize realistic data.

Summary

- Because of the versatility of GANs, they can be harnessed for a wide array of nonacademic applications and easily repurposed to use cases beyond the MNIST.
- In medicine, GANs produce synthetic examples that can improve classification accuracy beyond what is possible with standard dataset augmentation strategies.
- In fashion, GANs can be used to create new items and alter existing items to better match someone's personal style. This is accomplished by generating images that maximize preference score provided by a recommendation algorithm.

Looking ahead

This chapter covers

- The ethics of generative models
- Three recent improvements that we expect to be dominant in the years to come:
  - Relativistic GAN (RGAN)
  - Self-Attention GAN (SAGAN)
  - BigGAN
- Further reading for three more cutting-edge techniques
- A summary of the key themes and takeaways from this book

In this final chapter, we want to give you a brief overview of our thoughts about the ethics of GANs. Then we will talk about some important innovations that we expect to be even more important in the future. This chapter includes high-level ideas that we expect to define the future of GANs, but it does not feature any code. We want you to be prepared for the GANtastic journey ahead—even for advances that are yet to be published at the time of writing. Lastly, we will wrap up and say our teary-eyed goodbyes.

12.1 Ethics

The world is beginning to realize that AI ethics—GANs included—is an important issue. Some institutions have decided to not release their expensive, pretrained models for fear of misuse as a tool for generating fake news.[1] Numerous articles describe the ways in which GANs specifically may have potential malicious uses.[2]

We all understand that misinformation can be a huge problem and that GANs with photorealistic, synthetic images could pose a danger. Imagine synthesizing videos of a world leader saying they are about to launch a military strike on another country. Will the correcting information spread quickly enough to soothe the panic that will follow?

This is not a book about AI ethics, so we touch on this topic only briefly. But we strongly believe that it is important for all of us to think about the ethics of what we are doing and about the risks and unintended consequences that our work could have. Given that AI is such a scalable technology, it is vital to think through whether we are helping to create a world we want to live in.

We urge you to think about your principles and to go through at least one of the more evolved ethical frameworks. We are not going to discuss which one is better than the other—after all, humans have generally not yet agreed on a moral framework on much more mundane things—but please put the book down and read at least one of these if you have not already.

> **NOTE** You can read about Google's AI principles at https://ai.google/ principles. The Institute for Ethical AI & ML details its principles at https:// ethical.institute/principles.html. See also "IBM's Rometty Lays Out AI Considerations, Ethical Principles," by Larry Dignan, 2017, ZDNet, http://mng .bz/ZeZm.

For example, the technology known as *DeepFakes*—although not originally based on GANs—has been cited by many as a source for concern.[3] DeepFakes—a portmanteau of *deep learning* and *fake imagery*—has already proven controversial by generating fake political videos and synthetic involuntary pornographic content. Soon, this technology may be at a point where it would be impossible to tell whether the video or image is authentic. Given GANs' ability to synthesize new images, they may soon dominate this domain.

To say that everyone should think about the consequences of their research and code seems insufficient, but the reality is that there is no silver bullet. We should

---

[1] See "An AI That Writes Convincing Prose Risks Mass-Producing Fake News," by Will Knight, *MIT Technology Review*, 2019, http://mng.bz/RPGj.

[2] See "Inside the World of AI that Forges Beautiful Art and Terrifying Deepfakes," by Karen Hao, *MIT Technology Review*, 2019, http://mng.bz/2JA8. See also "AI Gets Creative Thanks to GANs Innovations," by Jakub Langr, *Forbes*, 2019, http://mng.bz/1w71.

[3] See "The Liar's Dividend, and Other Challenges of Deep-Fake News," by Paul Chadwick, *The Guardian*, 2018, http://mng.bz/6wN5. See also "If You Thought Fake News Was a Problem, Wait for DeepFakes," by Roula Khalaf, 2018, *Financial Times*, http://mng.bz/PO8Y.

consider these implications, even if the initial focus was entirely ethical, regardless of whether we are working in research or industry. We also do not want to give you a dull lecture nor unsubstantiated media-grabbing forecast, but this is a problem we care deeply about.

AI ethics is a real problem *already*, and we have presented three real problems here—AI-generated fake news, synthesized political proclamations, and involuntary pornography. But many more problems exist, such as Amazon using an AI-hiring tool showing negative bias against women.[4] But the practical landscape is complicated—some suggest that GANs have a tendency to favor images of women in face-genera-tion. Yet another angle is that GANs also have a potential to help AI be more ethi-cal—by synthesizing the underrepresented class in, for example, face-recognition problems in a semi-supervised setup, thereby improving the quality of classification in less-represented communities.

We are writing this book partially to make everyone more aware of the possibilities and possible misuses of GANs. We are excited by the future academic and practical applications of GANs and the ongoing research, but we are also aware that some appli-cations may have negative uses. Because it is impossible to "uninvent" a technology, we have to be aware of its capabilities. By no means are we saying that the world would be better off if GANs did not exist—but GANs are just a tool, and as we all know, tools can be misused.

We feel morally compelled to talk about the promises and dangers of this tech-nology, as otherwise misusing it becomes easier by a narrow group of the initiated. Although this book is not written for the general public, we hope that this is one stepping stone toward broader awareness—beyond the mostly academic circles that have dominated the field of GANs for now. Equally, much of the public outreach we are doing—we hope—is contributing to greater knowledge and discussions about this topic.

As more people are aware of this technology, even the existing malicious actors will no longer be able to catch anyone by surprise. We are hoping that GANs will never be a source of malicious acts, but that may be too idealistic. The next best thing is for knowledge of GANs to be available to everyone—not just academics and really invested malicious parties. We also hope (and all evidence thus far seems to point to this reality) that GANs will overall contribute positively to art, science, and engineer-ing. Furthermore, people are also working on DeepFake detection, incorporating ideas from GANs and adversarial examples, but we have to be cautious, because any classifier that can detect these with any degree of accuracy will lend all the more cred-ibility to an example that will manage to fool it.

In many ways, we are also hoping to start a more thorough conversation without any grandstanding—this is an invitation to connect with us through our book forums or our Twitter accounts. We are aware that we need a diverse range of perspectives to

---

[4] See "Amazon Scraps Secret AI Recruiting Tool That Showed Bias Against Women," by Jeffrey Dastin, 2018, Reuters, http://mng.bz/Jz8K.

keep checking our moral framework. We also are aware that these things will evolve over time, especially as use cases become clearer. Indeed, some people—such as Benedict Evans of a16z—argue that to regulate or talk about the ethics of AI does not make any more sense than to talk about the ethics of databases. What matters is the use case, not the technology.

12.2 GAN innovations

Speaking of use cases, we are aware that GANs are an ever-evolving field. In this section, we want to quickly update you on things that are not as robust in the community as some of the topics in prior chapters, but things we expect to be significant in the future. In the spirit of keeping this practical, we have picked out three GAN innovations that all have an interesting practical application: either a practical paper (RGAN), GitHub project (SAGAN), or artistic application (BigGAN).

12.2.1 Relativistic GAN

Not often do we get to see an update so simple and elegant that it could have been in the original paper, yet powerful enough to beat many of the state-of-the-art algorithms. *Relativistic GAN (RGAN)* is one such example. The core idea of the RGAN is that in addition to the original GAN (specifically, the NS-GAN that you may recall from chapter 5), we add an extra term to the Generator—forcing it to make the generated data seem more real than the real data.

In other words, the Generator should, in addition to making fake data seem more real, make real data seem comparatively less real, thereby also increasing the stability of the training. But of course, the only data the Generator has control over is the synthetic data, so the Generator can achieve this only comparatively.

The RGAN's author describes it as being a generalized version of the WGAN, which we discussed previously. Let's start with the simplified loss function from table 5.1 in chapter 5:

$$L_D = E[D(x)] - E[D(G(z))] \qquad \text{Equation 12.1}$$

$$L_G = E[D(G(z))] \qquad \text{Equation 12.2}$$

Recall that equation 12.1 describes the loss function for the Discriminator—where we measure the difference between the real data ($D(x)$) and the generated ones ($D(G(z))$). Equation 12.2 then describes the loss function of the Generator, where we are trying to make the Discriminator believe that the samples it is seeing are real.

To go to our closest predecessor, remember that the WGAN is trying to minimize the amount of probability mass we would have to move to get the generated distribution to look like the real one. In this sense, the RGAN has many similarities (for example, the Discriminator is frequently called the *critic*, and the WGAN is presented as a special case of the RGAN in this paper). Ultimately, both measure the current state of play as a single number—remember the earth mover's distance?

The innovation of the RGAN is that we no longer get the previous unhelpful dynamic of the Generator always playing catch-up. In other words, the Generator is trying to generate data that looks more realistic than the real data so that it is not always on the defensive. As a result, $D(x)$ can be interpreted as the probability that the real data is more realistic than the generated data.

Before we delve into the difference on a high level, we will introduce a slightly different notation, as to approximate the notation used by the paper, but simplify. In equations 12.3 and 12.4, $C(x)$ acts as a critic similar to a WGAN setup,[5] and you may think of it as a Discriminator. Furthermore, $a()$ is defined as log(sigmoid()). In the paper, $G(z)$ is replaced by x_f for fake samples, and x gets subscript r to indicate real samples, but we will follow the simpler notation from the earlier chapters.

$$L_D = E[a(C(x)] - C(G(z)))]$$ **Equation 12.3**

$$L_G = E[a(C(G(z)) - C(x))]$$ **Equation 12.4**

Importantly, in these equations, we see only one key difference in the Generator: the real data now adds into the loss function. This seemingly simple trick aligns the incentives of the Generator to not be at a permanent disadvantage. To understand this and two other perspectives in an idealized setting, let's plot the different Discriminator outputs as in figure 12.1.

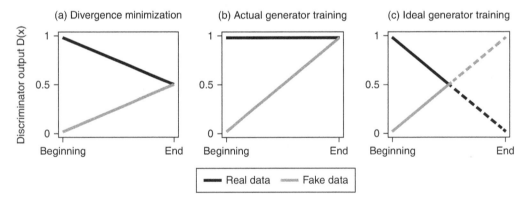

Figure 12.1   **Under divergence minimization (a), the Generator is always playing catch-up with the Discriminator (because divergence is always ≥ 0). In (b), we see what "good" NS-GAN training looks like. Again, the Generator cannot win. In (c), we can see that now the generator can win, but more importantly, the Generator always has something to strive for (and therefore recover useful gradient), no matter the stage of training.**

(Source: "The Relativistic Discriminator: A Key Element Missing from Standard GAN," by Alexia Jolicoeur-Martineau, 2018, http://arxiv.org/abs/1807.00734.)

---

[5] Because we are skipping over some details, we want to equip you with the high-level idea and keep the notation consistent so that you can fill in the blanks yourself.

You may be wondering, why should just adding this term be noteworthy? Well, this simple addition makes the training significantly more stable at a little extra computational cost. This is important, especially when you remember the "Are GANs Created Equal?" paper from chapter 5, where the authors argue that all the major GAN architectures considered so far have an only limited improvement over the original GAN when adjusted for the extra processing requirements. This is because many new GAN architectures are better only at huge computational cost, which makes them less useful, but the RGAN has potential to change GAN architectures across the board.

Always be aware of this trick, because even though a method may take fewer update steps, if each step takes two times longer because of the extra computation, is it really worth it? The peer review process at most conferences is not immune to this weakness, so you have to be careful.

APPLICATION

Your next question may be, why should this matter in practice? In less than a year, this paper has gathered more than 50 citations[6]—which is a lot for a new paper from a previously unknown author. Moreover, people have already written papers using the RGAN to, for example, achieve state-of-the-art speech (that is, best performance ever achieved) enhancement, beating other GAN-based and non-GAN-based methods.[7]

As you are reading this, the paper should be available, so feel free to take a look. Explaining this paper, with all the background necessary, however, is beyond the scope of this book.

12.2.2 *Self-Attention GAN*

The next innovation we believe is going to change the landscape is the *Self-Attention GAN (SAGAN)*. Attention is based on a very human idea of how we look at the world—through small patches of focus at a time.[8] A GAN's attention works similarly: your mind is consciously able to focus on only a small part of, say, a table, but your brain is able to stitch the whole table together through quick, minor eye movements called *saccades* while still focusing on only a subset of the image at a time.

The computer equivalent has been used in many fields, including natural language processing (NLP) and computer vision. Attention can help us solve, for example, the problem of convolutional neural networks (CNNs) ignoring much of the picture. As we know, CNNs rely on a small receptive field—as determined by the size of the convolution. However, as you may recall from chapter 5, in GANs, the size of the receptive field is likely to cause problems (such as cows with multiple heads or bodies), and the GAN will not consider them strange.

This is because when generating or evaluating that subset of the image, we may see that a leg is present in one field, but we do not see that other legs are already present in

---

[6] The following link names all the papers that cite the RGAN paper: http://mng.bz/omGj.

[7] See "SERGAN: Speech Enhancement Using Relativistic Generative Adversarial Networks with Gradient Penalty," by Deepak Baby and Sarah Verhulst, 2019, IEEE-ICASSP, https://ieeexplore.ieee.org/document/ 8683799.

[8] See *The Mind Is Flat: The Illusion of Mental Depth and the Improvised Mind* by Nick Chater (Penguin, 2018).

another one. This could be because the convolution ignores the structure of the object or because legs or leg rotations are represented by different, higher-level neurons that do not talk to each other. Our seasoned data scientists will remember that is what Hinton's CapsuleNets were attempting to solve, but they never really took off. For everyone else, the short story is that no one can say with absolute certainty why attention fixes this, but a good way to think about it is that we can now create *feature detectors* with a flexible receptive field (shape) to really focus on several key aspects of a given picture (see figure 12.2).

Figure 12.2 The output pixel (2 × 2 patch) ignores anything except the small highlighted region. Attention helps us solve that.
(Source: "Convolution Arithmetic," by vdmoulin, 2016, https://github.com/vdumoulin/conv_arithmetic.)

Recall that this is especially a problem when our images are, say, 512 × 512, but the largest commonly used convolution sizes are 7, so that is loads of ignored features! Even in higher-level nodes, the neural network may not be appropriately checking for, for example, a head in the right place. As a result, as long as the cow has a cow head next to a cow body, the network does not care about any other head, as long as it has at least one. But the structure is wrong.

These higher-level representations are harder to reason about, and so even researchers disagree as to exactly why this happens, but empirically, the network does not seem to pick it up. Attention allows us to pick out the relevant regions—whatever the shape or size—and consider them appropriately. To see the types of regions that attention can flexibly focus on, consider figure 12.3.

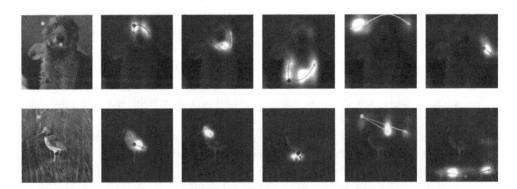

Figure 12.3 Here, we can see the regions of the image that the attention mechanism pays most attention to, given a representative query location. We can see that the attention mechanism generally cares about regions of different shapes and sizes, which is a good sign, given that we want it to pick out the regions of the image that indicate the kind of object it is.
(Source: "Self-Attention Generative Adversarial Networks," by Han Zhang, 2018, http://arxiv.org/abs/1805.08318.)

APPLICATION

DeOldify (https://github.com/jantic/DeOldify) is one of the popular applications of the SAGAN that was made by Jason Antic, a student of Jeremy Howard's fast.ai course. DeOldify uses the SAGAN to colorize old images and drawings to an amazing level of accuracy. As you can see in figure 12.4, you can turn famous historic photographs and paintings into fully colorized versions.

Figure 12.4   Deadwood, South Dakota, 1877. The image on the right has been colorized . . . for a black-and-white book. Trust us. If you do not believe us, check out the online liveBook on Manning's website to see for yourself!

12.2.3 BigGAN

Another architecture that has taken the world by storm is *BigGAN*.[9] BigGAN has achieved highly realistic 512×512 images on all 1,000 classes of ImageNet—a feat previously deemed almost impossible with the current generation of GANs. BigGAN achieved three times the previous best inception score. In brief, BigGAN builds on the SAGAN and spectral normalization and has further innovated in five directions:

- Scaling up GANs to previously unbelievable computational scale. The BigGAN authors trained with eight times the batch size, which was part of their success—giving already a 46% boost. Theoretically, the resources required to train a BigGAN add up to $59,000 worth of compute.[10]

- BigGAN's architecture has 1.5 times the number of channels (feature maps) in each layer relative to the SAGAN architecture. This may be due to the complexity of the dataset used.

[9] See "Large Scale GAN Training for High Fidelity Natural Image Synthesis," by Andrew Brock et al., 2019, https://arxiv.org/pdf/1809.11096.pdf.

[10] See Mario Klingemann's Twitter post at http://mng.bz/wll2.

- Improving the stability of the Generator and the Discriminator through controlling the adversarial process, which leads to overall better results. The underlying mathematics are unfortunately beyond the scope of this book, but if you're interested, we recommend starting with understanding spectral normalization. For those who are not, take solace in the fact that even the authors themselves abandon this strategy in later parts of training and let the mode collapse because of computational costs.

- Introducing a *truncation trick* to give us a way of controlling the trade-off between variety and fidelity. The truncation trick achieves better equality results if we sample closer to the middle of the distribution (truncate it). It makes sense that this would yield better samples, as this is where BigGAN has the "most experience."

- The authors introduce a further three theoretical advancements. According to the authors' own performance table, however, these seem to have only a marginal effect on the scores and frequently lead to less stability. They are useful for computational efficiency, but we will not discuss them.

APPLICATION

One fascinating artistic application of BigGAN is the Ganbreeder app, which was made possible thanks to the pretrained models and Joel Simon's hard work. Ganbreeder is an interactive web-based (free!) way to explore the latent space of BigGAN. It has been used in numerous artistic applications as a way to come up with new images.

You can either explore the adjacent latent space or use a linear interpolation between two samples of the two images to create new images. Figure 12.5 shows an example of creating Ganbreeder offspring.

BigGAN is further notable because DeepMind has given us all this compute for free and uploaded pretrained models onto TensorFlow Hub—a machine learning code repository that we used in chapter 6.

12.3 *Further reading*

We wanted to cover many other topics that seem to be gaining popularity in the works of academics and practitioners, but we did not have the space. Here, we will list at least three of them for interested readers. We hope we have equipped you with all that you need to understand these papers. We picked just three, as we expect this section to be changing quickly:

- *Style GAN* (http://arxiv.org/abs/1812.04948) merges ideas from GANs and "traditional" style transfer to give users much more control over the output they generate. This Conditional GAN from NVIDIA has managed to produce stunning full-HD results with several levels of control—from finer details to overall image. This work builds on chapter 6, so you may want to reread it before delving into this paper.

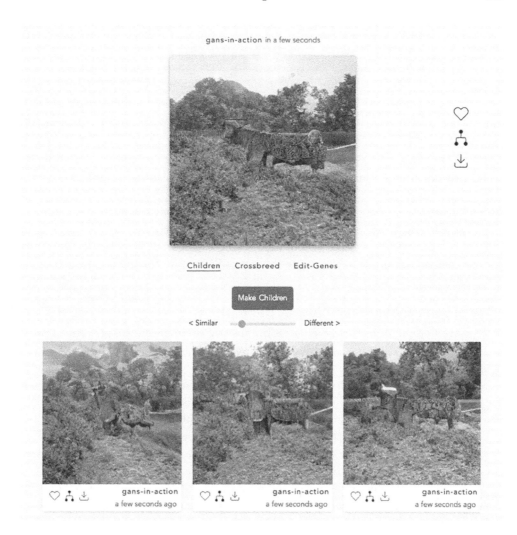

Figure 12.5 Every time you click the Make Children button, Ganbreeder gives you a selection of mutated images in the nearby latent space, producing the three images below. You may start from your own sample or someone else's—thereby making it a collaborative exercise. This is what the Crossbreed section is for, where you can select another interesting sample from other parts of the space and mix the two samples. Lastly, in Edit-Genes, you can edit parameters (such as Castle and Stone Wall, in this case) and add more or less of that feature into the picture.
(Source: Ganbreeder, http://mng.bz/nv28.)

- *Spectral normalization* (http://arxiv.org/abs/1802.05957) is a complex regularization technique and requires somewhat advanced linear algebra. For now, just remember the use case—stabilizing training by normalizing the weights in a network to satisfy a particular property, which is even formally required in WGAN (touched on in chapter 5). Spectral normalization acts somewhat similarly to gradient penalties.

- *SPADE*, aka *GauGAN* (https://arxiv.org/pdf/1903.07291.pdf) is cutting-edge work published in 2019 to synthesize photorealistic images based solely on a semantic map of the image, as you may recall from the start of chapter 9. The images can be up to 512 × 256 in resolution, but knowing NVIDIA, this may increase before the end of the year. This may be the most challenging technique of the three, but also one that has gathered the most media attention—probably because of how impressive the tech demo is!

There is so much going on in the world of GANs that it may be impossible to stay up-to-date all the time. However, we hope that in terms of both ethical frameworks and the latest interesting papers, we have given you the resources needed to look at the problems in this ever-evolving space. Indeed, that is our hope, even when it comes to the innovations behind the GANs presented in this chapter. We do not know whether all of these will become part of the routine bag of tricks that people use, but we think that they might. We also hope that this will be true for the most recent innovations listed in this section.

12.4 *Looking back and closing thoughts*

We hope that the cutting-edge techniques we've discussed will give you enough subject material to continue exploring GANs even as our book comes to an end. Before we send you off, however, it is worth looking back and recapping all that you have learned.

We started off with a basic explanation of what GANs are and how they work (chapter 1) and implemented a simple version of this system (chapter 3). We introduced you to generative models in an easier setting with autoencoders (chapter 2). We covered the theory of GANs (chapters 3 and 5) as well as their shortcomings and some of the ways to overcome them (chapter 5). This provided the foundation and tools for the later, advanced chapters.

We implemented several of the most canonical and influential GAN variants—Deep Convolutional GAN (chapter 4) and Conditional GAN (chapter 8)—as well as a few of the most advanced and complex ones—Progressive GANs (chapter 6) and CycleGANs (chapter 9). We also implemented Semi-Supervised GANs (chapter 8), a GAN variant designed to tackle one of the most severe shortcomings in machine learning: the lack of large, labeled datasets. We also explored several of the many practical and innovative applications of GANs (chapter 11), and presented adversarial examples (chapter 10), which are a challenge for all of machine learning.

Along the way, you expanded your theoretical and practical toolbox. From inception score and Fréchet inception distance (chapter 5) to pixel-wise feature normalization (chapter 6), batch normalization (chapter 4), and dropout (chapter 7), you learned about concepts and techniques that will serve you well for GANs and beyond.

As we look back, it is worth highlighting a few themes that came up time and time again as we explored GANs:

- GANs are tremendously versatile, in terms of both practical use cases and resilience against theoretical requirements and constraints. This was perhaps most apparent in the case of CycleGAN in chapter 9. This technique not only is unconstrained by the need for paired data that burdened its predecessors, but also can translate between examples in virtually any domain, from apples and oranges to horses and zebras. The versatility of GANs was also evident in chapter 6, where you saw that Progressive GANs can learn to generate equally well images as disparate as human faces and medical mammograms, and in chapter 7, where we needed to make only a handful of adjustments to turn the Discriminator into a multiclass classifier.

- GANs are as much an art as they are a science. The beauty and the curse of GANs—and, indeed, deep learning in general—is that our understanding of what makes them work so well in practice is limited. Few known mathematical guarantees exist, and most achievements are experimental only. This makes GANs susceptible to many training pitfalls, such as mode collapse, which you may recall from our discussion in chapter 5. Fortunately, researchers have found many tips and tricks that greatly mitigate these challenges—everything from input preprocessing to our choice of optimizer and activation functions—many of which you learned about and even saw firsthand in code tutorials thought the book. Indeed, as the GAN variants covered in this chapter show, the techniques to improve GANs continue to evolve.

In addition to difficulties in training, it is crucial to keep in mind that even techniques as powerful and versatile as GANs have other important limitations. GANs have been hailed by many as the technique that gave machines the gift of creativity. This is true to a degree—in a few short years, GANs have become the undisputed state-of-the-art technique in synthesizing fake data; however, they fall short of what human creativity can do.

Indeed, as we showed time and time again throughout this book, GANs can mimic the features of almost any existing dataset and come up with examples that look as though they came from that dataset. However, by their very nature, GANs will not stray far from the training data. For instance, if we have a training dataset of classical art masterpieces, the examples our GAN will produce will look more like Michelangelo than Jackson Pollock. Until a new AI paradigm comes along that gives machines true autonomy, it will be ultimately up to the (human) researcher to guide the GAN to the desired end goal.

As you experiment with GANs and their applications, bear in mind not only the practical techniques, tips, and tricks covered throughout this book, but also the ethical considerations discussed in this chapter. With that, we wish you all the best in the GANtastic journey ahead.

—Jakub and Vladimir

Summary

- We touched on AI and GAN ethics and discussed the moral frameworks, need for awareness, and openness of discussion.
- We equipped you with the innovations we believe will drive the future of GANs, and we gave you the high-level idea behind the following:
  - Relativistic GAN, which now ensures that the Generator considers the relative likelihood of real and generated data
  - SAGAN, with attention mechanisms that act similarly to human perception
  - BigGAN, which allowed us to generate all 1,000 ImageNet classes of unprecedented quality
- We highlighted two key recurring themes of our book: (1) the versatility of GANs and (2) the necessity for experimentation because, much like the rest of deep learning, GANs are as much an art as they are a science.

index